# You don't have to live in fear!

## Let your love of freedom be your guide.

Join this Revolution to restore honest, responsive and limited government in the United States of America which will restore and fulfill the letter and spirit of the Declaration of Independence and the Constitution of the United States of America as written and designed by America's founding fathers to protect the blessings of Liberty for all Americans.

Copyright © 2012
by David E. Robinson

All Rights Reserved
Parts of this book may be reproduced subject to due
and specific acknowledgment of their source.

MAINE-PATRIOT.com
3 Linnell Circle
Brunswick, Maine 04011

maine-patriot.com

*Office of The Maine free State, 3 Linnell Circle, Brunswick, Maine 04011*

# PREFACE

We are in a time of great change. **America's *Currency* was captured in 1913. America's *Government* was captured in 1933.** This explains why petitioning our government for grievances has been of no meaningful avail.

The *Corporations* that masquerade as our lawful government today, have almost *destroyed* America! Top people in our government — *including our military* — know this. They have been waiting for the "right time" to help *take America back to our lawful government.*

In the very near future, we can expect a major constructive change in our banking and currency system. We can expect to see contingents of Federal Marshals acting in the major seats of power — backed up by our Military.

These Military people are NOT any part of a military coup. They are backing up the Civilian *re-establishment* of our lost, lawful, government.

We can expect to see minor interruptions in our normal way of life.

This Transition has been designed to minimize interruptions in vital services in our economy — to minimize hardship.

This Transition will be accompanied by announcements in mainstream media. What we do *not* want is for people to become alarmed.

Our *so-called* "president" has been informed that he is *no longer* the Commander in Chief of our Military!

This is part of a worldwide operation whereby the non-aligned nations — *those nations that are not part of the G20* — will re-establish solid currencies.

There will be additional announcements to come — designed to slowly awaken the masses; to reduce panic.

Civil authority has been restored to the people of the United States.

The Military who exist now only through Civil authority, will be ready to assist the People whom they are sworn to protect in the effort to restore this nation to the Constitutional Republic it was created to be.

International Law has been unlawfully in effect in America since 1933. And *rescinding this law,* has been on the table since the 1950s.

We the People have regained Civilian Authority, in order to use the Military Services to support the ongoing effort to bring us back to true government *"of, for and by the people".*

Do *not* misread what is going on — they are *NOT* coming for the People. *The Cabal's time is up!*

Please prepare for *good* changes to come. Please share this information with others. The foundation has been laid. All that is needed now is YOU! — regular, everyday people. You will be needed for your insight, opinions and voice.

PLEASE SHARE THIS INFORMATION. EVERY AMERICAN MUST HEAR THIS TO KNOW WHAT IS HAPPENING TODAY!

# INTRODUCTION

Just before the end of last year, Pennsylvania — *as a state* — removed itself from the RuSA organization. After they did this, they put together a **Declaration of Notice to the World** stating that the Commonwealth of Pennsylvania had returned itself and its people back under its *de jur* Constitution *of the 1700s* and declared the People of Pennsylvania Free! — no longer recognizing *unlawful corporate government* within their state.

They did this *legally and properly.* They did not ask for permission, they simply went ahead and did it. And they received their acknowledgement receipt back from the Office of Private International Law at the Hague.

Shortly after that, an informed contact — who had been in touch with the various groups who had come forward in the beginning, concerning funding for RuSA and Rap, before changes were made and they withdrew their support — was contacted by the Pentagon and given a simple message; and that message was this:

**"It has come to our attention what Pennsylvania has done. How long would it take you to put together a simple majority of states to duplicate what Pennsylvania has done, for at such a time there could be monetary and military support?"**

They asked for a copy of the original documentation that Pennsylvania had submitted to the Office of Private International Law at the Hague, *so they could see who had been involved.*

Our contact had no problem with that, and neither did Pennsylvania. So they forwarded on the documentation that Pennsylvania had submitted. The answer was *"Yes! we'll just see how fast we can get that done!"*

So she sent out emails to everyone across the country that they knew, and had worked with all this time, that they knew to be capable, honorable, and honest Patriots, who would roll up their sleeves and actually get the job done, once they were told what had to be done.

And by the following day, at least one contact in 20-22 states had stepped up and volunteered to be a lead person in their state, to get it done!

The goal was for at least a simple majority — meaning 26 or more states to duplicate *exactly* what Pennsylvania had done.

It was later decided by those involved, to add *more strength* to the action by making the **Declaration of Notice to the World**, collectively as a united effort, so that the world will know we are not just free people in the various free states, but a Free People, *united as we were meant to be.*

We need no permission, recognition or opinion from foreign bodies or corporations to be what we are — Americans who claim our rightful heritage that was given to us by our founders in 1776.

This action should be seen as a *Declaration;* not just a notification — this is primary.

This action is interim; and we can't emphasize that enough.

A small group of elite people, have screwed things up — and in order to make sure that this doesn't happen again, all of the temporary aspects of this will be in writing.

After a period of about 120 days, free elections will be held. Paper ballots only; machines can be played with; paper ballots are a lot more difficult.

We've been told that old money people from before the Revolutionary War have been in contact with our military, and that some 80-90% of the military agree with the ideology found in our founding documents.

Everything we do is based on the principles in our 1787 Constitution and the Bill of Rights — including the *original 13th Amendment* that prohibits any foreign association, title of nobility, etc. — and the Oath of Service that everybody must take to *"support and defend the Constitution of the United States against all enemies, foreign and domestic."*

The U.S. Military has indicated to the financial people that they are willing to back us and that we have their recognition and support.

This gives the Military — *probably for the first time* — power to be used as a backup to federal Marshals who will take into custody all of the crooks and "fun-and-games people" on Wall Street, and so forth. There is going to be a tremendous house-cleaning.

The reorganizational portions of the government itself should be concluded in about 120 days. This 120 day period will begin with a formal announcement from the press-room of the White House.

This will give every reporter a clean shot at broadcasting the transition.

So these measures — *in terms of what the military wants* — they want to be the good guys. They're tired of being the bad guys. They would much rather be invited into a foreign country as a friend and an assistant.

You need some help? What do you need? Manpower? Bull-dozers? Food? We can come in and help you out.

Yes! we're the United States Military! but we're the *new* one. We're the good guys. BINGO!

We think this new approach will work quite well.

We are not putting together any interim government. We are not trying to overthrow anything. We are trying to revert back to law and order, and create the smallest amount of chaos *in the most peaceful fashion that we can*.

Our military cannot do this on their own for the simple reason that under the current structure Obama is considered to be the President — *we all know that he is not* — he is the CEO (Chief Executive Officer) of a Corporation called THE UNITED STATES.

The majority of the American people do not understand this.

So as long as the American people recognize a criminal corporation in Washington D.C. as having jurisdiction over them — *and they do not stand up and say otherwise* — our military's hands are somewhat tied. They have been taking orders from a fake Commander in Chief.

As far as the financial people are concerned, they will never bring forth the money that's been intended for this country these many years, until Washington is cleaned out, because if they did it would disappear down the black hole of theft almost immediately.

If the military are to once again take their orders from we the people, we have to be ready with a list of what we require it to do.

As pointed out above, this is temporary, and what gives the people the power and the authority and the standing to do this is simply that a majority of states filed the same paperwork that Pennsylvania filed, putting the world on Notice that they have gone back under their *de jur* Constitution.

They have reclaimed the Articles of Confederation which have never been rescinded.

The Declaration of Independence and the Articles of Confederation and the Bill of Rights are the basis of our freedom.

These arrests will mean the removal of the final obstacles that will allow for the implementation of the *new abundance systems* that are ready to free humanity from the current economy and its falsely imposed conditions of poverty and debt.

There are many men and women dedicated to this cause who have been working diligently in secret for years to bring us to this moment, who are eager to present to humanity the New System that will redistribute abundance to all, and release humanity from the mundane life it has known in the past.

Freedom is being returned to the people.

The release of withheld technologies and other suppressed elements will follow to assist this transition.

The news of these mass arrests will come sudden and come hard, and many who are unprepared with an understanding as to why, may feel shocked and confused to see so many people taken into custody.

Those people, however, have served to perpetuate our enslavement, and all have actively taken part in serious crimes against the people of the world.

Certain big media groups have agreed to cover these events and assist in the disclosure timeline.

These arrests will be televised and fully shared with you, for it is owed to the people of the world that they witness the very moments and actions taken that will mean their's and our release from the control of these people who have for so long worked to exploit and control humanity.

This manipulation will end and all humanity will enter into a new way of life.

True freedom is to be soon returned to you.


This is the link to a video posted on the Internet titled, *"MAKE THIS VIRAL! Freedom Reigns - Mass Arrests for the Cabal."*
http://tinyurl.com/7carxb7

# POINT OF ORDER

This writer became part of the RuSA movement during the latter part of 2010.

RuSA stands for the recently established *"Republic for the united States of America."* RuSA is a mirror government allegedly set up to operate parallel to the UNITED STATES OF AMERICA, INC., a for-profit corporation established in 1871, after the Civil War.

Upon realizing that a parallel government was not the lawful way to go, this writer and his many friends in the *Maine Assembly free State* withdrew their memberships from RuSA, and associated themselves with — *for want of better words* — the *"Nation-States Movement" (NSM)* that is the focus of this book.

In this *"Nation-States Movement"* there is no leader. There is no membership roster; — only an email list. And there is no parallel government parallel to the for-profit Corporation called the UNITED STATES.

The *"Nation-States Movement"* is comprised of any grass-roots, red blooded American who will stand up to the Fascist Government we are facing in America today, and say:

"No more!"

"I Object! We're not going to take it any more!"

"We Quit! And You're fired as of Now!"

## CONTENTS

| | | |
|---|---|---|
| 01 | Attention! DeJure Government is Restored!!! | 13 |
| 02 | The Restore America Plan | 15 |
| 03 | Deconstructing the sovereign United States: Is This Security? | 17 |
| 04 | New Educational Book Now Available | 19 |
| 05 | World Gripped By Anti-Government Riots; America Next? | 21 |
| 07 | Anti-Government Group Members Arrested For Money Laundering | 23 |
| 08 | Important Misunderstanding Clarified | 25 |
| 09 | Landmark Case To Stymie Legal System | 27 |
| 10 | First National Bank of Montgomery vs. Jerome Daly | 29 |
| 11 | The White Horse Prophecy | 31 |
| 12 | The Bigger Picture: Iraqi Dinar | 33 |
| 13 | Another Step Closer To a One World Religion | 35 |
| 14 | Acceptance For Value (A4V) VIA The IRS | 37 |
| 15 | Lyndon LaRouche Speaks Out | 39 |
| 16 | Geert Wilders Speaks Out | 45 |
| 17 | The United States Is A British Corporation | 47 |
| 18 | Rise of the 'Supertrees' [Money Talks] | 51 |
| 19 | Inflation, Interest & Taxation | 53 |
| 20 | Festo Launches SmartBird Robotic Seagull! | 55 |
| 21 | After Moving In For $16 He's Ready To Share Info | 57 |
| 22 | Republic Telephone Call - July 20, 2011 | 59 |
| 23 | Ground-breaking Supreme Court Ruling - July 16, 2011 | 63 |
| 24 | Benjamin Fulford on American Freedom Radio | 65 |
| 26 | Benjamin Fulford's Report | 69 |
| 27 | Emerging movement encourages Sheriffs to act as shield against federal tyranny | 71 |
| 28 | Open Letter To Benjamin Fulford & His Responses (questions on all our lips) | 73 |
| 29 | Ron Paul Is Secretly Taking Over The GOP — And It's Driving People Insane | 75 |
| 30 | A March Deadline Has Been Delivered To The Committee of 300 By The Illuminati Faction | 77 |
| 31 | The Countdown Has Begun | 79 |
| 32 | Geithner Gets a Subpoena: the fun will soon begin | 83 |
| 33 | What If...? (Judge Napolitano speaks) | 85 |
| 34 | U.S. Treasury Secretary arrested, questioned, and released | 87 |

| | | |
|---|---|---|
| 35 | MP means MicroPrint signature line | 89 |
| 36 | The Hunt is on, Cabal arrests accelerating | 91 |
| 37 | American Status Today | 93 |
| 38 | It is time to storm the Bastille, vive la Revolution | 95 |
| 39 | Mass Arrests of 10,000 Global Cabal Members | 97 |
| 40 | Rival Emperor stakes claim to Japanese throne, shows evidence he is the real deal | 99 |
| 41 | Warning! Major Changes ahead... | 101 |
| 42 | Over 200 senior bankers arrested last week as new banking system goes on line | 103 |
| 43 | National Emergency Committee Announcement Benjamin Fulford with Alexander Romanov and Chodoin Daikaku | 105 |
| 44 | A keen-Message for 'today' | 107 |
| 45 | More information about Drake | 111 |
| 46 | 'The Hunger Games' movie review | 113 |
| 47 | Japan's government formally agrees to set up 1000 trillion yen fund...geopolitical ramifications | 117 |
| 48 | The Pentagon wants this information to go viral | 119 |
| 49 | More information about Drake | 123 |
| 50 | The Bible... the story of our journey through the plane of duality... draws to a close | 125 |
| 51 | The Resurrection signifies humanity's awakening from the illusion | 131 |
| 52 | Obama Orders Press Blackout After US Credit Rating Cut | 133 |
| 53 | Sheriffs Bushwhacked | 135 |
| 54 | Update from "Drake" | 137 |
| 55 | A 'Teri Hinkle' Tough Talk | 139 |
| 56 | Bernanke and Geithner are still trying to cash bad checks | 141 |
| 57 | Epic Paradigm Shift Poised to Unfold Within US and World Imminently | 143 |
| 58 | What if the Government rejects the United States Constitution? | 147 |
| 59 | God is in the Details | 149 |
| 60 | <u>Major Event</u>: Liens Filed against all 12 Federal Reserve Banks | 151 |
| 61 | <u>Notice</u> to the world was delivered to the Office of Private International Law at the Hague! | 153 |
| | Freedom's Key | 157 |
| | The Declaration of Independence | 159 |

# Maine Republic Email Alert

No.1

"... that I should bear witness unto the truth." — John 18:33 // David E. Robinson, Publisher

"... if the trumpet give an uncertain sound, who shall prepare himself for battle?" — I Corinthians 14:8

## Attention! DeJure Government is Restored!!!

**The reinhabited <u>Republic for the united States of America</u> has been Restored circa 1791 per Constitutional Law.**

Conservative; Pro-small government; Securing our borders; Peace-loving; Honorable; Non-Confrontational; Non-Violent; Children Loving; Pro-Liberty; Pro-Freedom; Pro-Justice; Patriotic; Tax Paying; Hard-Working; God-Worshiping; Seekers of the Truth.

The year 1776 marked America's victory in the war for independence. The lawful right to "reinhabit" the Republic is inherent in The Declaration of Independence, circa 1776.

"To the Republic for which it stands... One Nation Under God."

The Declaration, one of our founding documents, declares our right to change, alter, or abolish any system of government that we believe is contrary to the safety and security of the American people.

In concern for all of humanity, "We the People" reinhabited our lawful *de jure* ("by right of legal establishment") government on March 30, 2010, by serving notice on the *de facto* Corporation known as the "UNITED STATES".

A lawful grand jury in each of the fifty Republics has created a new **Declaration of Independence** which was lawfully served on the corporate UNITED STATES informing them that the original *de jure* government of the Republic has been restored. We have claimed our right to exist as a free and independent People on our land, thus exercising our **God-given unalienable rights** as defined in our Constitution and the Bill of Rights.

On July 21, 2010, "We the People" of the *de jure* government, proclaimed our **"Declaration of Sovereignty for the Republic for the united States of America"** to The Hague (a.k.a. The International Court of Justice), the Universal Postal Union (UPU), and the United Nations (UN).

On September 23, 2010, the first Session of Congress was convened by the united free Republics of the reinhabited united States of America, and the seating of the Executive, Legislative and Judicial branches of the Republic government were successfully established.

This was completed by more than the required two-thirds majority vote of "We the People" on the land of the independent Republics.

Delegates from more than 42 free Republics (States) attended, and officers for all three branches of our government, having been officially sworn into office, lawfully electing interim President James Timothy Turner and interim Vice President Charles Eugene Wright, along with other cabinet members with a presiding majority vote of 94% approval.

Thus, the Republic Government is officially reinhabited and staffed for the first time since 1868 by the free will of "We the People".

**The *de facto* UNITED STATES CORPORATION** was unlawfully established by the 41st Congress in 1871 by deceptive means and without the proper consent of "We the People".

The American People were placed under involuntary servitude by a "legal" but not "lawful" system of laws that have continually violated **The "Constitution for the united States of America", "the Bill of Rights" and the "Declaration of Independence".**

The Corporate constitution was changed from the original form wherein Anti-bellam Amendments were unlawfully added and removed without the People's consent.

Our plan is to rebuild our economy and support other economies around the world, fulfilling humanitarian needs.

We will allow our military to withdraw from unnecessary conflicts around the world and promote world prosperity and peace.

We intend to follow the Creator-God's command to feed the hungry, clothe the naked, and care for the sick, irrespective of creed, religion or race.

Against such there is no law!

Office of The Maine free State, 3 Linnell Circle, Brunswick, Maine 04011

# Maine Republic Email Alert

*No.2*

"... that I should bear witness unto the truth." — John 18:33 // David E. Robinson, Publisher

"... if the trumpet give an uncertain sound, who shall prepare himself for battle?" — I Corinthians 14:8

## The Restore America Plan

The functional aspect and intent of the "Restore America Plan" was that in order to occupy the Republic a minimum level of individuals within a certain structure and context had to come together in every state.

The vehicle and focus of this was a de jure Grand Jury. De jure means: of law; based on law.

The corporate UNITED STATES is a de facto entity; it's of fact and operates factually but it's not lawful. It is not based on the original basis of law that was established by the foundational documents of this country.

The de jure Grand Jury is the 4th Branch of government. It is of, by and for the people. It is the ultimate authority. It is the highest form of law in this country in this forum. The other forms of government are constituted by the Constitutions, both state and federal, to be the servants of the people.

The people reserve their capacity and their authority, which is absolute, to hold and institute their law and the Grand Jury. The de jure of law Grand Jury is the body of the people, no matter how small in number, that were required to come together in each of the states to re-inhabit and reform the Republic. That number was minimally 27 individuals for each state, with 8 each alternative, making 35 individuals per state.

So by the end of March, 2010, all 50 states had properly formed the Grand Jury. Each individual signed an oath, which was put together and documented properly, to evidence the coming together and re-inhabiting of each of the State Republics.

When this was accomplished, by late March, the individuals who were leading the process then put together presentments which were presented, on March 29, 30, and 31 to all of the state governors of the corporate UNITED STATES, who were given 72 hours (3 days) to come in to and swear an oath to the de jure body of the restored Republic.

For the next 5 days, or so, there was actual public recognition of this in the media — TV News, CNN, Fox News, etc. — of this going on. Of course it was spun in the negative, as they always will do.

Other things occurred to try and demonize it, but it never got any traction on that basis, because it was all done properly and lawfully.

Quite a number of the people who took part in this were actually visited by the FBI; they were interviewed, and, in most cases, perhaps in all cases, those FBI agents actually left those interviews more enlightened than they were before.

Since that time, as this process has matured over the past months, more and more awareness within those entities and agencies, including the CIA, the NSA, and the FBI, has increased. So there is nothing untoward in terms of any legal background ramifications for what we are doing and have done. And why is that? Because we're doing it based on, and within the context of the law, the original structure of how this country was established.

In CONGRESS, July 4, 1776.
The unanimous Declaration of the thirteen united States of America
[in part]

"When in the Course of human events it becomes necessary for one people to dissolve the political bands which have connected them with another and to assume among the powers of the earth, the separate and equal station to which the Laws of Nature and of Nature's God entitle them, a decent respect to the opinions of mankind requires that they should declare the causes which impel them to the separation.

We hold these truths to be self-evident, that all men are created equal, that they are endowed by their Creator with certain unalienable Rights, that among these are Life, Liberty and the pursuit of Happiness. — That to secure these rights, Governments are instituted among Men, deriving their just powers from the consent of the governed. — That whenever any Form of Government becomes destructive of these ends, it is the Right of the People to alter or to abolish it, and to institute new Government, laying its foundation on such principles and organizing its powers in such form, as to them shall seem most likely to effect their Safety and Happiness. Prudence, indeed, will dictate that Governments long established should not be changed for light and transient causes; and accordingly all experience hath shewn that mankind are more disposed to suffer, while evils are sufferable than to right themselves by abolishing the forms to which they are accustomed. But when a long train of abuses and usurpations, pursuing invariably the same Object evinces a design to reduce them under absolute Despotism, it is their right, it is their duty, to throw off such Government, and to provide new Guards for their future security. — Such has been the patient sufferance of these Colonies; and such is now the necessity which constrains them to alter their former Systems of Government."

We have suffered long and we have abundantly enumerated the reasons by we are doing what we are doing.

We don't seek to change or overthrow the existing corporate de facto government. We are neutral to that government. We are at peace with that government and we operate as neutral and non-belligerent and at peace. That's important, both legally, morally, and lawfully, and all the rest.

We make that clear in everything we do. We are simply re-inhabiting that original form that never went away. We are reoccupying that Mansion in all 50 of its rooms and we are re-institution a structure that is recognized worldwide as a lawful and properly seated government.

# Maine Republic Email Alert

No. 3

*". . . that I should bear witness unto the truth." — John 18:33 // David E. Robinson, Publisher*

*". . . if the trumpet give an uncertain sound, who shall prepare himself for battle?" — I Corinthians 14:8*

## Deconstructing the sovereign United States: Is This Security?

*"While we allowed ourselves to be pre-occupied and entertained, while we became lazy and apathetic and allowed ourselves to be drawn into fictional political divides, our own government divided our country up, sold us off and are on the verge of the final coup' which will render us without land, freedom, wealth or country; or at the very least a country to call our own. "*

National security; this term has come to mean the terrorizing of legal US citizens by our own government. Any one or all of several spy agencies supposedly existing to protect us from terrorists, have made it evident that, "we the people" are the focus of their efforts. When speaking of national security I believe it is imperative to understand what that term in reality means:

National security is the protection of the corporate federal government, and by extension multi-national corporations that benefit from their unfettered access to the government, from the people of the (50) sovereign but united states. We the people are viewed as the greatest threat to a malevolent government and its partnering corporations and the expansion of what is becoming a full blown police state. The security the government desires is not from foreign terrorists, but rather, from us.

By now, any hopes any of us had that Obama was going to turn the tide, make things better for the country, or, that he would reverse the egregious laws passed by the neo-cons and executive orders issued by Bush the Dolt, have dissipated. Not only has Obama not undone the damage, he has carried it forward and continues the programs and plans unlawfully put in place by the previous administration and started a few of his own. We are in the end phase of a twenty year cycle of systematic deconstruction of the united States.

Laying the groundwork for programs to come was of course, the Bush 1 **Executive Order of 1992, #12803**. This executive order put the infrastructure of the states up for sale to anyone and everyone and began the wholesale selling off of our lands and structures to non-US interests.

While we are threatened continually with another possible 9/11 attack if we don't accept the assaults on our liberty perpetrated by our own government under the pretense of national security, our southern border remains unsecured allowing millions to enter the country at will. At the same time and since 1990 with the creation of **free trade zones**, now also being called what they trutly are, **foreign trade zones** (FTZ's), what can only be estimated at hundreds of thousands if not millions, of foreign nationals are transplanted into the US under the EB-5 visa program.

Quietly, out of sight of most of the public, the deconstruction of the sovereign United States is underway. Already at work was the **Security &** **Prosperity Partnership** begun by Bush which creates the **North American Union** and obliterates our borders with Canada and Mexico for the free movement of goods and people (referred to as "human capital") to benefit corporate business. It is this agreement that stands in the way of our southern border being secured. The **S&PP** is still rolling on out of the public's eye as working groups continue planning the evisceration of the US for corporate interests

Prior to the creation of S&PP was the **"Enterprise for the America's"** established in 1990 by George HW Bush which created the now prolific and pervasive **"Foreign/Free Trade Zones"** (FTZ's) that exist right here in virtually every state of the US. While these zones must obey local and state laws **special permission** must obtained and a request for entry into the FTZ has to be initiated in the event of any investigation. These can of course be denied by questioning jurisdictional authority as the FTZ has essentially been redefined and protected as foreign sovereign territory.

To accommodate these zones, **trans-model transportation centers** are being constructed at airports across the country. Billed as to centralize services, these airports also include taxi, bus, train and trucking and warehousing and manufacturing centers.

They also include something most people are not at all aware of; free trade zones **where the unemployed from other countries are ferried into the US under EB-5 visas**. Once here under the visa, the investor and his mobile work force can move unhindered into any other free trade zone in the US.

Free trade zones and the EB-5

Office of The Maine free State, 3 Linnell Circle, Brunswick, Maine 04011

Immigrant Investor (from the .gov site)

**"Visa Description**

The fifth employment based visa preference category, created by Congress in 1990, is available to immigrants seeking to enter the United States in order to invest in a new commercial enterprise that will benefit the US economy and create at least 10 full-time jobs. There are two ways to invest which you may use within the **EB-5 category** and they are: creating a new commercial enterprise or investing in a troubled business."

Purpose of **International Free Trade Zones** (as explained by Economy Watch.

The main idea behind creation of free trade zones is to facilitate cross-border trade by removing obstacles imposed by customs regulations.

Note: Translated this means that all the egregious rules, regulations, laws, statutes having passed or been implemented through the **unlawful "rulemaking"** by corporate federal agencies, and corrupt congresses do not apply to these zones. The obstacles referred to are environmental concerns, labor standards, business taxes, wage taxes and inspection of goods to determine their safety. You know….all those pesky things that a responsible business owner adheres to.

Free trade zones ensure faster turnaround of planes and ships by **lowering custom related formalities.** FTZs prove to be beneficial both for the importers and exporters, as these zones are designed to reduce labor cost and tax related expenditures.

Note: This means products from countries such as, but not limited to, China, notorious for its contaminated food products, can now be dumped into the US without going through the customs process. This also means that China can manufacture and produce here and ship its goods to other countries without paying duties, customs, fair wages, withholding taxes or any inspection of its notoriously shoddy and dangerous products.

This is a free pass zone. Few regulations, lowered standards, no customs inspections, tax "incentives", and they can fly in their own workforce to work for slave labor wages. **They only have to hire 10 American workers while importing thousands of impoverished Chinese** (or workers from any other country) **into the country sidestepping more stringent immigration laws and provisions for citizenship.**

Free trade zones help the traders to utilize the available business opportunities in the best possible way. FTZs promote export-oriented industries. These zones also help to increase foreign exchange earnings. Employ-ment opportunities created by free trade zones help to reduce unemployment problems in **the less developed economies.**

Note: The "less developed economies" and the reduction of unemployment in those economies is accomplished by importing their unemployed here. These FTZ's do not pay income, FICA, unemployment or any other tax. The employment opportunities mentioned do NOT have to be American workers. The foreign investor is required to hire only 10 American workers to meet guidelines. The remainder can be Chinese workers for instance, flown in to the FTZ's and housed there until they are moved quietly out into the surrounding communities and protected and given US citizenship through the use of the EB-5 visa.

None of the usual customs inspections, duties or fees will apply to the manufactured products leaving the FTZ unless those products are coming into the US markets. Products coming out of the free trade zones (sovereign foreign territory) and going out of the US to foreign markets are exempted from taxation, customs and inspections.

So what are the US areas targeted for these "no accountability" zones called FTZ's?

Turns out they are **rural areas for the most part.** At least now we know what they intend to do with all the agricultural land they are stealing. Or they will be focused on areas struck particularly hard with economic down turns and unemployment which encompasses virtually every part of the country.

**SUMMARY**

Since 1990 as a result of **Executive order #12803** selling off our infra-structure, and the **Enterprise for the America's** establishing the free trade zones, then the subsequent free trade agreements passed in the interim which are not lawful US treaties and, the creation of the **Security & Prosperity partnership** enacted by Bush 2, we have been sold off, parceled out and deprived of the ownership and control of what was once our country.

We allow ourselves to be assaulted by agents of the government who claim they are invading our privacy, our persons, our lives because it is the only way they can keep us safe. **These invasions have nothing to do with our safety or security, but rather, are the means by which the government protects itself from us.**

Those who believe the government is only trying to keep us safe, are fools. While we are harrassed, terrorized, assaulted and suffer the loss of our freedom at the hands of government sponsored agencies and agents, the unchecked flood of illegal immigrants and the transport of foreign nationals into the country goes on unabated. Eventually they will outnumber the legal US citizen.

**This is globalism.** This is the global economic model that has destroyed one country after another driving the populations into poverty while a select few at the top robbed the wealth and by extension, the viability of nations.

While we allowed ourselves to be pre-occupied and entertained, while we became lazy and apathetic and allowed ourselves to be drawn into fictional political divides, our own government divided our country up, sold us off and are on the verge of the final coup' which will render us without land, freedom, wealth or country; or at the very least a country to call our own.

# Maine Republic Email Alert

No. 4

"... that I should bear witness unto the truth." — John 18:33 // David E. Robinson, Publisher

"... if the trumpet give an uncertain sound, who shall prepare himself for battle?" — I Corinthians 14:8

## New Educational Book Now Available

The **Republic for the united States of America** (c.1791) has been reinhabited and restored per Constitutional Law.

Conservative; Pro-Smaller Government; Pro-Securing Our Borders; Peace Loving; Honorable; Non-Confrontational; Non-Violent; Children Loving; Pro-Liberty; Pro-Freedom; Pro-Justice; Patriotic; God Worship-ing; Hard Working; Tax Paying; Truth Seeking.

The year 1776 marked America's victory in the war for independence. The lawful right to "reinhabit" the Republic is inherent in The Declaration of Independence, circa 1776.

The Declaration, one of our founding documents, declares our right to change, alter, or abolish any system of government that we believe is contrary to the safety and security of the American people.

In concern for all of humanity, "We the People" reinhabited our lawful *de jure* ("by right of legal establishment") government on March 30, 2010, by serving notice on the de facto corporation, known as the corporate "UNITED STATES".

A lawful grand jury in each of the fifty republics has created a new Declaration of Independence which was lawfully served on the corporate UNITED STATES informing them that the original *de jure* government of the Republic has been restored. We have claimed our right to exist as a free and independent people on our land, thus exercising our God-given unalienable rights as defined in our Constitution and the Bill of Rights.

On July 21, 2010, "We the People" of the *de jure* government, proclaimed worldwide our "Declaration of Sovereignty for the Republic for the united States of America" to The Hague (a.k.a. the

### Manual of the United States Republic

International Court of Justice), the Universal Postal Union (UPU), and the United Nations (UN).

On September 23, 2010, the first session of Congress was convened by the united free Republics of the re-inhabited united States of America, and the seating of the Executive, Legislative and Judicial branches of the Republic government were successfully established.

This was completed by more than the required two-thirds majority vote of "We the People" on the land of the independent Republics.

Delegates from more than 42 free Republics (States) attended, and officers for all three branches of our government have been officially sworn into office, lawfully electing interim President James Timothy Turner and interim Vice President Charles Eugene Wright, along with other established cabinet members with a presiding majority vote of 94% approval.

Thus, the Republic government is officially re-inhabited and staffed for the first time since 1868 by the will of "We the People".

The de facto UNITED STATES CORPORATION was unlawfully established by the 41st Congress in 1871 by deceptive means and without proper consent from "We the People".

The American people were placed under involuntary servitude by a "legal" system of laws that have continually violated the "Constitution for the united States of America", "the Bill of Rights" and the "Declaration of Independence".

The corporate constitution was

changed from the original form, wherein Amendments were unlawfully added and removed without the people's consent.

Since 1871, the abuses of this corporation upon both the international community as well as the American people are inestimable and unconscionable. De facto Congress has repeatedly violated their Oaths of Office, fiduciary responsibilities, and in many cases, committed treasonous acts against "We the People" of the united States of America and the world.

We humbly come forward apologizing for the numerous atrocities we have unknowingly allowed the U.S. CORPORATION to carry out upon the international community. It is our mission to establish the American image of truth, honesty, integrity and honor around the world.

Our plan is to rebuild our economy and support other economies around the world, fulfilling humanitarian needs. We will allow our military to withdraw from unnecessary conflicts around the world and promote world prosperity and peace. We intend to follow the Creator God's command to feed the hungry, clothe the naked, and care for the sick, irrespective of creed, religion or race. There is no law against these things.

We are calling on the support of all Nations around the world to help us end the tyranny that has been perpetrated by the unlawful actions of the UNITED STATES corporate government. We shall achieve this goal PEACEFULLY AND LAWFULLY, with boldness, integrity and truth, so help us God.

The Republic of the united States
http://republicoftheunitedstates.org/

The 50 Great Seals of the free States
http://tinyurl.com/6jnx3yc

The Maine Republic Free State
http://maine-republic-free-state.ning.com/

# Maine Republic Email Alert

No. 5

*". . . that I should bear witness unto the truth."* — John 18:33 // David E. Robinson, Publisher

*". . . if the trumpet give an uncertain sound, who shall prepare himself for battle?"* — I Corinthians 14:8

## World Gripped By Anti-Government Riots; America Next?

**Global unrest causing spiraling food prices as regimes are toppled.**

The planet is in a never-ending cycle of anti-government revolt as riots that plagued Europe last year now spread like wildfire through the Middle East and beyond, threatening to accelerate bloody clashes and force the hand of authorities as the risk of a new Tiananmen Square-style massacre grows ever likelier. Is America next in line to experience unrest that has touched almost every corner of the globe?

Predictions three years ago, were based on UN documents, which were made six months before the collapse of Lehman brothers, that the world would be hit by massive food riots and anti-government unrest in the aftermath of an economic collapse, is now unfolding at an astonishing pace.

The latest countries to be enveloped by the chaos are Tunisia, Egypt, and now Yemen, whose population are demanding the ouster of 30-year President Ali Abdullah Saleh in a protest against poverty and lack of political freedom.

The unrest in Yemen was inspired by a popular uprising in Tunisia earlier this month that led to the ejection of President Zine al-Abidine Ben Ali, figurehead of a government accused of abusing their power to enrich themselves while the poverty gripped the rest of the country. Ben Ali was forced to flee the country and the interim government has now issued an international arrest warrant for the President and his wife.

Riots in Tunisia were quickly followed by mass protests in Egypt demanding an end to President Mubarek's regime. Four people have died as demonstrators

engaged in violent clashes with police and set fire to government buildings.

Besides America there has barely been an area of the globe that hasn't been hit by riots and unrest in the last six months, as the fallout from the economic collapse begins to be felt amongst the victims of the financial terrorists that launched an assault characterized by falling wages, high unemployment, spiraling inflation and food prices as well as crippling austerity cuts.

The cost of staples like wheat, corn and soybeans is going through the roof as countries increasingly rely on imports from the U.S. to offset the impact of global unrest.

"In emerging markets, it's leading to rising inflation, to reduction in disposable income, it's leading to riots, demonstrations and political instability," New York University economist Nouriel Roubini said in an interview in Davos, Switzerland, today with Tom Keene on Bloomberg Television's "The Pulse." "It's really something that can topple regimes, as we have seen in the Middle East."

Back in early 2008, before the collapse of Lehman Brothers and the start of the financial crisis, we warned that inflation and economic uncertainty would cause inflation to skyrocket and food prices to explode, which would lead to riots globally.

In June of last year, shortly before mass unrest hit Europe in countries like France, Italy and the United Kingdom, we forecast that, "The imminent onset of so-called austerity measures, which in reality represent nothing more than an elevated phase of government-run looting of the taxpayer, would herald an "age of rage," leading to "riots and even revolutions as people react with fury in response to their jobs, savings, basic public services, pensions and welfare money being seized by the financial terrorists who caused the economic collapse in the first place."

That "age of rage" is now playing out across the planet, with governments being toppled left, right and center as economic turmoil forces desperate people to revolt in a bid to rescue any kind of decent living standard.

We didn't have the privilege of a crystal ball when we made these predictions, we were merely reading what globalist bodies and the elite themselves were saying would be the consequences of their agenda to eviscerate any kind of middle class and re-impose an archaic caste system of haves and have nots.

The only question left to be answered is if and when similar scenes will unfold on the streets of America, as notoriously accurate trend forecaster Gerald Celente warned would happen several years ago. Celente put the time frame on "tax rebellions and food riots" sweeping the US by 2012.

With even the likes of Time Magazine seriously entertaining the probability of social dislocation as a backlash to the

Office of The Maine free State, 3 Linnell Circle, Brunswick, Maine 04011

crumbling economy leading to "civil war" in the United States, as we stand on the precipice of bedlam.

In November 2008, right as the economic implosion was unraveling, the U.S. Army War College released a white paper called Known Unknowns: Unconventional 'Strategic Shocks' in Defense Strategy Development. The report warned that the military must be prepared for a "violent, strategic dislocation inside the United States," which could be provoked by "unforeseen economic collapse," "purposeful domestic resistance," "pervasive public health emergencies" or "loss of functioning political and legal order." The "widespread civil violence," the document said, "would force the defense establishment to reorient priorities in extremis to defend basic domestic order and human security."

A British Ministry of Defence report struck a similar tone when it predicted that within 30 years, the growing gap between the super rich and the middle class, along with an urban underclass threatening social order would mean, "The world's middle classes might unite, using access to knowledge, resources and skills to shape transnational processes in their own class interest," and that, "The middle classes could become a revolutionary class."

If the violent scenes we now witness unfolding across the planet are anything to go by, we won't have to wait too long to find out whether or not the United States will become engulfed in the crisis, or whether the global elite will move to prevent such a scenario by coming to the realization that their war on the middle class and the poor threatens to provoke a reaction that even they may be unprepared to deal with.e

# Maine Republic Email Alert

No. 7

"... that I should bear witness unto the truth." — John 18:33 // David E. Robinson, Publisher

"... if the trumpet give an uncertain sound, who shall prepare himself for battle?" — I Corinthians 14:8

## Anti-Government Group Members Arrested For Money Laundering

By Mary Manning
Published Friday, March 6, 2009 | 3:51 p.m. Updated Friday, March 6, 2009 | 5:28 p.m.

**Sun coverage**
Four arrested in Las Vegas on federal charges (3-5-09)

Four members of an anti-government movement, known as the "Sovereign Movement," have been arrested after a three-year investigation by the Nevada Joint Terrorism Task Force on allegations of money laundering, tax evasion and possessing unregistered machine guns.

The four men were arrested Thursday in the Las Vegas area, said Greg Brower, U.S. Attorney for Nevada.

Samuel Davis, 54, of Council, Idaho; Shawn Rice, 46, of Seligman, Ariz.; Harold Call, 67, of Las Vegas; and Jan Lindsey, 66, of Henderson, were taken into custody, Brower said.

Davis and Rice are charged in a federal indictment with one count of conspiracy to commit money laundering and 30 counts of money laundering. If convicted, they face up to 20 years in prison and a $500,000 fine on each count.

Call is charged in a federal indictment with two counts of possession and transfer of a machine gun and three counts of possession of an unregistered machine gun. If convicted, Call faces up to 10 years in prison and a $250,000 fine on each count.

Undercover agents working for the FBI infiltrated the anti-government group, which often met at a Denny's restaurant at Fremont Street and Boulder Highway, and for $750 purchased parts from Call to turn guns into machine guns, the search warrants said.

Call in one phone conversation said he phoned the IRS to see whether his account had been credited. He said that after asking a woman IRS four times for his account balance, Call learned the IRS had not credited his account. In the phone call with the undercover FBI agent, Call said, "Every time I talk to the IRS, I just want to go kill somebody."

In addition to the STEN machine gun, the task force seized a mill and other equipment that allowed Call to transform weapons into machine guns and he demonstrated an AR-15 rifle he had converted to allow for fully automatic firing.

Lindsey is charged in a federal indictment with one count of evasion of payment of tax and four counts of tax evasion. If convicted, Lindsey faces up to five years in prison and a $250,000 fine on each count.

The indictments were returned by a federal grand jury Tuesday and unsealed on Thursday. The defendants were to appear before U.S. Magistrate Judge Lawrence R. Leavitt on Friday.

From March 2008 through the date of the indictment, Davis and Rice allegedly laundered about $1.3 million for FBI undercover agents, court records show. Davis and Rice were told by the undercover agents that the monies were proceeds of a bank fraud scheme, specifically from the theft and forgery of stolen official bank checks.

Davis and Rice laundered the money through a nominee trust account controlled by Davis and through an account of a purported religious organization controlled by Rice. The men took about $74,000 and $22,000, respectively, in fees for their money laundering services before handing the rest of the funds to the undercover FBI agents.

Davis is allegedly a national leader of the anti-government movement, traveling nationwide to teach different theories and ideologies of the movement, court records said. Rice allegedly claims that he is a lawyer and Rabbi, and uses his law school education and businesses to promote his sovereign ideas and to gain credibility in the community.

Call allegedly possessed and transferred an "auto sear" or "lightning link," a combination of firearm parts designed to convert a weapon from a single-shot manual one to automatic use, on Sept. 11, 2008, and Jan. 20, 2009, the court records said. Call allegedly possessed a STEN machine gun on Oct. 9, 2008, which was not registered to him in the National Firearms Registration and Transfer Record.

Lindsey is a retired FBI agent. He and Call are leaders of the Nevada Lawmen Group for Public Awareness, a group that is associated with the sovereign movement.

Lindsey allegedly failed to timely file or pay federal income tax for the years 1999 through 2006, and committed various acts designed to hide his income and assets from the IRS, including filing false tax returns, making false statements to the IRS, placing funds and property in the names of nominees, using fake negotiable instruments to attempt to pay his taxes and filing false documents with the IRS and Clark County.

In a detailed search warrant unsealed Friday, authorities said Lindsey underwent and passed a background investigation in 2000 for his work conducting FBI background checks, but in 2005 he revealed he had not filed his income taxes. The FBI's Security Division determined he was a security risk and did not grant him clearances.

The search warrant said Lindsey owes the IRS $333,397.78 for unpaid taxes from 1999 to 2002.

On May 7, 2008, Lindsey filed a false tax form for 2000 saying his wife earned $13,638.33 from Azurix and $7,249.77 from Enron, when IRS wage records show she earned $169,109 and $174,142, respectively, from the two companies.

Unsealed search warrant affidavits allege that Rice, Davis, Lindsey and Call are heavily involved in the "Sovereign Movement," an extreme anti-government organization whose members attempt to disrupt and overthrow government and other forms of authority by using "paper terrorist" tactics, intimidation, harassment and violence, court records said.

Members of the group believe they do not have to pay taxes and believe the federal government deceived Americans into obtaining Social Security cards, drivers' licenses, car registrations and wedding licenses, among other official records. The group believes that if these contracts are revoked, persons are "sovereign citizens."

Members of this group also believe that U.S. currency is invalid. They widely use fictitious financial instruments, such as fake money orders, personal checks and sight drafts, and participate in "redemption" schemes where the false financial documents are used to pay creditors.

The FBI-led Nevada Joint Terrorism Task Force includes the Alcohol, Tobacco, Firearms and Explosives, Henderson Police Department, IRS Criminal Investigation, Metro Police, the Nevada Department of Public Safety and the North Las Vegas Police Department in addition to other federal, state and local law enforcement agencies in Nevada, Council, Idaho, and Flagstaff and Seligman, Ariz.

# The Maine free State - email alert  No.008

*". . . that I should bear witness unto the truth."* — John 18:33 // David E. Robinson, Publisher

*". . . if the trumpet give an uncertain sound, who shall prepare himself for battle?"* — I Corinthians 14:8

## Important Misunderstanding Clarified

**CORPORATE/COMMERCIAL/ PUBLIC LAW VS. CONSTITUTION-AL/ COMMON/PUBLIC LAW**

Many aware Americans mistakenly believe that the UNITED STATES CORPORATION operates under Corporate/Commercial/Public Law rather than Constitutional/Common/Private Law.

This is a common misunderstanding; whereas neither operation is correct.

Actually . . .

The UNITED STATES CORPORATION operates under private Corporate Law rather than public Common Law.

Corporate Law is Private.
Common Law is Public.

We do not have to obey The McDonalds-Corporation's *private* corporate laws, regulations and rules.

From the standpoint of the de jure Republic, corporate law is *private* law.

**RE: COMMERCIAL LAW**

Commercial Law is neutral with respect to the CORPORATION and the Republic.

Commercial Law relates to commercial transactions which are common to both the CORPORATION and the Republic.

*"The underlying purpose of commercial law is to simplify and modernize the law governing commercial transactions."* (UCC, Article I, Section 1-102(2)a).

Commercial transactions are common to both the CORPORATION and the Republic.

For more, see ***Policies, Procedures & Protocols***, Chapter 4, *The Hierarchy Of Law*, pages 21-24.

Commercial Law - a derivative of Natural Law - is basic to Common Law. Next in the hierarchy of law - after common law - comes Regulatory Law - followed by Political Law, the copyrighted private policy of foreign corporations such as the UNITED STATES CORPORATION and its subdivisions, such as corporate States, Cities and Towns, etc.

**FOR EXAMPLE**

See ***Policies, Procedures & Protocols***, Chapter 3, *Courts Of Record*, pages 15-17.

"Whether the issue is large or small, — to right a wrong, or to achieve justice and reparation for damage or loss, questions have to be asked and answered and faithfully recorded in a Book of Records.

Hearsay is disregarded as off public face, i.e. Hearsay is not to be written down.

Oaths are not useful in Courts of Record. What you want to create is an ***Affidavit***. (See Maxims 5 & 6 below.)

**10 MAXIMS
of Commercial Law**

1. A workman is worthy of his hire.
2. All men are equal under the law.
3. In commerce truth is sovereign.
4. Truth is expressed in the form of an affidavit.
5. **An unrebutted affidavit stands as truth in commerce.**
6. **An unrebutted affidavit becomes judgement in commerce.**
7. A matter must be expressed to be resolved.
8. He who leaves the field of battle first loses by default.
9. Sacrifice is the measure of credibility
10. A lien or claim can be satisfied only through rebuttal by counter affidavit point by point, resolution by jury, or payment or performance of the claim.

All law is contract. Contract makes the law. ***To make a contract valid, the consent of the parties must be free, mutual, and communicated.*** Consent is not real or free when obtained through duress, menace, fraud, undue influence, or mistake.

The crucial and incurable flaw in all contracts is the absence of **full disclosure** and a true **meeting of the minds**, and **mutual good faith**. This absence constitutes fraud.

In order for a contract to be valid it must be entered into with **full disclosure**, **good faith** and **clean hands**.

**EXAMPLE TWO**

See ***Manual For The United States Republic***, Chapter 3, *Initial Proceedings*, page 13.

When Claim Documents were presented to the fifty state governors of the de facto United States, and they failed to timely respond, this gave the People of the Republic the opportunity to institute their own lawful Remedy, — ***according to commercial law***.

Office of The Maine free State, 3 Linnell Circle, Brunswick, Maine 04011

*Office of The Maine free State, 3 Linnell Circle, Brunswick, Maine 04011*

# The Maine free State - email alert   No.009

*". . . that I should bear witness unto the truth." — John 18:33 // David E. Robinson, Publisher*

*". . . if the trumpet give an uncertain sound, who shall prepare himself for battle?" — I Corinthians 14:8*

## Landmark Case To Stymie Legal System

**If everyone** began using this defense the entire legal system could be brought to its knees in a matter of weeks if not days.

John Anthony Hill, the Producer of the documentary film "7/7 Ripple Effect", was acquitted, on the 12th of May 2011, of the ridiculous and politically-motivated charge of attempting to "pervert the course of justice".

For more details about this extraordinary case and the trial itself, please visit the following links:

   http://mtrial.org
   http://jamesfetzer.blogspot.com
   http://terrorontheltube.co.uk/2011/05/12/muaddib-acquitted/

Two very important precedents were established based upon the jurisdiction and the sovereignty of Elizabeth Battenberg/Mountbatten.

The first point being that she was knowingly, and with malice afore-thought, coronated on a fake stone in 1953 and thus has never been lawfully crowned.

Elizabeth II has been pretending to be the monarch for over 58 years. In actual fact the Coronation is a binding oath and a contract, requiring the monarch's signature.

Which brings us to the second point.

At that Coronation ceremony, Elizabeth signed a binding contract, before God and the British people, that she would do her utmost to maintain The Laws of God. This she solemnly swore to do, with her hand placed on the Sovereign's Bible, before kissing The Bible and signing the oath and contract.

In The Law of God, found in the first five books of The Bible, man-made legislation is strictly prohibited.

The very first time that she gave "royal assent" to any piece of man-made legislation, she broke her solemn oath with God and with the British people, and she ceased to be the monarch with immediate effect.

To date, she has broken her oath thousands and thousands of times, which is an undeniable, iron-clad FACT. She is, therefore and without question, not the monarch, but is instead, a criminal guilty of high treason, among her other numerous crimes.

All of the courts in the U.K. are referred to as HM Courts or "Her Majesty's" Courts.

This means that every judge draws their authority from her. All cases brought by the state are "Regina vs. Xxxxxxx", which means they are all brought in the name of the queen. So if she isn't really the monarch, then she doesn't have the authority or the jurisdiction to bring a case against anyone else. And neither do any of "her majesty's" judges or courts.

Since "No man can judge in his own cause", no judge in the Commonwealth could lawfully rule on a challenge to the jurisdiction and sovereignty of the monarch.

It is a question of their own authority, so they are obviously not impartial to the outcome.

This is why the ONLY way the question of jurisdiction can lawfully and impartially be decided is by a jury.

And that is exactly why John Anthony Hill requested a jury trial to decide his challenge to the jurisdiction and sovereignty of Elizabeth II.

No judge under any circumstances can deny someone their right to request a jury trial.

No judge can lawfully rule in their own cause.

This doesn't mean they won't try, it only means that when they do, they are committing a criminal act (just as Judge Jeffrey Vincent Pegden did at John Anthony Hill's trial) and that their decision is immediate grounds for an appeal and for a citizen's arrest.

The fact that the court and its corrupt judge tried to ignore this particular point is proof that they are well aware they have no lawful authority. This is one of the reasons why this is a landmark case.

If everyone began using this defense tomorrow, in all of the Commonwealth courts and in the courts of the United States, the entire legal system could be brought to its knees in a matter of weeks if not days.

The signed E2 Coronation oath (Exhibit 1) and the Bible she swore on at that Coronation (Exhibit 2) clearly orders judges and lawyers to obey the Laws of God.

These two factual pieces of evidence ought to be presented as defense at the start of every single victimless case where someone has been wrongfully charged, and to proceed forth Lawfully.

The two pieces of evidence require the use and application of only God's Laws which demand a trial by jury, to proceed forth maintaining only God's Laws with judges roles clearly defined.

Whilst Elizabeth II is committing

*Office of The Maine free State, 3 Linnell Circle, Brunswick, Maine 04011*

treason, explained in full detail in the Lawful Argument, the signed oath orders all subjects to obediently maintain only the Laws of God.

Judges and lawyers have taken an oath (BAR), so they're ordered to comply to Exhibit 1, and Exhibit 2 (Bible), and it is as simple as that.

People were unaware of that which was in place for them to use, but we know now.

For those of us in the United States who may be thinking "hey, we aren't a Commonwealth country, why would this affect us?" you need to know that these three little letters, BAR stand for the British Accreditation Registry.

It doesn't matter whether it is the Australian BAR; or the Canadian BAR; or the American BAR association; they ALL report to the British monarch, who is the head of the BAR.

So thanks to John Anthony Hill and this amazing precedent, we now all know a peaceful way to bring the system down. If enough people ACT and use this simple, bullet-proof defense, we can put an end to the insanity and injustice of the courts.

All that is required is for YOU to spread the word to as many as possible so that this peaceful rebellion can begin right now!

Or you can watch the last remnants of your freedoms being swept away as the Global Elite plunge the entire world into bankruptcy and WW3; to usher in their "New World Order".

By now some of you may be beginning to see the Light at the end of a very dark tunnel and are so enthusiastic about putting this simple plan into motion that you may have forgotten there was a second precedent set during this landmark case.

While the official reason for this trial was to address this trumped-up and frivolous charge of attempting to "pervert the course of justice", the real reason for this trial was so the authorities could punish John Anthony Hill for making the "7/7 Ripple Effect" which, in less than an hour and using strictly mainstream media reports, completely dismantles the official government conspiracy theories, such as the London Bombings and the so-called 911 Terrorists' Attack.

The film is so credible that even the prosecution at the trial, after showing it in its entirety to the jurors, admitted that the film was made in such a way that it "changes the minds of people who see it." This is how powerful the truth really is.

This was the first time this information was shown at an official proceeding and the results were impressive. At least 83% of the jurors felt the film accurately depicted what happened in London on July 7th, 2005, and that John Anthony Hill did the right thing in presenting these facts.

For those unfamiliar with the case, JAH forwarded copies of the "7/7 Ripple Effect" to the Kingston Crown court in 2008 in the hope of correcting misleading statements made by the judge and the QC at the outset of the first trial of the supposed "7/7 helpers" (who were also found not guilty).

John Anthony Hill was also able to enter into the official record his testimony about what happened on September 11th, 2001 in the United States and that both 9/11 and 7/7 were false flag attacks.

Hill went on to show the jurors the now infamous BBC report by Jane Standley of the collapse of the Salomon Brothers building (WTC7) on 9/11/2001. She reported the collapse 25 minutes before the collapse actually occurred, and with the building clearly visible, still standing in the window behind her left shoulder, leaving no doubt that the BBC had foreknowledge of the event.

As a result of the "7/7 Ripple Effect" being shown to the jurors by the prosecution and John Anthony Hill's testimony about 9/11, the truth that those two events were false flag attacks, and that the mainstream media is nothing more than a government propaganda machine is now officially on record.

And the "Not Guilty" verdict by the jury is a ringing endorsement of that official record.

This case brings with it a New Hope and the opportunity for a new beginning, where liberty, justice, and peace aren't just nice sounding words, but a reality. This could be heaven on earth instead of the hell we have let it become by allowing all of this evil to grow up around us.

Just as John Anthony Hill has shown us by example, all it takes is a dauntless faith that good will always triumph over evil and the courage to take action to do the right thing, regardless of the personal cost.

For additional details about this bullet-proof defense, please visit: http://jahtruth.net/britmon.htm#crimes

"7/7 Ripple Effect" - in 7 Parts
http://tinyurl.com/2scg6j

*"ad Christi potentium et gloriam"*
*(for the power and glory of Christ)*

# Maine Republic Email Alert

*No. 010*

"... that I should bear witness unto the truth." — John 18:33 // David E. Robinson, Publisher

"... if the trumpet give an uncertain sound, who shall prepare himself for battle?" — I Corinthians 14:8

# First National Bank of Montgomery vs. Jerome Daly

The **First National Bank of Montgomery v. Jerome Daly** (Justice Court, Credit River Township, Scott County, Minnesota), known as the **Credit River Case,** was tried before a Justice of the Peace in Minnesota, Dec. 9, 1968. The decision in this case is sometimes cited by opponents of the United States banking system.

In that case the jury found that:

1. That the Plaintiff (meaning the Bank) is not entitled to recover the possession of Lot 19...
2. That because of *the failure of a lawful consideration* the Note and Mortgage dated May 8, 1964 are null and void.
3. That the Sheriff's sale of the above premises is null and void, and of no effect.
4. That the Plaintiff has no right title or interest in said premises of lien thereon as is above described.

**Sections 50, 51 and 52 of Am Jur 2nd** (American Jurisprudence 2nd Edition) **under "Actions"** on page 584 states that:

"**No action will lie to recover on a claim based upon, or in any manner depending upon, a fraudulent, illegal, or immoral transaction or contract to which Plaintiff was a party.**"

**No bank ever loans money.**

In it's unlawful conversion they take your promissory note and convert it into so-called "money" which the didn't tell you about, and give you your "money" (your credit) back to you, and so **there's no lawful consideration,** there's no risk, and **without any risk there's no contract.** And no contract means that all these foreclosures that are going on today in America are fraudulent, null and void.

**The trial**

Jerome Daly was the **defendant** in a civil case in Credit River Township, Scott County, Minnesota, heard on December 9, 1968.

The **plaintiff** was the First National Bank of Montgomery, *which had foreclosed on Daly's property for nonpayment of the mortgage, and was seeking to evict him from the property.*

Daly based his defense on the argument that the bank had not actually loaned him any money but had simply created credit on its books. Daly argued that *the bank had thus not given him anything of value and was not entitled to the property that secured the loan.*

The jury and the justice of the peace, Martin V. Mahoney, agreed with this argument. **The jury returned a verdict of not guilty for the defendant,** and the Justice of the Peace declared that the mortgage was "null and void" and that the bank was not entitled to possession of the property.

The Justice admitted in his order that his decision might run counter to provisions in the Minnesota Constitution and some Minnesota statutes, but *contended that such provisions were "repugnant" to the Constitution of the United States and the Bill of Rights in the Minnesota Constitution.*

**The result**

The immediate effect of the decision was that Daly did not have to repay the mortgage or relinquish the property.

However, the bank appealed the next day, and the decision was ultimately nullified on the grounds that a Justice of the Peace did not have the power to make such a ruling beyond the limits of the jurisdiction of a justice of the peace.

**The juries verdict was totally ignored !**

This nullified case and its reasoning have nevertheless been cited by groups opposing the Federal Reserve System and in particular the practice of fractional-reserve banking.

That such groups argue the case demonstrates **that the Federal Reserve System is unconstitutional.**

**Jerome Daly's disbarment and criminal conviction**

The defendant, Jerome Daly, was convicted of willfully failing to file federal income tax returns for the years 1967 and 1968. In rejecting his appeal, the United States Court of Appeals for the Eighth Circuit noted:

"That defendant's fourth contention involves his seemingly incessant attack against the federal reserve and monetary system of the United States. His apparent thesis is that the only 'Legal Tender Dollars' are those which contain a mixture of gold and silver and that only those dollars may be constitutionally taxed. This contention is clearly frivolous."

Daly had been an attorney, but was disbarred by a decision of the Minnesota Supreme Court in a case similar to the **Credit River** case involving the same justice of the peace.

# Maine Republic Email Alert

No. 011

*". . . that I should bear witness unto the truth."* — John 18:33  //  David E. Robinson, Publisher

*". . . if the trumpet give an uncertain sound, who shall prepare himself for battle?"* — I Corinthians 14:8

## The White Horse Prophecy

The **White Horse Prophecy** is a statement made in 1843 by Joseph Smith, Jr., founder of the Latter Day Saint movement, regarding the future of the Latter Day Saints (Mormons) and the United States of America.

The Latter Day Saints, according to the prophecy, would "go to the Rocky Mountains and ... be a great and mighty people", identified figuratively with the White Horse described in the Revelation of John.

The prophecy further predicts that the United States Constitution will one day "hang like a thread" and will be saved "by the efforts of the White Horse".

### Origins

Joseph Smith, Jr., first leader of the Latter Day Saints (Mormons) and purported source of the White Horse Prophecy.

Latter Day Saint movement founder Joseph Smith went to Washington D.C. seeking help for his persecuted followers but received nothing but frustration. Pat Bagley of the *Salt Lake Tribune* writes that from then on Smith and his followers "considered themselves the last Real Americans, (and) the legitimate heirs of the pilgrims and Founding Fathers", who would be called upon one day to save the U.S. Constitution. Smith responded that when the Constitution hangs by a thread, Latter Day Saint elders will step in on the proverbial white horse to save the country.

In 1844, Smith rejected the platforms of the major candidates for President of the United States and decided to conduct his own third-party campaign for the Presidency. At the time of his death on June 27 of that year, the Latter Day Saints were headquartered in Nauvoo, Illinois. Following a succession crisis in which Brigham Young was seen as Smith's successor by the majority of the Latter Day Saints, the Mormon migration to the Intermountain West began under Young's

Joseph Smith, Jr., first leader of the Latter Day Saints (Mormons) and purported source of the White Horse Prophecy.

direction in February 1846.

### Historical use

Brigham Young, who assumed the leadership of The Church of Jesus Christ of Latter-day Saints after the death of Joseph Smith.

Joseph Smith's successors attribute the phrase "hang by a thread" to him, and continue to make theological references to it. In 1855 Brigham Young reportedly wrote that "when the Constitution of the United States hangs, as it were, upon a single thread, they will have to call for the Mormon Elders to save it from utter destruction; and they will step forth and do it."

A compilation of statements of leaders' in The Church of Jesus Christ of Latter-day Saints (LDS Church) by *BYU Studies* also shows that a number of them spoke of its importance. Orson Hyde for instance, a Smith contemporary, wrote that Smith believed "the time would come when the Constitution and the country would be in danger of an overthrow", while the LDS Church's fifth presiding bishop Charles W. Nibley, stated:

"the day would come when there would be so much of disorder, of secret combinations taking the law into their own hands, tramping upon Constitutional rights and the liberties of the people, that the Constitution would hang as by a thread. Yes, but it will still hang, and there will be enough of good people, many who may not belong to our Church at all, people who have respect for law and for order, and for Constitutional rights, who will rally around with us and save the Constitution."

Years later in 1928, the LDS Church Apostle Melvin J. Ballard remarked that:

"The prophet Joseph Smith said the time will come when, through secret organizations taking the law into their own hands the Constitution of the United States would be so torn and rent asunder, and life and property and peace and security would be held of so little value, that the Constitution would, as it were, hang by a thread. This Constitution will be preserved, but it will be preserved very largely in consequence of what the Lord has revealed and what this people, through listening to the Lord and being obedient, will help to bring about, to stabilize and give permanency and effect to the Constitution itself. That also is our mission."

### Authenticity

Eliza R. Snow, noted LDS poet, writer, and leader of the church's women's auxiliary (the Relief Society).

The authenticity of the White Horse Prophecy is debated by the LDS Church. It was made public after his death by one of his associates, Edwin Rushton. Rushton's manuscript was written around 1900. Although some elements of the statement were confirmed by contemporary LDS Church leaders as having been taught by Smith, the prophecy as a whole has never been officially acknowledged or accepted, and has been repudiated by the LDS Church since 1918 though it is often cited by followers of the Church.

In early 2010, the LDS Church issued a statement saying that "the so-called 'White Horse Prophecy' is based on accounts that have not been substantiated by historical research and is not embraced as Church doctrine."[5] In 2010 the journal *BYU Studies* also published an article establishing Edwin Rushton as the author of the prophecy and that it was not reliable. It claimed Rushton had embellished on Brigham Young's (in 1854) and Eliza R. Snow's (in 1870) reminiscences that Joseph Smith had once said the U.S. Constitution would hang by a thread. It also noted the prophecy's claims that the Latter Day Saints in the Rocky Mountain were supposed to stand against worldwide financial and political disaster, and the foreign nations led by the Russian Czar. The prophecy remains a salient feature of the LDS perspective on the relationship between religion and government, evidenced by many popular references to it, including Glenn Beck and Sen. Orin Hatch.

### Interpretation

Many people outside the LDS Church have speculated, on the basis of the White Horse Prophecy, that Mormons expect the United States to eventually become a theocracy dominated by the LDS Church. This question has arisen periodically as prominent Mormons have sought political office in the United States — such as during the 2010 campaign of Rex Rammell for the governorship of the state of Idaho.

### Glenn Beck

LDS conservative commentator Glenn Beck, speaking at the Restoring Honor rally in 2010.

On November 14, 2008, following President Barack Obama's election, conservative personality and 1999 Mormon convert Glenn Beck told Bill O'Reilly while a guest on *The O'Reilly Factor*, that "we are at the place where the Constitution hangs in the balance, I feel the Constitution is hanging in the balance right now, hanging by a thread unless the good Americans wake up." *Washington Post* journalist Dana Milbank, who authored the 2010 critical polemic *Tears of a Clown: Glenn Beck and the Tea Bagging of America*, has written on Beck's perceived affinity for the prophecy and thus described Beck's views as essentially "White Horse Prophecy meets horsemen of the apocalypse". In discussing whether Beck's wording was coincidental, Milbank noted that ten days earlier, Beck was interviewing U.S. Senator Orrin Hatch of Utah, also a Mormon, and remarked: "I heard Barack Obama talk about the Constitution and I thought, we are at the point or we are very near the point where our Constitution is hanging by a thread." Milbank also notes that two months later when Beck's Fox show started in January 2009, Beck had Hatch on, and again prompted him by declaring "I believe our Constitution hangs by a thread."

LDS blogger and religious commentator Joanna Brooks, who has written extensively on the importance of Mormonism to Beck's political worldview, has also alluded to the potential connection of Beck's proclamations and the White Horse Prophecy.

# Maine Republic Email Alert

No. 012

*". . . that I should bear witness unto the truth."* — John 18:33 // David E. Robinson, Publisher

*". . . if the trumpet give an uncertain sound, who shall prepare himself for battle?"* — I Corinthians 14:8

## The Bigger Picture: Iraqi Dinar

The Babylonian system intends to use the revaluation of the dinar to infuse a huge amount of cash into its near-collapsed world-wide banking system. They are essentially monetizing Iraq's natural resources by printing up debt notes to buy the Iraqi's oil and natural gas that is yet in the ground.

This was possibly the plan of the bankers and oil companies from the start . . . trick Saddam Hussein into attacking Kuwait so that there would be an excuse to put Iraq under UN Sanctions.

Then make a two-pronged attack on Iraq: first by the military taking over the country. Second by the banks taking over the country's oil and natural gas.

The military phase is now finished for all practical purposes. Once "stability" is established, Phase II can occur.

The Fed has, reportedly, bought about **$7 trillion Iraqi dinar** at very low prices, probably $2-3 billion in all, and when the dinar is revalued, The Fed (those who own the banks that own the Fed) has incentive to push for a high rate of exchange, to increase its profit.

Secondly, The Fed has, apparently, agreed to not dump Iraq's dinar on Iraq all at once, but to use them to purchase oil at the predetermined low rate of about $40 per barrel (some have stated $32 per barrel).

With the price of oil now about $90 per barrel, this means that the Fed's dinars, whatever the revalued rate turns out to be, will be worth at least double to them than what the dinar will be for us in actual purchasing power.

If the revaluation comes in at, say, $5/dinar, then the Fed's $7 trillion worth of dinar would be worth $35 trillion toward the purchase of Iraqi oil and gas. They will get to purchase Iraq's natural resources at a low, low rate, essentially doubling the purchasing power of their dinar to the equivalent of $70 trillion or more. Hence, for a mere 2-3 billion, of their own Federal Reserve Notes, The Fed has a mortgage claim on Iraq's entire wealth in the ground for the next century.

Militarily securing these resources cost them nothing, because the US Treasury paid the troops to do their work. The US Treasury paid for this by borrowing "money" (Federal Reserve Notes) from The Fed, that was created at no cost to them, and was then loaned to the US Government, plus interest.

Certain men have been doing such things for a long, long time, and America, too, has been a victim of this kind of *takeover by monetary manipulation*. Such is the nature of the Beast of Babylon.

Some may ask, then, why should we buy Iraqi dinar?

First, there are, supposedly, about 3 million American "little guys" who have purchased about $1.6 trillion Iraqi dinar. Most other nations have prohibited the sale of Iraqi dinar within their countries.

The Fed has *limited* the sale of dinars to Americans by publicizing the purchase of dinars as a scam. Along with banks that do not want their employees to become millionaires and quit their jobs — which the bank trained them to do — not because they like us so much, but because when we cash in the revalued dinars at the bank (exchange dinars for bank credits or Federal Reserve Notes) the dinars make their way to the Fed's bank vaults!

The Fed pays the banks for the dinar with credits or Federal Reserve Notes, but the dinar are worth at least twice as much to The Fed in purchasing Iraqi oil and gas (which is then sold to whom? and for what price?).

Those who own The Fed are using us Americans to legitimize their plan to enhance their balance sheets.

The real question is: "What is The Creator's divine plan in all of this?"

When we look at the prophetic history of Babylon and see Iraq as a type of Babylon the plan unfolds perfectly. When the kings of the East conquered Babylon in the days of Daniel, they diverted the Euphrates River and walked into the city on the dry river bed. They killed the king (Belshazzar) and the city fell to them intact.

The drying up of the Euphrates is mentioned in Isaiah 44, as well as in Revelation 16, where it pictures part of the prophetic sequence of events. The Euphrates is the *life blood* of Babylon and prophetically represents cash flow liquidity — river of currency — the *life blood* of modern Mystery Babylon.

When the Iraqi dinar revalues, it becomes prophetic of the diversion of the Euphrates, before Babylon falls, i.e., a type of Babylon: meaning Iraq today.

We will have a short time in which to cash in/exchange dinars before "the city falls". We do not suggest holding Iraqi dinar to await an increase in value.

Let The Fed do that, because their greed will be their downfall.

Iraq's Prime Minister is Mr. Maliki. The Hebrew word for "king" is Melek. Maliki prophetically represents the "king of Babylon" - Belshazzar of old. It appears that Mr. Maliki will be overthrown at some point. This would inflame the entire country in a civil war.

An assassination would split Iraq into

three parts. When this happens, none of those three parts will honor the dinar but will begin printing their own currencies.

"The Fed" will then be caught with close to $9 trillion dinar that will be the worthless pieces of paper they once were. This will cause Mystery Babylon to collapse. In other words, the "type" (Iraq) will be a regional picture of a much bigger collapse of the entire Babylonian system worldwide. The final outcome of the great conspiracy of The Fed against Iraq will backfire because they do not know that YHWH is running a *counter-conspiracy* to catch them in their own trap, and will use this situation to help fund the Kingdom.

There will be a short window of opportunity that may only last a few months or a year. So, if you find yourselves with Iraqi dinar that are worth something, do not plan to hold them hoping they will increase in value, as you might if they were "precious metal". Use them to help build the Kingdom and to prepare for the overthrow of "that great City" that will come.

Use the money to buy things of real value that will be useful in the times ahead, so that you will be part of the solution, rather than be destroyed along with that which has been the problem.

*"ad Christi potentium et gloriam"*
*(for the power and glory of Christ)*

# Maine Republic Email Alert

*No.013*

*". . . that I should bear witness unto the truth." — John 18:33 // David E. Robinson, Publisher*

*". . . if the trumpet give an uncertain sound, who shall prepare himself for battle?" — I Corinthians 14:8*

## Another Step Closer to a One World Religion

June 27, 2011: **50 U.S. Churches To Read From The Quoran On Sunday.**

The three main pillars of the "New World Order" that the global elite want to bring about are a one world economy, a one world government and a one world religion.

A lot of attention gets paid to the development of the first two pillars, but the third pillar gets very little attention. But the truth is that a one world religion is getting closer than ever.

"Interfaith" conferences and meetings are being held with increasing frequency all over the globe. Major global religious leaders are urging all of us to focus on our "shared" religious traditions.

The belief that all religions are equally valid paths to the same destination is being taught in houses of worship and at religious institutions all over the globe. This "interfaith movement" is being promoted by NGOs, "charitable foundations" and top politicians and it is being backed by big money all over the planet.

Now some U.S. churches are trying to take things to another level. On June 26th, the National Cathedral in Washington D.C. and approximately 50 other churches in 26 U.S. states will publicly read from the Quran during their Sunday worship services.

This is all part of an interfaith project being promoted by the Interfaith Alliance and Human Rights First. The theme of this Sunday is "Faith Shared: Uniting in Prayer and Understanding", and the goal is apparently to show how much Christian churches in the United States respect Islam.

The following are some of the other prominent U.S. churches that will be doing Quran readings this Sunday....
• **Christ Church in New York City**

• **All Saints Church in Pasadena, California**
• **Park Hill Congregational in Denver**
• **Hillview United Methodist in Boise, Idaho**
• **First United Lutheran in San Francisco**
• **St. Elizabeth's Episcopal Church in Honolulu**

In all, churches in 26 U.S. states will be participating.

But these Quran readings are just supposed to be the beginning of something bigger. The following is from a description of the Quran reading project on the website of Human Rights First....

*At its core, this project will bring together Christian, Jewish and Muslim clergy to read from and hear from each other's sacred texts. In doing so, they will serve as a model for respect and cooperation and create a concrete opportunity to build and strengthen working ties between and among faith communities moving forward.*

The truth is that all Americans have the freedom to read the Quran whenever they want. But should Christian churches be reading from it during Sunday worship and should they be seeking to "build and strengthen working ties" with Islamic groups that are seeking to promote the spread of another religion?

Obviously, many Christian leaders are not pleased with this development. Worldview Weekend President Brannon Howse recently made the following comment regarding the reading of the Quran in U.S. churches....

***"They have denied the exclusivity of Jesus Christ. They have denied the inerrancy of Scripture; they've denied the inspiration of Scripture."***

Sadly, this is not a new trend. The truth is that the "interfaith movement" has been building momentum for decades and some of the most prominent religious leaders in the world are involved.

For example, the following excerpt from a CNS article talks about a huge "interfaith event" hosted by the Pope when he visited Washington D.C. in 2008...

***When Pope Benedict XVI comes to the Pope John Paul II Cultural Center in Washington for an early-evening interfaith meeting April 17 with Buddhists, Hindus, Jews, Muslims and representatives of other religions, space will be at a premium.***

Many top U.S. Christian leaders have been very involved in the "interfaith movement" as well.

For example, Brian McLaren, one of the top leaders of the emerging church movement, actually celebrated Ramadan back in 2009.

Rick Warren, a member of the Council on Foreign Relations, has been a guest speaker at the national conference of the Islamic Society of North America.

Some time ago, a virtual "who's who" of evangelical Christian leaders that

that included Rick Warren, Robert Schuller, Brian McLaren, Richard Cizik and Bill Hybels all signed a letter to the Islamic community that was entitled "Loving God And Neighbor Together". This letter made it abundantly clear that these Christians leaders consider Allah and the Christian God to be the same entity.

Let's take a quick look at a couple of quotes from the letter….

**Before we "shake your hand" in responding to your letter, we ask forgiveness of the All-Merciful One.**

In Islam, "the All-Merciful One" is one of the key names for Allah.

So in this letter the Christian leaders were praying to Allah and were asking for his forgiveness and were acknowledging that he is God.

Here is another quote from the letter….

**If we fail to make every effort to make peace and come together in harmony you correctly remind us that "our eternal souls" are at stake as well.**

Very strangely, in the letter the Christian leaders claim that their "eternal souls" are at stake if they do not make every effort to "come together in harmony" with the Islamic community.

Once again, people in America are free to believe whatever they want, but Christian leaders should not be trying to develop religious ties with Islam.

The truth is that Jesus would not have wanted anything to do with this one world religion that the New World Order is trying to bring in.

In John 14:6, Jesus made the following statement…..

**I am the way, the truth, and the life: no man cometh unto the Father, but by me.**

You would think that would be so clear that no Christian leader would ever be able to misunderstand it.

In fact, the very first two of the Ten Commandments are about how no other gods should ever be worshipped except for the one true God.

In Exodus 20:3-6 it says the following….

**Thou shalt have no other gods before me. Thou shalt not make unto thee any graven image, or any likeness of any thing that is in heaven above, or that is in the earth beneath, or that is in the water under the earth. Thou shalt not bow down thyself to them, nor serve them: for I the LORD thy God am a jealous God, visiting the iniquity of the fathers upon the children unto the third and fourth generation of them that hate me; And shewing mercy unto thousands of them that love me, and keep my commandments.**

But today everybody wants to be "politically correct". This is especially true of religious leaders.

But this is exactly what the global elite want. They want everyone herded into one giant "global religion" that they will be able to take charge of and control.

Of course once the global religion is established, they won't have much use for the real Jesus Christ or for the Bible.

Even if you are not a Christian, you should be deeply troubled by these developments.

Yesterday, I read about Agenda 21 and the radical population control agenda of the global elite. The reality is that they want to use "climate change" and environmentalism as social engineering tools in order to reconstruct society in the way that they see fit.

I have also previously read about the globalization of the world economy. The global elite eventually want to merge us all into a one world economic system that they will totally dominate.

So even if you are not of any particular faith, you should be alarmed when you see attempts being made to merge the major religions of the world into one global faith.

# Maine Republic Email Alert

*No.014*

"... that I should bear witness unto the truth." — John 18:33 // David E. Robinson, Publisher

"... if the trumpet give an uncertain sound, who shall prepare himself for battle?" — I Corinthians 14:8

## Acceptance For Value (A4V) VIA The IRS

**When you receive a presentment** from a corporation it is not really a bill, it is a credit instrument that you can use as a money order per HJR 192 of June 5, 1933.

Since 1933, no one in America has been able to "pay" a debt with money backed by silver or gold.

Payment of debt with money backed by silver or gold is against Public Policy established by Congress. Henceforth, every "charge" of debt shall be "discharged."

The United States went bankrupt, by filing Chapter 11, in 1933. There is no gold to back up our money supply, so they used our birth certificates, which represent the future labor of our bodies, to create needed funds.

We are creditors of the United States who can turn any "debt" into a "credit instrument" with which we can "pay" our debts; by endorsing it with our signature.

Federal Reserve Notes (FRNs) are "debt instruments". And you cannot "pay" a debt with more debt. It just increases the debt.

Negative 10 dollars, minus negative 10 dollars = negative 20 dollars.

We create money with our signature. We can discharge all debts with our signature; backed by the future commercial energy that we will produce.

When you get a "presentment" — a traffic ticket, a bill, or a summons, etc. — you can "discharge" the presented "charge".

The bill (the presentment) is like a check. "Accept (the presentment) for Value", and endorse it on the back as you would a check, and send it to the IRS, because they know what to do with it. They are pros at handling this stuff.

**This is what you can do . . .**
When you get a presentment, you look at it and see a bill, but what it really is, is a check.

So **"Accept it for Value"** which is your right. It is *your credit* being returned to you.

Write the following **eight items** on the presentment at an angle:

ACCEPTED FOR VALUE
EXEMPT FROM LEVY
DEPOSIT TO US TREASURY
*Your name in cursive in blue ink*
*Exemption 123456789*
*Date of signature*
*Charge to STRAWMAN Name*
*SSN 123-45-6789*

And endorse the back
*Your name in cursive in blue ink*
*Authorized Representative*

This is discharging the debt with your signature — your "credit sign." The bill they have sent you is not really a bill; it's *a credit return*.

Say someone give you a $200 dollar bill. Cool! Right? That's a $200 dollar credit — *your* credit — what Uncle Sam owes *you* in return for his use of your credit.

So why not *accept the return*? Why not **Accept** [the return of your credit] **For** [its] **Value**? (AFV or A4V).

**Or fill out the voucher** as a Money Order as shown.

Write the following **eight items** anywhere on the voucher-face:

MONEY ORDER
Pay to the US Treasury
*Write out the amount in cursive*
*Add the numerical figures*
*Your name in cursive in blue ink*
*Authorized Representative*
*Exemption 123456789*
*Date of signature*

And endorse the back
*Your name in cursive in blue ink*
*Authorized Representative*

**Send with a Form 1099-A to the IRS to one of the addresses below:**

IRS - Treasury UCC Contract Trust
1500 Pennsylvania Avenue, NW
Washington, D.C. 20220

IRS - Stop 4440
P. O. Box 9036
Ogden, Utah 84201

IRS - CID
Box 192
Covington, KY 41012

Every time you see a bill, see it as **your credit being returned to you.**

You can discharge any public debt that you see: **credit cards, school loans, mortgages; etc.**

Processing may take 60-90 days.

See: **Give Yourself Credit: Money Doesn't Grow On Trees**
http://tinyurl.com/39eoywm

**Don't purchase anything with A4V.**
*A4V is not for creating debt;*
*A4V is only for discharging debt.*

Office of The Maine free State, 3 Linnell Circle, Brunswick, Maine 04011

# Maine Republic Email Alert

No. 015

"... that I should bear witness unto the truth." — John 18:33 // David E. Robinson, Publisher

"... if the trumpet give an uncertain sound, who shall prepare himself for battle?" — I Corinthians 14:8

## Lyndon LaRouche Speaks Out

**THIS IS A TRANSCRIPT** of a 72 minute interview of former presidential candidate **Lyndon LaRouche**, by Alex Jones, which is archived on Alex Jones' PrisonPlanetTV show of June 30th, 2011, where Mr. LaRouche [now 89] gives us his view of the state of the world as it is right now.

**Alex:** The Financial Times of London is talking about the end of dollar hegemony; the Chinese said that we already have a technical default. Do you agree with that?

**LLR:** Well, it's worse than that. We are in a general breakdown crisis. Everything is about to go down. There are remedies, but as long as this president remains president, there's no chance that these remedies will be supplied. He has committed an act with a lie, which makes him impeachable.

Now, the question is whether the impeachment rage will be strong enough to put him out or not.

First of all: We have a problem with the British. They are, in a sense, controlling our destiny, because we have a president who is nothing but a British asset. And he's not really a very stable person, and he has some very bad policies.

The entire trans-atlantic system is now coming down. We've reached a point where the last attempt at bail-out has created a situation which Europe has not yet corrected, which means that, right now, Europe and also the United States is on a slide down toward breakdown, as early as sometime this coming month [July].

There are remedies, of course, but the question is, if this guy remains president, is it possible to apply any of these remedies which do exist?

Repeatedly Wall Street always fails,

because it is a thief. They're more interested in what they can extract from people than the economy of production for the State.

China today is absorbing the industries we have shut down inside the United States, and this means that we are becoming more and more helpless because we no longer have the food supply, the production we had, the production upon which our economy depends. We are now in a very grave crisis.

We cannot have a thermo-nuclear war. And you cannot have a war between nations that would not be thermo-nuclear.

There's a long term trend situated on certain people in the United Kingdom, which is the desire to reduce the human population to Two billion, some say even One. And recently, the One is preferred.

The policy of the so-called green-revolution people — that is, the anti-technology people — is precisely that, and the worst case right now happens to be in Germany where the green-change is heading, and it means a disaster for the whole population of Germany.

At this point, with this president, who is nothing but a British Puppet, they created him, how do you think all the money which was cooked up under suspicious circumstances to overwhelm the presidential campaign — with him — with money to hide him.

Some of the people using this money should have gone to prison. They overwhelmed the legitimate campaign for the presidency.

On the basis of his debt to the British, who put him into office inside the United States, with this load of money, he now actually has control over the presidency.

There are people in the United States, the older people and less institutional, who understand this. And we are prepared to dump this bum from office.

Now we have the perfect ground of doing so. We had the ground under the 25th Amendment earlier [*that the president is unable to discharge the powers and duties of his office*] which should have been exercised. It was not.

Now we have caught him in the outrage of an impeachable offense against the United States in his fraudulent policy on warfare in Libya.

We have him there, but some weaklings in the United States are afraid to close in on this guy.

But I know if he is not thrown out of office very soon, and I mean in the weeks immediately ahead, this United States cannot survive the kind of conditions which we are going into in the month of July. It doesn't mean we're going to collapse in July, but we are going through a process where we will collapse some time along summer time.

Twitter operates a riot creating operation. Twitter as an organization is controlled from the top. You have an arrangement of youths who have a very poor arrangement of life — that isn't their fault — it was given to them.

We're heading for a general collapse throughout the trans-atlantic region, centered of course in Europe and Canada, and it extends throughout the

Office of The Maine free State, 3 Linnell Circle, Brunswick, Maine 04011

United States and Africa and through parts of Asia. This is the area that's in trouble. Right now it's coming down.

One problem is, you have the European system with its own currency — the Euro. A system of globalization in which the nations are losing their sovereignty at a rapid rate in order to become members of a blob of an assortment of nations. Their thing is now in the process of coming down.

The breakdown of the process was established in New York City by a gentleman called Strauss Khann who was, at that point, the head of the IMF. And he was caught in the attack of a woman — which was considered rape — and for that he was picked on plane-side, before he could board the plane to France. He then spent some time at Rickers Island, the famous prison in the New York City area, and he's now sitting on parole with a little special attachment to his leg, awaiting trial, which will be at some duration.

[*He has now been released due to circumstantial evidence that the woman has lied on many occasions in the past*].

Strauss Khann's elimination from the operation killed the bail-out operation which was intended.

Now the inability of our crowd to get a bail-out going again resulted in a deterioration. Because what they're getting is a bunch of money which is not money. They're getting electronic money, not even electronic — fake money — which is in our appearance a bail-out. This stuff has no redeemable value, except to collect debts from victims, including countries that are victims, including the United States.

We are being looted as a nation . . . four States are on the verge of bankruptcy right now, because they can't meet the debt requirements, to bail themselves out.

Other parts of the nation are being crushed at an accelerating rate. For example, our military is under threat right now. The military of the United States is going to be sliced massively if something is not done about it. And that's going to leave us in a very strange degree of vulnerability. Not because of foreign wars, or such, but simply because our military is one of the final institutions which is still functioning.

Everyone of our institutions is crumbling. If we do not get this bum out of office now, on the grounds existing on the 25th Amendment, which of course is violation of the War Powers Act, for which he should be thrown out of office, for the crime against the nation, along with what ever other crimes of office go with that.

But he's not. And as long as this bum remains in office, he will do everything to destroy these United States.

If we don't get him out, you can kiss the United States good-by while you are still able to kiss. That's where it stands.

Now, there are many options. We have wonderful options in the United States, if we chose to use them. We could rebuild our entire central water system in the United States.

We could create industry, and develope agriculture where it does not exist, or where it is being destroyed. The destruction of Agriculture by the storms which have hit in the recent period, have destroyed the food supply of the United States to a critical degree for the immediate period ahead, and there are no plans to restore it. The farmers are bankrupt. They have no credit available to meet the crops.

The whole region . . . the Mississippi River . . . the Ohio basin . . . the Missouri basin . . . The food supply is being destroyed.

**Alex:** Again we're talking live to Lyndon LaRouche: Twenty years ago you said that NAFTA and GATT would do this to us. But what is the British model of this Corporate Imperium going to do when it's built up? China and others are still standing. And when their main command base, their main Titan, the United States, is accelerating its debilitation, what is the method to that madness?

You have a report out, of Obama being in violation of the War Powers Act. Why are they becoming so arrogant? In his speech yesterday he was saying, "I don't even have to discuss the Constitution any more."

What is he getting us ready for?

**LLR:** What you have to remember is that our system of government was unique when founded. At the time we had won the Revolutionary War we had a great problem of debt. The debt of what became the respective States of that period.

There was apparently no solution because each of these States of the United States was vulnerable to this debt, in danger of going into bankruptcy, and the British were just waiting to come back in and take us over.

Alexander Hamilton, who was a protege really of Benjamin Franklin, introduced a reform which established our Republic under a Constitutional system rather than a collection of States.

In other words, they're part of old European standard of States . . . with a centralized form of government . . . and went to a system of national credit.

This was the basis on which the Constitution was written. Therefore, our system in contrast to the European monetary system, our system is corporate by virtue of our Constitution — a credit system — not a monetary system.

Roosevelt put us back on the monetary system in his presidency. It was undermined, and in 1999 it was destroyed by the repeal of the Glass-Steagall Act which had been the bulwark of the entire recovery through the 1970's and thereafter. So that destruction in 1999 of the Glass-Steagall Act opened the gates for a complete take-over by the British International Monatarist Interests. That today is our problem.

Now, we *could* get out of this mess. All we have to do is to reenact the original Glass-Steagall Act of 1933 which was functioning more or less until about 1999. Once that is done then all the phony money, the Wall Street money and the British money goes into a different department of banking, not part of the Federal Debt. It's a part of the market, or speculative investment. The Wall Street Market.

Therefore, once we pass the Glass-Steagall Act — and there's a strong movement for that now — we are then able to get rid of tens of trillions of dollars of phony debt which the nation is now carrying, which is ruining our States, and destroying our population. We can reverse that process.

Obama is the advocate of the British interest. He's a tool of the British, they own him, they control his mind, he's just an agent who was bought by a vast influx of drug money and other corrupt currency. But for this drug money fund, which brought Obama into the presidency, he would not have been president.

The policies of Obama are the enemy of the United States. The enemy of our existence. We could be destroyed irreparably within a few weeks from now. It's not a long term enemy, it's a short term enemy.

**Alex:** Explain the technicals of that, of how in a few weeks this is bound to accelerate.

**LLR:** If you acknowledge . . . if you try to collect what the British essentially control, which is a worthless massive debt of many trillions of dollars, and more — there are actually quadrillions of phony value out there — clamoring for being fed. All we have to do is pass Glass-Steadgall again, now, with the understanding of what we've been through. If we do that now, these guys will go bankrupt with their phony claims against the United States.

**Alex:** . . . because that will further implode the current ponzi scheme they've got. They've created 1.5 billion dollars in derivatives. They bought off our government to buy into that debt, and it's a black hole, and if we don't pull out of it there's no hope.

**LLR:** Exactly!

**Alex:** What do we do when they hold us hostage as they openly do and implode the Stock Market? Do we then just arrest them for financial terrorism, because they're on record in Europe and the United States threatening to implode things if they can't hold us hostage. It's truly us or them, and they are the fraudsters. But any government . . . any Congress person, as you know, they get busted for something, or their plane blows up, so how do you stop them?

**LLR:** Very simply. Glass-Steagall. If we re-enact the 1933 Glass-Steagall Act which was cancelled in 1999, we are immediately in a new situation in which the only credit system operating is the United States Govern-ment's Treasury system.

We then have to use the powers of the Treasury under those conditions to issue credit — not money — but credit — and give the credit to projects we consider worth placing public investment in them, we support private industry, etc. . . the secretary of Agriculture.

We have a crisis in agriculture in the United States. We have a food supply which is totally insufficient for our total population, right now. We can get that back if we put the investment back into the Mississippi River areas, alone. These areas will give us a growth in our food supply.

We have major projects — infrastructure projects — not what they call infrastructure projects, but real ones. Like water. We can change the character qualitatively simply by using public credit to loan it out. Simply by bringing public credit into the places where it will do the most good from the States' standpoint.

For example, Take for instance the State of California. The State of California is dying under these conditions. We can rescue it. We have other States. Three other States that are dying right now under the terms of the present administration.

**Alex:** And that's what the banksters want because — and we have the IMF documents — when their policies explode things further, they come in and buy things for pennies on the dollar and then they implode it more and more and more.

**LLR:** It's intentional. Their intent is to reduce the population. That's why they buy into the Malthusian view, and the social Darwinistic view that they're psychopathic activity is a favor for humanity.

**Alex:** Of course they adopt these bankrupt game-theory philosophies, and RAND corporation ideas, because it feeds in as a rationale for what they're doing, but in the end of the day, they're destroying the very civilization that they've fed off — they're actually in danger of killing their host. If they are successful in the end, won't they destroy their system as well? . . . but their predatorial instinct can't be stopped?

**LLR:** This is all intentional. The intend is to reduce the world population to no more than 2 billion people, to One, in the shortest possible time. If you understand that, then you know what's going on. If you don't understand that, then you really don't know what's going on.

When your looking at the whole system, the whole system was born with the founding of the Roman Empire. The Roman Empire collapsed, thus then it was reborn with the founding of Byzantium. That collapsed. It was revived as a Crusader system. That collapsed, and then after a whole series of wars in Europe, it was established as a new Empire, with William of Orange, who caused the flag of a new Venetian Party, from the Netherlands into England and Ireland, and did a lot of killing, and this is the outcome of his actions when the 7-years War, concluded in 1763, established the British Kingdom as an Imperial power on the Planet, including his control of India, Nova Scotia, Canada, etc.

**Alex:** So basically, we're considered as weevils who have invaded their grain base so we all need to be exterminated, and that's what they all say. That's their philosophy, their religion, driving their system, and its all admitted.

Look at California going into total implosion. 38% unemployment. Their answer is to ram through a 20%+ carbon tax on California.

If that isn't proof of the economic genocide, what is?

**LLR:** That's what your getting. There is real genocide. And it's intentional. And the Obama administration is an instrument of that policy of genocide. If you look at the policies that are admitted by the Obama administration as apart from any other policy inside the United States you find that only Obama — what he represents and his immediate cronies — are the people who are behind in the health-care and other fields, to increase the killing rate of what is considered an excessively large human population.

So we're not involved in a physical quarrel, we're involved in an existential issue. Are we going to be human? Or are we going to be cannibals? That is where we are. Go with Obama, look for the cannibal class. And that's where we're headed for.

**Alex:** And is that why they've put him in, because he is black and they thought they could give him political cover, because its admitted that the carbon tax that was introduced at Copenhagen would kill at least a billion people in five years if it were implemented, and that was just the first roll-out, and they told the 3rd World, for this, we're going to tax the West, and give it to you, and then they got the treaty, and it was double the taxes that the West would pay on people making less that $2 dollars a day. It was a death sentence.

**LLR:** I know, I know

**Alex:** How do we stop these people? They are mad men!

**LLR:** They are criminals! And we have to understand that. We have to salvage our government free of the Obama syndrome and also the George W. Bush Jr. syndrome which is almost as bad.

**Alex:** What is your view of the political field right now in the United States?

**LLR:** What we have now is, among some senators, and among members of the House of Representatives, and in terms of the elite institutions, the system has a lot of good people in it.

We're pushing for the Glass-Steagall reenactment, and it's a very serious and growing movement, right now. We're moving to re-install Glass-Steagall. And that will change things.

We in the United States, with our government, as long as we control it, have the capacity to create credit. We could put the United States back to work. They could turn it around anytime they wanted to.

Obama is impeachable on the grounds of the War Powers Act. He's impeachable because he is also insane, and he couldn't be what he is if he wasn't insane. This man is a mental case of a certain type. He's crazy. But he's — like the famous Nero — he's got the same syndrome of the Emperor Nero, psychologically.

**Alex:** I'm concerned about the False Flag terror. What are some of the tricks that the ruling class may use to block the people from removing them from power?

**LLR:** Well, lets take the case of 911 as a good example of exactly how this whole system works today.

What happened was that the British system, through a certain bunch of its operatives, together with the Saudi Kingdom, set up an operation, a secret operation, which would take oil prices in the Gulf — at Gulf prices — then move it up to the coast of Europe. Then they would sell it on the market at a European price that is much above the Saudi price.

This created a large fund.

The largest available fund for dirty operations, military and otherwise, in the world at that time.

This funding was used for what was called 911. And the whole operation was based on this. The 911 operation.

Now, this was well known. The evidence of a direct relationship of the Saudi Ambassador to Washington, and his involvement in recruiting and backing and funding some of the pilots who actually flew those planes, was conclusive evidence which was buried under the pressure of the then Bush administration. But that is the truth.

The Truth was never told publicly But so many of us knew it. The evidence existed. We knew it. Other people knew it. But it was never presented in the press.

Even the people who were on the Commission, who were investigating precisely this line of investigation were pressured not to open their mouths. The same was kept a national secret.

It was the alliance of the Saudi Kingdom with this faction of the British system which funded, created, and directed the 911 Attack. And that's a fact we have to remember.

We're in this kind of mess because the Bush administration obtained dictatorial power over the presidency and over the Congress through the terror caused by this incident. And that's a thing that's still harassing us today. And we should make the record clear.

Now, the main thing here is, we have a bunch of Congressmen — good ones — the normal members of Congress — but to the extent that they are fragmented and are not working together on a common cause, they are not effective in dealing with a president who is an enemy of the United States.

**Alex:** Well, Mr. LaRouche, bottom line you're saying 911 was an inside job!

**LLR:** Yup! It was a totally inside job. It involved Bush all over the place. Remember the whole family was there in Texas at the time when Ben Laden was functioning.

**Alex:** Talking about the world plan for population reduction, the British Empire through the corporate system, the Corporatocracy, the Kleptocracy, a total inside job! Some are concerned that they may stage newer events as their flagging system goes forward. Can you finish with that?

**LLR:** Yes. The Glass-Steagall Act will unite enough members of Congress to create a force which will be able to face up to the threat of the Obama administration.

If we succeed in pushing the Glass-Steagall Act through, in at least one House, we will then have crippled the Obama dictatorship, and that will lead to the elimination of him from the presidency.

Under those conditions, the American people — thinking they've got their nation back — will be able to mobilize themselves in an organized force and take the measures needed to save our nation.

We can do it. We need a sense of emergency in enough of our people to unite around the bright people of

Congress as a force of government to get our country back now. If we don't do it, we're going to lose it. So now we've got to mobilize around the best political choice of strategy.

If we restore a sense of unity among a majority of the US members of Congress, I guarantee you we can win this fight, in short order. That's what we have to do.

I'm out to organize this as a life and death objective.

# Maine Republic Email Alert
*No.016*

*". . . that I should bear witness unto the truth." — John 18:33  //  David E. Robinson, Publisher*

*". . . if the trumpet give an uncertain sound, who shall prepare himself for battle?" — I Corinthians 14:8*

## Geert Wilders Speaks Out

**Geert Wilders is a Dutch Member of Parliament.**

In a generation or two, the US will ask itself: 'Who lost Europe ?'

Here is the speech of Geert Wilders, Chairman, Party for Freedom, the Netherlands, at the Four Seasons, New York, introducing an Alliance of Patriots and announcing the 'Facing Jihad Conference' in Jerusalem.

**Dear friends,**

Thank you very much for inviting me.

I come to America with a mission: All is not well in the old world. There is a tremendous danger looming, and it is very difficult to be optimistic.

We might be in the final stages of the Islamization of Europe. This not only is a clear and present danger to the future of Europe itself, it is a threat to America and the sheer survival of the West. The United States as the last bastion of Western civilization, facing an Islamic Europe.

First I will describe the situation on the ground in Europe. Then, I will say a few things about Islam. To close I will tell you about a meeting in Jerusalem.

The Europe you know is changing.

You have probably seen the landmarks. But in all of these cities, sometimes a few blocks away from your tourist destination, there is another world. It is the world of the parallel society created by Muslim mass-migration.

All throughout Europe a new reality is rising: entire Muslim neighborhoods where very few indigenous people reside or are even seen. And if they are, they might regret it. This goes for the police as well.

It's the world of head scarves, where women walk around in figureless tents, with baby strollers and a group of children. Their husbands, or slave-holders if you prefer, walk three steps ahead.

With mosques on many street corners.

The shops have signs you and I cannot read. You will be hard-pressed to find any economic activity. These are Muslim ghettos controlled by religious fanatics.

These are Muslim neighborhoods, and they are mushrooming in every city across Europe.

These are the building-blocks for territorial control of increasingly larger portions of Europe, street by street, neighborhood by neighborhood, city by city.

There are now thousands of mosques throughout Europe. With larger congregations than there are in churches. And in every European city there are plans to build super-mosques that will dwarf every church in the region. Clearly, the signal is: we rule.

Many European cities are already one-quarter Muslim: Amsterdam, Marseille and Malmo in Sweden.

In many cities the majority of the under-18 population is Muslim. Paris is now surrounded by a ring of Muslim neighborhoods. Mohammed is the most popular name among boys in many cities.

In some elementary schools in Amsterdam the farm can no longer be mentioned, because that would also mean mentioning the pig, and that would be an insult to Muslims.

Many state schools in Belgium and Denmark only serve halal food to all pupils. In once-tolerant Amsterdam gays are beaten up almost exclusively by Muslims. Non-Muslim women routinely hear 'whore,' 'whore'. Satellite dishes are not pointed to local TV stations, but to stations in the country of origin.

In France school teachers are advised to avoid authors deemed offensive to Muslims, including Voltaire and Diderot; the same is increasingly true of Darwin. The history of the Holocaust can no longer be taught because of Muslim sensitivity.

In England sharia courts are now officially part of the British legal system. Many neighborhoods in France are no-go areas for women without head scarves. Last week a man almost died after being beaten up by Muslims in Brussels, because he was drinking alcohol during the Ramadan.

Jews are fleeing France in record numbers, on the run for the worst wave of anti-Semitism since World War II. French is now commonly spoken on the streets of Tel Aviv and Netanya, Israel. I could go on forever with stories like this. Stories about Islamization.

A total of fifty-four million Muslims now live in Europe. San Diego University recently calculated that a staggering 25 percent of the population in Europe will be Muslim just 12 years from now. Bernhard Lewis has predicted a Muslim majority by the end of this century.

Now these are just numbers. And the numbers would not be threatening if the Muslim-immigrants had a strong desire to assimilate. But there are few signs of that. The Pew Research Center reported that half of French Muslims see their loyalty to Islam as greater than their loyalty to France. One-third of French Muslims do not object to suicide

*Office of The Maine free State, 3 Linnell Circle, Brunswick, Maine 04011*

attacks. The British Centre for Social Cohesion reported that one-third of British Muslim students are in favor of a worldwide caliphate. Muslims demand what they call 'respect'. And this is how we give them respect. We have Muslim official state holidays.

The Christian-Democratic attorney general is willing to accept sharia in the Netherlands if there is a Muslim majority. We have cabinet members with passports from Morocco and Turkey.

Muslim demands are supported by unlawful behavior, ranging from petty crimes and random violence, for example against ambulance workers and bus drivers, to small-scale riots.

Paris has seen its uprising in the low-income suburbs, the banlieus. I call the perpetrators 'settlers'. Because that is what they are. They do not come to integrate into our societies; they come to integrate our society into their Dar-al-Islam. Therefore, they are settlers.

Much of this street violence I mentioned is directed exclusively against non-Muslims, forcing many native people to leave their neighbor-hoods, their cities, their countries. Moreover, Muslims are now a swing vote not to be ignored.

The second thing you need to know is the importance of Mohammed the prophet. His behavior is an example to all Muslims and cannot be criticized. Now, if Mohammed had been a man of peace, let us say like Ghandi and Mother Theresa wrapped in one, there would be no problem. But Mohammed was a warlord, a mass murderer, a pedophile, and had several marriages; at the same time. Islamic tradition tells us how he fought in battles, how he had his enemies murdered and even had prisoners of war executed. Mohammed himself slaughtered the Jewish tribe of Banu Qurayza. If it is good for Islam, it is good. If it is bad for Islam, it is bad.

Let no one fool you about Islam being a religion. Sure, it has a god, and a here-after, and 72 virgins. But in its essence Islam is a political ideology. It is a system that lays down detailed rules for society and the life of every person. Islam wants to dictate every aspect of life. Islam means 'submission'. Islam is not compatible with democracy and freedom, because what it strives for is sharia. If you want to compare Islam to anything, compare it to communism or national-socialism, these are all totalitarian ideologies.

Now you know why Winston Churchill called Islam "the most retrograde force in the world", and why he compared *Mein Kampf* to the *Quran*.

The public has wholeheartedly accepted the Palestinian narrative, and sees Israel as the aggressor I have lived in this country and visited it dozens of times. I support Israel. First, because it is the Jewish homeland after two thousand years of exile up to and including Auschwitz. Second because it is a democracy. Third because Israel is our first line of defense.

This tiny country is situated on the fault line of jihad, frustrating Islam's territorial advance. Israel is facing the front lines of jihad, like Kashmir, Kosovo, the Philippines, Southern Thailand, Darfur in Sudan, Lebanon, and Aceh in Indonesia. Israel is simply in the way. The same way West-Berlin was during the Cold War.

The war against Israel is not a war against Israel. It is a war against the West. It is jihad. Israel is simply receiving the blows that are meant for all of us. If there would have been no Israel, Islamic imperialism would have found other venues to release its energy and its desire for conquest. Thanks to Israeli parents who send their children to the army lay awake at night, while parents in Europe and America sleep well and dream, unaware of the dangers looming.

Many in Europe argue in favor of abandoning Israel in order to address the grievances of our Muslim minorities. But if Israel were, God forbid, to go down, it would not bring any solace to the West It would not mean our Muslim minorities would all of a sudden change their behavior, and accept our values.

On the contrary, the end of Israel would give enormous encouragement to the forces of Islam. They would, and rightly so, see the demise of Israel as proof that the West is weak, and doomed. The end of Israel would not mean the end of our problems with Islam, but only the beginning. It would mean the start of the final battle for world domination.

If they can get Israel , they can get everything.

So-called journalists volunteer to label any and all critics of Islamization as a 'right-wing extremists' or 'racists'. In my country, the Netherlands, 60 percent of the population now sees the mass immigration of Muslims as the number one policy mistake since World War II. And another 60 percent sees Islam as the biggest threat.

Yet there is a greater danger than terrorist attacks, the scenario of America as the last man standing. The lights may go out in Europe faster than you can imagine. An Islamic Europe means a Europe without freedom and democracy, an economic wasteland, an intellectual nightmare, and a loss of military might for America - as its allies will turn into enemies, enemies with atomic bombs.

With an Islamic Europe, it would be up to America alone to preserve the heritage of Rome, Athens — and Jerusalem.

# Maine Republic Email Alert

No.017

*". . . that I should bear witness unto the truth." — John 18:33 // David E. Robinson, Publisher*

*". . . if the trumpet give an uncertain sound, who shall prepare himself for battle?" — I Corinthians 14:8*

## The United States Is A British Corporation

**This is a transcript of a 10 minute video on "YouTube" about the United States as a corporation not a country, operating in commerce on the world scene. The title of the video will not be mentioned because of some inappropriate language that is used.**

United States code, Title 28 3002 (15)(A)(B)(C) "The United States is a corporation.

**Cornell University Law School LII/Legal Information Institute**
Title 28 > PART VI > CHAPTER 176 > SUBCHAPTER A > 3002 § 3002. **Definitions.**
(15) "United States" means —
   (A) a Federal Corporation;
   (B) an agency, department, commission, board, or other entity of the United States;
   (C) an instrumentality of the Corporation.

Obama is the president of the Corporation. And the citizens are the employees of the Corporation.
America is a British Colony.

"The United States is a corporation not a land mass and it existed before the Revolutionary War, and the British Troops did not leave until 1796". — *Respublica v. Sweers 1 Dallas 43, Treaty of commerce 8 Stat 116, The Society for Propagating the Gospel, &c v. New Haven 8 Wheat 464, Treaty of Peace 8 Stat 80, IRS Publication 6209, Articles of Association, October 20, 1774.*

The King of England financially backed both sides of the Revolutionary War. — *Treaty at Versailles, July 16, 1782, Treaty of Peace 8 Stat 80.*

The United States corporation did not declare Independence from Great Britain or King George.
In 1604 a corporation called the

Virginia Company was formed in anticipation of the imminent influx of White Europeans, mostly British at first, into the North American continent. Its main stock holder was King James 1 and the original charter for the company was completed by April 10th 1606.

"... Virginia Company of London, also called London Company Commercial trading company, chartered by King James 1 of England in 1606 with the object of colonizing the eastern coast of North America between latitudes 34° and 41° N. Its shareholders were Londoners, and it was disting-uished from the Plymouth Company, which was chartered at the same time and composed largely of men from Plymouth.

The Virginia Company owned most of the land of what we now call the USA.

The Virginia Company (the British Crown and the bloodline families) had rights to 50%, yes 50%, of all gold and silver mined on its lands, plus percentages of other minerals and raw materials, and 5% of all profits from other ventures.

The lands of the Virginia Company were granted to the colonies under a Deed of Trust (on lease) and therefore they could not claim ownership of the land. They could pass on the perpetual use of the land to their heirs or sell the perpetual use, but they could never own it. Ownership was retained by the British Crown.

**HUMAN BEING.** See monster. Ballentine's Law Dictionary, 1930.

**Hypothecate.** ["Hypotheca was a term, of the Roman law, and denoted a pledge or mortgage..." — *Black's 1st.*] **1.** to pledge to a creditor as security without delivering over; mortgage. **2.** to put in pledge by delivery, as stocks given as security for a loan. ACED. to pledge something as security without turning over possession of it.

**MONSTER.** A human being by birth, but in some part resembling a lower animal. **A monster hath no inheritable blood and cannot be heir to any land.** — *Ballentine's Law Dictionary, 1930.* A prodigious birth; a human birth or offspring not having the shape of mankind: which cannot be heir to any land, albeit it be brought forth *in marriage.* — *Black's 1st. See Note.*

Note: under "human being" Ballentine's says only "See **monster**." Neither of the above major law dictionaries defines "human being" only "**monster**."

You own no property, slaves cannot own property. Read the Deed to the property that you think is yours. You are listed as a Tenant. — *See Document 43, 73rd Congress, 1st Session.*

After the first 21 years from the formation of the Virginia Company, all "duties, imposts, and excises" paid on trading activities in the colonies had be paid directly to the British Crown through the Crown treasurer.

Queen Elizabeth controls and has amended U.S. Social Security. — *S.I. 1997 No. 1778, the Social Security.*

Statutory Instrument 1997 No. 1778. The Social Security (United States of America) Order 1997. Statutory Instruments printed from this website are printed under the superintendance and the authority of HMSO being the Queen's Printer of Acts of Parliament.

A 1040 form is for tribute paid to Britain. — *IRS Publication 6209.*

Americans are slaves to the Queen and own absolutely nothing. — *Tillman v. Roberts 108 So. 62, Van Koten v. Van Koten 154 N.E. 146, Senate Document 43 & 73rd Congress 1st Session, Wynehammet v. People 13 N.Y. REP 379, 481.*

Social Security is not insurance or a contract, nor is there a Trust Fund. — *Helvering v. Davis 301 US 619, Steward Co. v. Davis 301 US 548.*

The criminal courts on the lands of the Virginia Company were to be operated under Admiralty Law, the law of the sea, and the civil courts under common law, the law of the land. This is a crucial point which I will address below.

The United States of America is not a country, it is a corporation owned by the same bloodlines who owned the Virginia Company because the USA *IS* the Virginia Company!

I wouldn't chop the Queen's head off. She should go to prison with her bloodline dogs.

You see, there are two USA's, or rather the USA and the usA. The united states of America with the lower case "u" and "s" are the lands of the various states. These lands, as we have seen, are still owned by the British Crown as the head of the old Virginia Company.

Then there is the United States of America, capital "U" and "S", which is the 68 square miles of land west [*actually east*] of the Potomac River on which is built the federal capital, Washington, D.C. and the District of Columbia. It also includes the US protectorates of Guam and Puerto Rico.

The Act of 1871 created a NEW altered Constitution. The title was Capitalized and the word "for" was changed to the word "of".

The original Organic American Constitution for the united states of America reads:
THE CONSTITUTION OF THE UNITED STATES OF AMERICA".

You cannot use the Constitution to defend yourself because you are not a party to it. — *Padelford Ray & Co. v. The Mayor and Aldermen of the City of Savannah 14 Georgia 438, 520.*

"The People" does not include U.S. Citizens. — *Barron v. Mayor & City Council of Baltimore 32 U.S. 243.*

The Act of 1871 also created a separate form of government for the District of Columbia, which is now a 68 square miles square parcel of land and is governed with British Admiralty Law, UCC. — *"Acts of the 41st Congress", Section 34, Session III, chapters 61 & 62. "An Act to Provide A Government for the District of Columbia".*

When Americans agree to have a Social Security number the citizens of the United States surrender their sovereignty and agree to become franchisees of the United States: the Virginia Company of the British Crown. Americans are led to believe that there is only one United States and the Federal government is the rightful government.

The use of lower/upper case, is making a legal statement. Have you noticed that when you receive correspondence relating to the government, law, or anything to do with finance, including taxation, your name is always spelled in all upper case, as in JOHN DOE. You're CAPITALIZED?

No. Your upper case name is not you. It is a corporation/trust setup by the "government" corporation through the treasury department at you birth. Every time a child is born a corporation/trust is created using his or her name in all upper case letters.

**person.** n. **1.** a human being. **2.** a corporation treated as having the rights and obligations of a person. Counties and duties can be treated as a person in that same manner as a corporation.

**natural person.** n. a real human being, as distinguished from a corporation , which is often treated at law as a fictitious person.

**corporation.** n. an organization formed with state governmental approval to act as an artificial person to carry on business (or other activities), which can sue or be sued.

Everything in the "United States" is "For Sale", roads, bridges, schools, hospitals, water, prisons, airports, etc. — *Executive Order 12803.*

Americans are Human Capital. — *Executive Order 13037.*

(Executive Order 13307 of March 3, 1997. Commission To Study Capital Budgeting.)

The U.S. has two flags, a military flag and a civil flag for peacetime. Why do you think that the U.S. is constantly flying the military flag?

**MILITARY.** Pertaining to war or to the army; concerned with war. — *Black's 6th. See Note.*

Note: The Amendatory Act to the Trading With The Enemy Act of October 6, 1917 — namely the Emergency Banking Relief Act of March 9, 1933 — defined the American people as the enemy, legally, of the United States Government because of the US bankruptcy, through which the private, international Federal Reserve System " became the Government": Creditor of the United States. — *See "Ramifica-tions of the Bankruptcy — The nature of Federal Reserve Notes."*

You may have noticed that the national flag of the United States always has a gold fringe when displayed in court or federal buildings, and you see this also in federally funded schools and on the uniforms of US Troops. Under the International Law of the Flags, a gold fringe indicates the jurisdiction of commercial law, also know as British Maritime Law, and in the US, as the Uniform Commercial Code, or UCC.

Bush launched a "war on terrorism" on behalf of a private corporation to further the goals of that Corporation. It had nothing to do with "America" or "Americans", because these are very different legal entities. The United States Corporation which owns the United States military and everything else that comes under the term "federal".

It is not the duty of the U.S. police to protect Americans! Their job is to protect the Corporation and arrest code breakers. — *Sapp v. Tallahassee, 348 So.2nd. 363, Reiff v. City of Philadelphia, 477 F.Supp. 1262, Lynch v. N.C. Department of Justice 376 S.E.2nd , 247.*

There are no Judicial courts in America and there has not been since 1789. Judges do not enforce Statutes and Codes, Executive Administrators enforce Statute and Codes. — *FRC v.*

GE 281 US 464, Keller v. PE 261 US 428, 1 Stat. 138-17.

**COMMERCE.** Sexual intercourse. — *Webster's*. Commerce is a term of the largest import. It comprehends intercourse for the purpose of trade in any and all its forms.

The most powerful court in America is not the United States Supreme Court but the Supreme Court of Pennsylvania. — *42 Pa. C.S.A. 502*.

Pennsylvania is the Keystone state.

The FCC, CIA, FBI, NASA, and all of the other alphabet gangs were never part of the United States government even though the US Government" holds shares of stock in the various Agencies. — *U.S. v. Strang, 254 US 491, Lewis v. US, 680 F.2nd, 1239*.

Americans may think that their government is pegged in some way to the Constitution, but it is not. The United States, like Britain and elsewhere, is ruled by commercial law to overcome the checks and balances of common law. It's another monumental fraud.

Britain is owned by the Vatican. — *Treaty of 1213*. The Vatican courtyard is St. Peter's Square. This is where we get the term "double-crosses"; The Pope and the Queen of England of Rome.

The words "Brit - ish", in Hebrew, mean a contract, or writ, a holy writ. So the word for "Brit" is contract, or covenant. And the word in Hebrew for man is "ish". Therefore "Brit - ish" is the covenant man, or holy man. That is where we get the idea that the King of England is so holy, because he is "Brit-ish", or a "holy man".

But that is Hebrew. Then when you find out where this whole idea of the holiness came from, this is considered a very serious thing because the King of England is considered to be one of the holiest men in the world.

(Research the Divine Rite of Kings & God's United Kingdom.)

The Pope can abolish any law in the United States. — *Elements of Ecclesiastical Law, Volume 1, 53-54*.

The Pope's laws are obligatory on everyone. — *Benedict XIV., De Syn. Dioed, lib, ix., c.vii., n.4 Prari, 1844. Syllabus, prop 28, 29, 44*.

Americans are the cows, the IRS is the company that milks the cows. The UNITED STATES Corporation is the Veterinarian who takes care of the herd and the British Crown is the Owner of the farm. The farm is held in allodium by the Pope.

All this is founded on Roman law, which goes back to the Babylonian and Sumerian law. The Illuminati bloodlines have been playing this same game throughout the centuries. It was brought into England in 1066 and has been enforced by the Pope, Kings, and the Christian Churches ever since. It is total and relentless mind control, people are taught to believe in things that do not exist: the New World Order and the Fourth of July.

**Voice over by Jordan Maxwell:**

When you begin to look at this way our government operates and the words that are used, and the symbols, you begin to see that the most powerful law in the world . . .

There are two basic kinds of law on the earth. One is called Civil law, which goes back to the Latin word "civili". The "ili" is where, in the ancient world the gods, civil means the people of God, so we have something called Civil law.

Civil law is different, for you can do things in America that you can't do in Russsia; you can do things in China that you can't do in Africa. Because the civil law is based on the culture of the people who live on the land.

But there's a far, far more powerful law that the Kings and the powerful men of this planet live by, and it has nothing to do with Civil law; it's called the Law of Water. Because on the earth there are only two things: land and water.

There is 3 times more water than there is earth. So the Law of Water is 3 times more powerful than the law of the land" Civil law. It's called the Law of the High Seas. The Law of Water. This is why the Vatican is call the Holy See. The Sea is considered holy by the masters of this planet; the waters of the earth.

Consequently, based on that idea that the Law of the Sea is the most powerful law on the earth, it is referred to as banking law, the Law of Money is the Law of the Sea. The Cash-flow.

And once you understand that you can get a credit card in China and use it in Africa; you can open up a bank account in New Zeland and use it in Alaska. Why? Because it's banking, and now you're talking money.

Consequently, money is run around the world in one operation. Banking is one thing.

Once you understand that the law of the land is the people's law of the culture, but the law of money is called the law of water.

This is why, incidently, the Statue of Liberty could not be put on American land. It was put in the harbor [of New York City] because the Statue of Liberty is a Maritime/Admiralty symbol.

It's called the Statue of Liberty; not the Statue of Freedom.

There's a world of difference between freedom and liberty. Liberty means that you ask your father if you can use the car. If he says No, you don't use it. Liberty is what a sailor gets when he pulls into a harbor; he asks the captain if he can leave [the ship]. If the captain says Yes — and he is more than likely to say No — that means you have liberty; you don't have freedom.

America is not the land of the free and the home of the brave; we're not free, nor brave. We're ill informed, entertained, and totally ignorant of the powers-that-be on this earth, and how it works.

Let me give you an example of how the Law of Water works. When you go into a court; why do you have to go into a court? You play tennis and basketball on a court. The whole idea on a court is to put the ball back in the other guy's court.

Consequently, this team stands up and throws the ball at that team and that team stands up and throws the ball back. And the Judge sits there, and that's what he is, the Referee. He doesn't care who wins or loses; somebody's going to pay the court. And *he's* going to be payed, so he doesn't care who wins or loses. He's only there to make sure that the game is played correctly. It's called "commerce". Commerce, because the whole world is commerce.

Look up the word commerce in the law dictionary and it tells you sexual intercourse. Marriage is a partnership. Partner is a term used in business. And consider, if your "business" with your partner doesn't work out, you're not going to God, you're going to court, and you bring your check, and all your property, and your house, with you. Cause it's just business — nothing personal.

You need to understand that there's a world of difference between the United States, and America as a country. The corporation headquarters is in Washington D.C.

You also need to understand that Maryland is Mary - land, and that Virginia gives us the word Virgin or vagina. Virginia: Virgin Mary Land. The two together is a sense of power, the Virgin Mary; Virginia Maryland.

What does this have to do with anything? Well it's the central power in America under the Virgin Mary. Once you begin to look at the Vatican.

Now it's going to get serious . . .

We live under the Vatican in this country. The Vatican system, of course, is based one the ancient Roman system. And then, Rome, the seat of power for Caesar, was called Capitol Hill. Capital is a Latin word for money. You either have the Capital or you don't.

Consequently, in the Capitol Hill, Caesar would meet with the Senate. We have a Senate. The symbol for the ancient Senate was two crossed Fasces. The crossing of the Fasces; that's the symbol of the United States Senate.

When you see the president of the United States standing in the Senate and speaking to an audience, look on both sides of the podium, look at the symbols. For many will look with their eyes, but will not see. And listen with their ears, but will not hear. And with the heart, not get the sense of it.

You need to open your eyes and look at the symbols on both sides of the podium which is about an 8 or 9 foot high Fasces: A bundle of sticks with an axe head, the symbol of royal power in Rome. Our system is under Rome. It doesn't matter what you think of the Roman Catholic Church, it doesn't matter what you think of the Religion of the Roman Catholic Church. All you need to know is that you're country is dominated by the Pope: Period!

*"ad Christi potentium et gloriam"*
*(for the power and glory of Christ)*

# Maine Republic Email Alert

*No. 018*

"... that I should bear witness unto the truth." — John 18:33 // David E. Robinson, Publisher

"... if the trumpet give an uncertain sound, who shall prepare himself for battle?" — I Corinthians 14:8

## Rise of the 'Supertrees' [Money Talks]

The island's skyscrapers can be seen behind the trees while to the left, a smaller real real tree struggles to reach the same heights

**People are dwarfed by a clump of "Supertrees" seen against the financial skyline of Singapore on June 29.**

According to AP, Singapore's "Supertrees" are environmentally sustainable vertical gardens displaying tropical flowering climbers, ferns and epiphytes. Ranging from 25 to 50 meters in height, the construction of the trees is part of a government effort to make the city center greener.

• Giant concrete and metal 'plants' create a manmake woodland.
• Trunks are made from concrete while canopies alone weigh up to 80 tonnes.
• Vast structures will house international plants in 'botanical capital of the world.

Towering in front of tall skyscrapers, these enormous trees appear to be thriving in the middle of the city. But the vast woodland in Singapore is actually entirely manmade, stretching up to 50 metres into the sky.

The imposing trees have colossal concrete trunks weighing hundreds of tonnes. While thousands of thick wire rods have been used to create artificial branches and canopies.

The entire structure will house a cluster of green conservatories when it is completed by the end of 2011. Inside the trees there will be plants from around the world. The park will also become home to the Singapore Garden Festival.

http://tinyurl.com/5us74zl

http://tinyurl.com/6yh2heo

http://tinyurl.com/65d69vb

Office of The Maine free State, 3 Linnell Circle, Brunswick, Maine 04011

Hanging gardens and rainwater catches will be added to the trees and a 22 metre high walkway will be made between two of the canopies allowing guests to take in a view of the scenery.

The Gardens at Marina South is one of three waterfront garden projects under the massive Gardens by the Bay initiative, with the other two in Marina East and Marina Center.

Leaders want to create a continuous ring of greenery, with the three gardens wrapping around the Marina Bay area.

'They have to be lightweight, they have to be maintainable and hardy, and a great amount of effort has gone into looking for plants that can actually be sustained on this living skin,' Kenneth Er from Gardens by the Bay told Channel News Asia.

Read more: http://www.dailymail.co.uk/news/article-2009458/Singapore-supertrees-How-giant-concrete-metal-woodland-towering-horizon.html#ixzz1RS1Z1paT

# Maine Republic Email Alert

No.019

"... that I should bear witness unto the truth." — John 18:33 // David E. Robinson, Publisher

"... if the trumpet give an uncertain sound, who shall prepare himself for battle?" — I Corinthians 14:8

## Inflation, Interest & Taxation

*Recorded by California Republic Chief Justice Ken Cousens, Republic Call, July 13, 2011.*

There are **three things** in our current monetary system that are purely scientific, and systematically designed to steal all of the wealth of all the people today, and what we're living in, in our social economic structure, is based on those three things: **Inflation, Interest,** and **Taxation.**

With these **three things,** and with an elastic monetary system, the complete draining of virtually 98% of the wealth created by the people of America, by the banks, is taking place.

The fundamental of what we need to do in restructuring a balanced and a grounded foundational monetary system, with a currency, a treasury, and all of that, is to remove the things that basically lead to this stealing of the wealth.

So let me define elastic monetary currency. Elastic means that it is not fixed; it's not on a par (common level) with one-to-one direct value.

That word "par" is very important to understand, because there is something in the study of monetary structure called a "parity" system ("parity" meaning *equal* or *equivalent*). That means that one unit measurement of value, like a dollar, or a pound, or anything that measures value, is on par, equal one-to-one with a unit of wealth creation.

And there are only four main components of wealth creation: *Labor, Intellectual property, Natural resources* or *raw materials,* and *Manufacturing:* taking Labor, Intellectual property, and Raw materials; and producing a product, such as furniture, houses, automobiles, and all the rest of that.

So we have this term called Gross Natural Product (GNP), or Gross Domestic Product (GDP).

If we're in a parity system, then we create a unit of value, whether we call it a dollar, a sovereign, a beany, or whatever, and we issue that as money; because money is continually being created.

Once that unit of value is produced by human effort and natural resources, and a unit of measure is created, then we're on a parity system; one-to-one.

If those three incremental negative functions, **Inflation, Interest,** and **Taxation** are no longer part of the monetary system, since these are what create elasticity, we have a parity system where the wealth that is being created is retained by the people in the communities, and is building an economic basis that becomes stronger and stronger, is balanced, and does not involve the vast amounts of undermining forces that we're all experiencing today.

So where did we get an elastic monetary system? That's not how the founders started it. We started with what is called **standard weights** and **measures.**

We had a **bi-metal system** where gold and silver were pegged or fixed in a special ratio so that it could not be manipulated against paper.

So all through the 1800's the system was progressively eroded, silver was taken out as a monetary standard in the 1870's, and then into the early 1900's.

In 1913, the Federal Reserve Act was created, and within two years the United States corporation was put into bankruptcy, and the creditor was the Federal Reserve System — the 12 Federal Reserve Banks and their foreign owners who had put the United States into Bankruptcy, and required as part of the bankruptcy reorganization, the implementation of something called **legal tender,** with legal tender laws based on commerce.

And by 1965, the silver was removed as a circulating medium of coins, and in 1966, the international, Uniform Commercial Code (UCC) was introduced, creating a purely elastic currency.

From that point on, an ever-expanding and contracting of the monetary base, caused a steady reduction of the purchasing power of each individual unit of value, or dollar.

And through those three mechanisms, **Inflation, Interest,** and **Taxation,** a progressive eroding of the wealth of the people of the United States to the foreign owners of the non-federal Reserve is taking place.

So that elasticity is very important to understand, since during the history of the last 60-90 years, we see cycles of recessions and expansions at work.

When the bubble expands, the people go to work because of the fluidity of currency and the credit. We saw that in the 1990's in what became known as the "Dot-Com" bubble. The Stock Market created mere paper, along with the creation of capital and stock, and it expanded, then it contracted. Then in the 2000's we had the housing bubble and the mortgage bubble, to boot.

If you look back decade by decade, there were bubbles in mortgages, in farmland values, in commodities, etc. And when the bubbles would expand, the

Office of The Maine free State, 3 Linnell Circle, Brunswick, Maine 04011         53 people would go to work, they would build houses, create farms, build manufacturing facilities, and when that elasticity pulled in and the bubbles broke, this would literally sweep away the wealth, like a windshield wiper that sweeps the water off with every motion, to be redistributed to the big corporations, until where we are fiscally today.

So, the Republic gives us now the ability to create a sound monetary policy through a balanced system that will create parity in the people's wealth, so that we can build and maintain that wealth, and can go back to the America that honored and supported innovation, the emergence of technology, education, and everything else that built this country to be what we knew it to be when we were growing up.

It is all too apparent, the corporate UNITED STATES is no longer the Leader of this world. So that's what we're doing in the Republic: creating a *lawful basis,* a *lawful enclave* to reintroduce a sound monetary policy and enable us to keep that wealth that we build.

California Republic
Chief Justice Ken Cousens

# Maine Republic Email Alert

*No.020*

"... that I should bear witness unto the truth." — John 18:33 // David E. Robinson, Publisher

"... if the trumpet give an uncertain sound, who shall prepare himself for battle?" — I Corinthians 14:8

## Festo Launches SmartBird Robotic Seagull!

On Thursday, March 24, 2011, Festo unveiled their 2011 Bionic Learning Network projects, the most awesome of which is definitely their SmartBird Robotic Seagull. Watch it fly in the videos below.

Unlike many of Festo's prior flying robots, SmartBird doesn't rely on lifting gas at all. It weighs less than half a kilo, and is capable of autonomous **take-off, flight,** and **landing** using just its two meter-long wings.

SmartBird is modeled very closely on the herring gull, and controls itself the same way birds do, by twisting its body, wings, and tail. For example, if you look closely in the videos, you can see SmartBird turning its head to steer.

### Aerodynamic lightweight design

SmartBird is an ultralight but powerful flight model with excellent aerodynamic qualities and extreme agility. With SmartBird, Festo has succeeded in **deciphering the flight of birds** – one of the oldest dreams of humankind.

This bionic technology-bearer, which is inspired by the herring gull, can start, fly and land autonomously – with no additional drive mechanism. Its wings not only beat up and down, but also twist at specific angles. This is made possible by an active articulated torsional drive unit, which in combination with a complex control system attains an unprecedented level of efficiency in flight operation. Festo has thus succeeded for the first time in creating an energy-efficient technical adaptation of this model from nature.

### New approaches in automation

The functional integration of coupled drive units yields significant ideas and insights that Festo can transfer to the development and optimisation of hybrid drive technology.

The minimal use of materials and the extremely lightweight construction pave the way for efficiency in resource and energy consumption.

Festo already today puts its expertise in the field of fluid dynamics to use in the development of the latest generations of cylinders and valves. By analysing **SmartBird's flow characteristics** during the course of its development, Festo has acquired additional knowledge for the optimisation of its product solutions and has learned to design even more efficiently.

Festo SmartBird
http://tinyurl.com/44ywbgl

Bird Flight Deciphered
http://tinyurl.com/3h9b6ud

Festo SmartBird Animation
http://tinyurl.com/3qprmvj

( Maine Patriot Books )
http://tinyurl.com/3ovmxds

Office of The Maine free State, 3 Linnell Circle, Brunswick, Maine 04011

*Office of The Maine free State, 3 Linnell Circle, Brunswick, Maine 04011*

# Maine Republic Email Alert

No. 021

*". . . that I should bear witness unto the truth."* — John 18:33 // David E. Robinson, Publisher

*". . . if the trumpet give an uncertain sound, who shall prepare himself for battle?"* — I Corinthians 14:8

# After Moving In For $16 He's Ready To Share Info

WFAA Bio by CASEY NORTON, July 14, 2011, Updated Saturday, Jul 23.

FLOWER MOUND TEXAS — **A little-known Texas law and a foreclosure could have a man in Flower Mound living on Easy Street.**

Flower Mound's Waterford Drive is lined with well-manicured $300,000 homes. So, when a new neighbor moved in without the usual sale, mortgage-paying homeowners had a few questions.

"What paperwork is it and how is it legally binding if he doesn't legally own the house?" asked Leigh Lowrie, a neighboring resident. "He just squats there."

Lowrie and her husband said the house down the street was in foreclosure for more than a year and the owner walked away. Then, the mortgage company went out of business.

Apparently, that opened the door for someone to take advantage of the situation. But, **Kenneth Robinson** [not related to publisher: publisher is white] said he's no squatter. He said he moved in on June 17 after months of research about a Texas law called **"adverse possession."**

"This is not a normal process, but it is not a process that is not known," he said. "It's just not known to everybody."

He says an online form he printed out and filed at the Denton County courthouse for $16 gave him rights to the house. The paper says the house was abandoned and he's claiming ownership.

"I added some things here for my own protection," Robinson said.

The house is virtually empty, with just a few pieces of furniture. There is no running water or electricity.

But, Robinson said just by setting up camp in the living room, Texas law gives him exclusive negotiating rights with the original owner. If the owner wants him out, he would have to pay off his massive mortgage debt and the bank would have to file a complicated lawsuit.

Robinson believes because of the cost, neither is likely. The law says if he stays in the house, after three years he can ask the court for the title.

He told News 8 his goal is to eventually have the title of the home and be named the legal owner of the home.

"Absolutely," he said. **"I want to be owner of record. At this point,** because I possess it, **I am the owner."**

Robinson posted "no trespassing" signs after neighbors asked police to arrest him for breaking in.

Flower mound officers say they can't remove him from the property because home ownership is a civil matter, not criminal.

Lowrie and her neighbors continue to look for legal ways to get him out. They are talking to the mortgage company, real estate agents and attorneys. They're convinced he broke into the house to take possession, but Robinson told News 8 he found a key and he gained access legally.

"If he wants the house, buy the house like everyone else had to," Lowrie said. "Get the money, buy the house."

Robinson said he's not buying anything. As far as he's concerned, the $330,000 house is already his and he has the paperwork to prove it.

**PUBLISHER'S COMMENTS**
Right on! This guy filed an Affidavit of Adverse possession and now is staying in the house, legally. This ought to renew some interest in the **adverse possession** topic.

Most folks commenting about adverse possession don't understand it.

According to the law the person taking possession (a **"disseisor"**) has a claim of possession as soon as he moves in with intent to claim it as his own. His claim doesn't ripen into "perfect title" until the statutory period has elapsed (usually 7-10 years depending on the state), in this case apparently three years.

**But he does have a claim of title, and the only person with a better claim is the mortgage company.** That means the mortgage company is the only **"person"** who can legally kick him off the property now.

Hmm, so how do you defend against the mortgage company?

I think one should demand to see the **original promissory note**, since without it the lender has no standing to bring a lawsuit. And considering that most mortgages between 2002 and 2008 were sold to investors, the lenders probably no longer have that note.

But naturally the only reason the neighbors are so mad is that they are ignorant enough to pay for mortgages that they do not have to pay for. **If they looked into the retrieval of the original promissory note or the fact that no consideration was given for the mortgage thereby no legally binding contract.**

"Ignorance is bliss" is not always the rule. This case shows what a little knowledge can do for you; and in this case score yourself a house for $16.

This will teach people that being a willfully ignorant slave in the system seldom pays.

Since he has possession he can file a Common Law Lien against it, and a Labor/Mechanics Lien, under Common Law.

These will put him in the position where he will be very tough to remove. Anybody coming against him will have to pay those liens before any title insurance will bind. Before the bank can do much, it has to undo all that and pay off the liens. These liens, if done right, are testimony to his **Affidavit of Adverse Possession.**

No equity judge can lawfully overturn testimony or alter such facts as recorded in commerce under common law.

This looks like a much better way to go than buying a home — unless you can A4V the debt away fast — even then this looks cheaper, **less down payment in FRN's.**

See video:
http://tinyurl.com/4xry4wl

Here's the Affidavit the guy filed one week after he moved in:

http://www.fatwallet.com/static/attachments/102594_affidavitofadversepossession.pdf

**Public Insurance Policy HJR 192 of 1933** provided a **REMEDY** for the victims of President Roosevelt's crime. This **REMEDY** is the basis of lawful **mutual offset credit exemption exchange.** This **CONVERSION** created the **EXEMPTION** upon which **mutual offset credit exemption exchange** is based.

http://tinyurl.com/39eoywm

# Maine Republic Email Alert

No. 022

"... that I should bear witness unto the truth." — John 18:33 // David E. Robinson, Publisher

"... if the trumpet give an uncertain sound, who shall prepare himself for battle?" — I Corinthians 14:8

## Republic Telephone Call - July 20, 2011

**Republic Weekly Update** 7-20-2011 Kelby Smith-Host/Moderator. This call is a great starter call for the brand new party to the Republic.

http://tinyurl.com/4xtvrqg

Republic Calls are Open to Public Wednesdays 6:00 P.S.T. / 9:00 E.S.T. Conf.No: (424) 203-8000 Code: 819054.

**Kelby speaks on the specific history and fraud from 1776 to 1871.**
Some key Definitions:
When a word is implied in a contract "person" also means "corporation."
"De-facto" means "not by right and not by law."
"De-jur" means "according to law, by right, or lawful and original."

The Obama administration does not exist by right or law, and in fact has no right to exist.

The Republic for the united States of America re-seated the government that was vacated in 1860.

The Call that you are on tonight is the rightful lawful government on the land.

Between 1776 and 1860, the United States was a collection of sovereign republics in a Union, and the federal government did not control the States; it had very little authority

In 1860 Congress was adjourned sine dia (without day; to reconvene). This was the very last time that the rightful, lawful de-jur Congress convened. No Congress has lawfully convened since that date.

In 1860, the Southern States seceded from the Northern Union States while James Buchanan was President. Most people think that slavery was the reason, but the reason was taxation.

In 1861, war was declared on the Southern States, violating states rights by a taxation without representation. Sla-

very was propaganda to keep the North's support of the war.

In 1861, President Lincoln declared a national emergency and established martial law. This gave the president massive powers, and withdrew power from the other branches. This emergency has never been reversed.

People think that a war, like the Civil War, is only for four or five years. In fact, World War I lasted for 90 years!

Because Germany was found liable, they had to repay the people they went to war against. It took Germany 90 years to pay the cost of World War I, so technically it was a 90 year war.

Why is this component important?
**To maintain martial law, you have to be in an active war.**

You know you're in an active war because of the flag that is flown; because presidents have been declaring Executive Orders ever since 1861.

The flag with the gold fringe is a war flag. It is flown in every courthouse, and in every state building, and in every government school, and it is flown behind the president in the presidential office.

**In 1861, habeas corpus was suspended.** Habeas corpus means "You have the body." The term represents an important right granted to citizens in America. It is a traditional mandate requiring the prisoner to be brought before the court; and when the government has a right to continue retaining them, the individual being held there can petition the court for such a writ.

**In 1863, the Lieber Code,** also known as **General Order 100,** better-known as **the first Executive Order, was introduced by the Secretary of War,** with **instructions for the government of the armies of the United States in the Field.**

Article III declared that martial law in a hostile country consists of **the suspension by the occupying military authority of the criminal and civil law.** This Executive Order declared a suspension of the criminal and civil law.

**This is Key: there has never been a peace treaty ending the Civil War.** We are still under martial law, and we have no property rights.

**In 1865, the capital was moved to Washington, DC.** The District of Columbia is not a part of this country. Like Vatican City in Rome, and the City of London in London, England, **Washington DC is a separate and individual city-state. It is not a part of these United States.**

**In 1871, the United States Corporation was established by a de-facto Congress that had no rights or authority to do this.**

Using the leverage of bankruptcy and the federal government's debt, and its desperate need for funds, the international bankers finally got their foot in the door; the 41st Congress, without constitutional authority to do so, passed **an act to provide the government for the District of Columbia.**

A corporation was formed called the **United States Corporation of Washington, DC.** This placed the corporate government on the 10 square mile area

Office of The Maine free State, 3 Linnell Circle, Brunswick, Maine 04011

of land where it is today: **the United States Corporation,** under commercial public law, rather than private common law.

**Their Constitution is different from our Constitution. It is the same Constitution** of 1791 (the 1787 Original with the Bill of Rights added in 1791) **but withour the Bill of Rights.**

It needed to be ratified by the people according to the original Constitution, but **their Constitution was never ratified.**

This Corporate Constitution, operating in economic capacity, is being used to fool you, the American people, into thinking it is the same parchment that governs the original Republic. It absolutely is not. **The whole process was established behind closed doors.**

**The United States was incorporated on February 21, 1871.** You can find that in **16 Stat. 419, ch. 62, 41st Congress, 1st. Sess.** The purpose being **"an Act to provide a Congress for the District of Columbia."**

United States means federal Corporation, **28 USC § 3002 Definitions (15)(a).** The location of the United States Corporation is in the District of Columbia. One of the meanings of "Columbia" is "Goddess of death and destruction."

The United States Constitution is a foreign corporation with respect to the states. 19 CJS 541.

**In 1871, the original constitutional government was vacated** basically until 2010. The de-jur and de-facto juries that existed and overall had governmental power no longer was the de-jur power. It operates under common private law and **with the Act of 1871 our constitution was defaced;** the title was block capitalized, and the word "for" was changed to the word "of" in the title.

The original Constitution drafted by our Founding Fathers was written this way in the Preamble, the first paragraph of the Constitution. It calls itself **the Constitution "for" the United States of America.** The altered Constitution for the Corporation reads the Constitution "of" the United States of America.

**Go to House.gov**, the website for the legislative body of the de-facto government, **and search the word "Constitution"** and you will find brackets around the numbers of the first 12 Amendments.

Something in brackets is omitted and not to be considered.

This is saying that we're showing you the first 12 amendments, but we don't consider them, because we didn't adopt them. This is done to fool the American people into thinking that they have those rights, whereas they really don't.

It is important to understand just how God and the enemy plays into this whole picture, and how straight forward the dark and light issue really is.

In the 1800's a private corporation took over this country without the majority of the people ever knowing it.

In the late 1800's, when the 41st Congress gave the District of Columbia the 10 square miles for the seat of government, they had to structure and lay out the streets of the city.

In 1860 everything that those politicians and bankers did was to clearly mock man and God.

When they laid out the streets of Washington, DC (the District of Columbia) they layed out the streets in a design that framed what is called the "goat head": an upside down star.

The goat is a beast of the field. So in Washington, DC, they built the streets so that there world be an upside down star with the White House at the bottom of the star. The mouth of the goat head is located at the bottom of the star. That is said to be the mouthpiece of the beast.

13 streets directly north of the White House is the 33rd degree Mason Church. 13 is a number that is commonly used in the Occult. They serve the enemy, not the God of the Bible.

The place where this church is located is where the brains of the goat head would be, to show you who actually is running things.

And the top 3 points of this star are Scott, Logan, and DuPont traffic circles, which have 6 avenues running into them. So across the forehead of the head of the beast are the numbers 666.

Go to Google and click on "images" and type in **"pentagon Washington, DC"** (or go directly to http://tinyurl.com/4xdnbjv). And you can actually see where the Mason Church continued in putting their mark by putting the compass and ruler that the Masons used into the streets as well.

In 1066, William the Conqueror established the "City of London." on the Thames River, to be known as London.

Everything we're dealing with today, how America has been bled dry of its wealth over the past 200 years; and we are now literally being dispossessed from all of our homes, or virtually all of them. But the fundamental, underlying legal structural principles were actually laid down soon after the conquering of the southern area of England in 1066.

**The Crown of England is** naturally **held by the sovereigns, and was passed on by lines of succession.**

In 1213, King John was in fear of his mortal soul and wished to make amends. And for hundreds of years the Catholic Church was accepting payments from the wealthy in one form or another to pay off their sins, obeisances, allowances, and things like that.

**Well, King John,** having a very large and disproportionate debt to pay, and decided to relinquish and grant. irrevocable and incontestably, all of his rights, titles, lands, and hereditaments to his and his successors, forever **the claim and rights to the Crown of England to the Vatican and the Pope.**

So to this day **the Crown of England is held and retained by the Vatican and the Popes.** That was in the year 1213 and from that time forward, progressively into the 1600's, culminating with the building of the formal, organized, jurisdictional area known as the City of London, about the 1660's.

In fact, if you will recall the history of the Great Fire of London, **the City of London is a separate distinct jurisdiction. It has nothing to do with London, England; just as Vatican City has nothing to do with Rome, Italy; just as Washington, DC, has nothing to do with the rest of the contiguous states of the Union of States in North America.**

What I am outlining here as in reference to the establishment of **three city-states; Vatican City, the City of London, and Washington, DC.**

The City of London was established

to be the banking establishment of the world to control the banking wealth and the gold and the commercial extensions of the crown — the crown being held by the City of London, as agent for its owner, the Vatican.

The extension of the City of London for commercial terms was the establishment by corporate charter of the British East India Company in the early part of the 1600's, and extending out from the British Empire, from the 1600's to the 1900's, throughout the world, establishing at one time virtually 25% or more of the known lands and political entities of the world, controlled by the British East India Company as a corporate monopoly that started as a commercial extension of the crown of England for the purposes that I am outlining.

When the Constitution for the united States was established, it established a relationship for the social/economic compact between the sovereign, nation-state of the Republic, the 13 original Republics, from 1776 though 1787. The commercial interests of the crown were retained in that contract. You can look at Article 6 where it says that [henceforth] "All debts contracted and engagements entered into, before the adoption of this Constitution, shall be as valid against the United States" as under the Confederation.

That meant that the crown of England, through the British East India Company, as a commercial extension representing both the commercial and economic interests of the City of London and the owner of the Crown, was established as a link to the United states.

The United States Corporation was established to return all of the authority and sovereign capacity of the people to the crown; and the Sovereign Republics inside out and upside down. To create a federal overlay so that eventually, by 1933, all of the states' rights, and all of the people's capacities both in sovereign and in economic and legal terms would be separated and subjugated by contract into that corporate United States.

So if you look at Vatican City, the City of London, and Washington, DC, as the equivalent of those three points of the Confederation that Kelby described laid out in the street diagram of Washington, DC,

it's the concept of a tri-partide co-ownership of the world. And in law we have a hierarchy of what is considered the highest laws, or forms of law, at least from their point of view. The highest is Common law, that's the Church; below that is Kingdom law, that's the Crown, and below that is Commercial law, and that's Washington, DC, through commerce and through the attachment by contract of everything I've described.

Of course we could go on and on, but I just wanted to summarize this, that if we move forward in history to the 1860's and 1870's, that Corporation was put into bankruptcy on March 6, 1933. Three days later, on March 9, 1933, President Franklin Delano Roosevelt declared a state of emergency. He asked Congress to grant him the war-powers to continue on the basis of martial law, so from that going forward we have been in a continuous state of declared emergency and declared martial law. And in this state the President is a Dictator who controls the structure that we were taught in school was the separation and balance of power between three branches of government, Executive, Legislative, and Judicial, where in fact those 3 branches are under the authority of the president.

Everything we watch unfold these days is, for the most part, a dog-and-poney-show to keep the public thinking that we have some form of say in the government; and we don't.

In 1933 when all this happened, everything was brought under that corporate United States and attached as pledged collateral, and from that point forward everything is collateralized, as what is known in insurance and legal terms, as a pledge of surety, a guarantee, against what? Against debt.

The system we have today is an ever expanding uncollectible and unretireable structure of debt that basically is designed, and has been designed, to bond the people to that surety attachment to a status of perpetual debt, and enslavement to that debt.

That's to you, and your children, and your grandchildren, and your great, great grandchildren — except for one caveat — there's a hierarchy of those laws. What supersedes that is the law of the land, and we hold the law of the land, and the

law of the land supersedes all of that.

And we have the capacity and the authority to do what we need to do.

I now yield the floor.

**From 1933 on what has been built** is the New World Order; and the subjugation of the Sovereignty of the United States into a global system.

I'd like to present 4 quotes from the statute codes and other bodies of codified statutes:

1. **On December 26, 1933, 49 Statute 3097**, Treaty Theories 881, **Convention on Rights and Duties of States:** Congress replaced statutes with international law placing all states under the Uniform Commercial Code (UCC).

2. **On December 9, 1945, the International Organization Immunities Act** relinqushed every public office of the United States **to the United Nations.** 22 CFR The implementing regulations that come out of the federal register. 92.12 through 92.31 that an oath is required to take office.

3. **Title 8 USC 1481: Once and oath of office is taken citizenship is relinquished** thus one becomes a foreign entity or agency or state. This means that **every public office in the United States has been pledged to be in the United Nations** and is acting as a public office or officer as a foreign state including all political subdivisions and every public officer is a foreign agent, including **every court in the system is considered to be a separate foreign entity.** All of the courts are **administrative courts functioning within their admiralty international law adjudicating the ongoing bankruptcy of the debtor corporation** and setting the commercial requirements under that context **with all the people being the bonded surety.** In other words, we are hamsters on a wheel creating more debt, more attachment and perpetual debt and enslavement.

4. Finally, **Title 27 USC, Foreign Relations and Intercourse Chapter One, Identification,** All public officials as foreign agents. **The corporate United**

States is a foreign country. Foreign to who we are; and now we have re-inhabited the original Republic and are re-establishing the law and the capacity and standing of the people in Republic on the land, and re-establishing our sovereign rights, authority, and capacity.

We invite you to educate yourself to all of this and to make that choice, if you want to begin to re-build a true secure state with all of the protections that are available within the Republic for yourself and your children.

I now yield the floor.

## SPECIAL NEWS
http://tinyurl.com/3upf9kv

**On June 16, 2011, the US Supreme Court** overturned a US Court of Appeal ruling; and, believe it or not, **reasserted not only State sovereignty but individual sovereignty as well.** And we thought the government was going to hell in a hand basket! **This unanimous decision,** as I see it, **is a major turning point, a visible shift in consciousness of the ruling elite.** All things are possible. Watch for miraculous reversals in the remainder of **this 9th wave.**

http://www.supremecourt.gov/opinions/10pdf/09-1227.pdf

# Maine Republic Email Alert

*No.023*

*". . . that I should bear witness unto the truth." — John 18:33 // David E. Robinson, Publisher*

*". . . if the trumpet give an uncertain sound, who shall prepare himself for battle?" — I Corinthians 14:8*

## Ground-breaking Supreme Court Ruling - July 16, 2011

On June 16, 2011, the United States Supreme Court overturned a US Court of Appeals ruling, and believe it or not, reasserted not only State sovereignty but individual sovereignty as well.

**By Ron Van Dyke**, Melbourn, Florida. Good morning. You know, my mood just keeps getting better and better. I just have so much joy in my heart. The Spirit keeps revealing more thing to me.

Because of the legal action of which I'm involved, I subscribe to a lot of Alerts and e-mail groupings, and stuff like that keeps me abreast of what's happening in the world of law and courts, because I'm... like it or not, I have to be concerned, because I'm involved myself in these matters, and for may of you who are not involved with matters of the court, it may not make any difference because where we're in, in this 9th wave, is a shift in consciousness that is changing the entire world.

The title of a message that I just received by e-mail is, Groundbreaking US Supreme Court Ruling, that on June 16, 2011, that's a little over a month ago, the United States Supreme Court overturned a US Court of Appeals ruling, and, believe it or not, reasserted not only State sovereignty but individual sovereignty as well. And we thought the government was going to hell in a handbasket.

This unanimous decision, as I see it, is a major turning point, a visible shift in consciousness of the ruling elite. All things are possible. Watch for miraculous reversals in the remainder of this 9th wave.

Here is what some of what was said by Kennedy on the Supreme Court, and Ginsburg filed a concurring opinion, and Bryer joined in.

They completely reversed and remanded the lower court which is not a very low court: the US Court of Appeals is a pretty high court and the UN

**Ron Van Dyke**

Supreme Court overturned it. This is wonderful news.

Let me read a few paragraphs from this ruling. This is *Carol Anne Bond vs. United States*. 09-1227; 564 US Supreme Court, etc., that came to me in the e-mail.

It's amazingly good news!

### BEGIN QUOTES

"The Court of Appeal held that because a State was not a party to the federal Criminal proceeding, petitioner had no standing to challenge the statute as an infringement upon the powers reserve to the States. Having concluded that petitioner does have standing to challenge the federal statute on these grounds, this Court now reverses that determination"

"The federal balance is, in part, an end in itself, to ensure that States function as political entities in their own right."

"State sovereignty is not just an end in itself: 'Rather, federalism secures to citizens the liberties that derive from the diffusion of sovereign power.'"

"Federalism secures freedom of the individual. It allows States to respond, through the enactment of positive law, to the initiative of those who seek a voice in shaping the destiny of their own time, without having to rely solely upon the political processes that control a remote central power. ...the individual liberty secured by federalism is not simply derivative of the right of the States."

"Federalism also protects the liberty of all persons within a State by ensuring that laws enacted in excess of delegated governmental power cannot direct or control their actions."

"By denying any one government complete jurisdiction over all the concerns of public life, federalism protects the liberty of the individual from arbitrary power. When government acts in excess of its lawful power, that liberty is at stake."

"The limitations that federalism entails are not therefore a matter of rights belonging only to the States. States are not the sole intended beneficiaries of federalism."

"An individual has a direct interest in objecting to laws that upset the constitutional balance between the National Government and the States when the enforcement of those laws causes injury that is concrete, particular, and redressable. Fidelity to principles of federalism is not for the States alone to vindicate."

"The public policy of the Commonwealth of Pennsylvania, enacted in its capacity as sovereign, has been displace by that of the National Government."

"Impermissible interference with state sovereignty is not within the enumerated powers of the National Government, and

*Office of The Maine free State, 3 Linnell Circle, Brunswick, Maine 04011*

and action that exceeds the National Government's enumerated powers undermines the sovereign interests of States."

"Bond, like any other defendant, has a personal right not to be convicted under a constitutionally invalid law."

"Due process ... is a guarantee that a man should be tried and convicted only in accordance with valid laws of the land."

"In this case, Bond argues that the statute under which she was charged, 18 USC §229, exceeds Congress' enumerated powers and violates the Tenth Amendment. Other defendants might assert that a law exceeds Congress' power because it violates the Ex Post Facto Clause, or the Establishment Clause, or the Due Process Clause."

"Whatever the claim, success on the merits would require reversal of the conviction. 'An offence created by [an unconstitutional law],' the Court has held, 'is not a crime.' A conviction under [such a law] is not merely erroneous, but is illegal and void, and cannot be a legal cause of imprisonment. If a law is invalid as applied to the criminal defendant's conduct, the defendant is entitled to go free."

"A court has no 'prudential' license to decline to consider whether the statute under which the defendant has been charged lacks constitutional application to her conduct. And that is so even where the constitutional provision that would render the conviction void is directed at protecting a party not before the Court."

"Reversal required even if, going forward, Congress would cure the unequal treatment by extending rather than invalidating the criminal proscription."

"In short, a law 'beyond the power of Congress,' for any reason, is 'no law at all.' The validity of Bond's conviction depends upon whether the Constitution permits Congress to enact §299. Her claim that it does not must be considered and decided on the merits."

END QUOTES

And then this e-mail that I received said that this would mean that the following were also reversed: *Madbury vs. Madison* (1803):

"The very essence of civil liberty certainly consists in the right of every individual to claim the protection of the laws whenever he receives an injury. One of the first duties of government is to afford that protection. In Great Britain, the King himself is sued in the respectful form of a petition and he never fails to comply with the judgment of this court. A law repugnant to the Constitution is void. And act of Congress repugnant to the Constitution cannot become a law. The Constitution supersedes all other laws, and the individual's rights shall be liberally enforced in favor him to clearly an expressly designated beneficiary."

Folks, do you understand anything of what I just read to you? I mean, this is enormously powerful!!!

At a time when we thought the government, as I said, was going to hell in a handbasket, that the powers were being concentrated in the federal government and in the state, and in the Elite's power-grab for a New World Order, all of a sudden, the US Supreme Court which has made some horrible decisions in the past, makes this decision in June of 2011 during the 9th wave of the Myan Calendar. Reasserting for each of us our individual rights.

And you better believe, this will be in my brief before the Court of Appeals. Because spirit is bringing to me syncrinistically that which I need and I am invoking principles of mate Masonic principles that have been long established and most of these judges, who are going to be hearing my case, if not all three of them, are probably 33rd Degree Mason.

And there is a spiritual foundation for Masonry, folks, like it or not, and they have left the markings in plain view.

I mean, I am so encouraged by what I see happening, because this is conscientiousness folks. This is a shift in conscientiousness — this is a reversal of the power-grab of the Elite — by the Elite!!!

Listen to me! . . . This is the United States Supreme Court! . . . And other courts will be following suit. And people that have cases before the court would be foolish not to use this newest ruling less than a month old, in their own case, to get the lower courts to pay attention,

as I am going to be doing in my brief. And I totally changed the way I am doing my brief. I mean my brief is being revolutionized, just in the past few days. Because of the new information that's coming in to me.

And I was fretting and beside myself with worry, and trying to fit, as I said... into a box that I didn't fit into, studying all these laws, and looking into all these laws, and all of a sudden, I get this ruling that reaffirms divine law, natural law, constitutional law, higher law, and reaffirms sovereignty; my sovereignty; your sovereignty.

This is a sovereignty issue folks. And the Elite — the Elite of the government of the United States — just reaffirmed it for each of us. This is powerful, powerful information. And you may think that politics and stuff like this has nothing to do with you.

My friend, It has *everything* to do with everyone of us; *everything* to do. There is no division. There is no division between spritiual and political, or between spirit and anything else. Spiritual encompasses the whole thing.

I've been saying that. I hope you're getting it. I'm getting it, folks. I'm getting it And I invite you to get it too, because this is part of the change that is happening that's shifting the entire world, and it is a change of conscious-ness. Consciousness drives reality, folks; not the other way around.

Well, when *un*-consciousness is in the drivers seat you get what we *had,* but now consciousness and awakening is happening. It's shifting everything, as the Supreme Court Ruling indicates.

It's a beautiful thing. And a beautiful time to be alive!

Thank you for listening, and I hope you're as excited about what I shared as I am. Namistad.*

http://tinyurl.com/3upf9kv

*Not sure if it's spelled correctly, or what it means, but it *sounds* good.

# Maine Republic Email Alert

*No.024*

"... that I should bear witness unto the truth." — John 18:33 // David E. Robinson, Publisher

"... if the trumpet give an uncertain sound, who shall prepare himself for battle?" — I Corinthians 14:8

## Benjamin Fulford on American Freedom Radio; *01-31-12*

**Moderator:** [Sean David Morton] Most of the people in my audience are very familiar with my guest, Benjamin Fulford. Hi, Ben. How are you?

**Ben:** Yeah. Fine, fine.

**Sean:** Every time I read your post it seems like the tide is turning, that the whole point of 2012 is that there are more of us than there is of them. I love the fact that you're thinking big. That you're looking at the whole globe being reshaped, so give us the update. What's the good news from behind the scenes?

**Ben:** Yeah. Things are happening for sure.

**Sean:** And all good things, I'm sure.

**Ben:** Well, first of all, here in Asia, the secret history, Ah, has come out, you know, and we find out that Korea and Japan were ruled in secret by two competing Korean dynasties, the Northern and the Southern.

And it goes back so far...

For example, during World War II the Japanese ground Army was run by the Northern dynasty, and the Navy was run by the Southern dynasty.

The southern dynasty was allied with the House of Windsor and the British, and the Northern dynasty was run by the Nazis.

And to this day, George Bush, Sr. is considered to be the boss of some of the ??? groups, and he supplies them, or some of his groups, with drugs, through the 7th Fleet.

So that situation has been going on for...

What happened was, there was a coup de tat in the North. And North Korea was run by the leftovers of the Japanese Imperial Army. It was like the Japanese World Way II government in exile. That's what North Korea really was.

But now that's changed. Their leader Kim Jong Un is willing to accept some kind of a ceremonial post, and what this will mean, is that...

The thing being discussed now, and a lot of the Japanese right wing types, and everybody else who have the actual men, the guns, and the goons, and all that kind of stuff, are saying that they want to join North and South Korea with Japan and then move the capital of the new entity west of Osaka around Nara, the oldest city there.

**Sean:** To Henry City which is the center of religion called Tenrikyo started by Oyasama [Nokayama Miki], a woman who was channeling extra terrestrials in the 1840's. So it's a very sacred city and it's a perfect place for them to start, sort of a whole new system.

**Ben:** One other thing is...

The Japanese people for 50 years have been sending stuff to America — cars, tv's, radios, whatever — and a lot of the times they've been sending it on credit, and what that means is that they're the largest colonial creditors in the world. That means they have a lor of trust. A lor of people trust them and have good will towards them because they got stuff from them — physical stuff that they can use.

So what's happening is, the plan being pushed is that we're going to set up long term investments for everbody, a life agency with an initial budget of ten million yen, or about $125,000 for every man, woman, and child on earth, for development projects, canals, irrigation projects, schools, holpitals, nature preserves, and that kind of stuff.

And that's gonna lead to huge projects. Discussion are going on now. We're at the level where we're down to a few people.

For example, the man now in charge of the yen prinring press is a guy called ???. He's the top beaueaucrat of administrative finance.

And that's the cutting edge of what's going on back over here. OK?

Now in the West, it's still more complicated. The Pentagon and the military types are really trying to isolate the Federal Reserve Board thugs, and that process is still taking time. You still don't see it on the corporate media. You still see these people running around, and as long as you do, you still con't be 100% opportunistic, but what I am hearing, though, is that what the Pentagon proplr have decided is that they're going to end the FED. They're gonna bust up the big corporation that were adquired by these people through their printing press.

For example, Microsoft will finally dease to exist as it is now, according to these people, and there's gonna be a lor of money freed for the United States and for Europe, but only after these criminals are removed.

And of course they're stubbornly clinging to power. But they're trying to join us now, and they're being told, "NO. Because you guys are not trustworthy. You've broken every promis you've made for the past hundreds of years."

I mean, they lie through their teeth constantly. They don't know how to make an honest deal. So they've lost what's know as Trust, in the world.

That's what's going on.

We don't trust you anymore. You're murderers and liers. And you've never kept any of you're promises.

So they're slowly being isolated. And that process is what you can see in the corporate news when the IMF is saying that they have no money. When Greece is telling Germany to buzz off. When Sicily's on strike. This is the process of cutting them off, to get them out.

Now, you need to understand that what the Asians, and their Allies in the West and the rest of the world, have to their advantage is that they control the physical stuff. The actual ships with stuff in them, as opposed to the money printing presses in dollars and euros.

And at the end of the day, you can eay a ship load of wheat; you cannot eaty a ship load of dollars. You know what I mean?

And that's the process. We're isolating them on the physical economy so that their virtual finacial economy is like Wile E. Coyote after he's run off the cliff, you know, and it's taken him this long to figure out that he can't fly!

# Maine Republic Email Alert

No. 025

*". . . that I should bear witness unto the truth." — John 18:33 // David E. Robinson, Publisher*

*". . . if the trumpet give an uncertain sound, who shall prepare himself for battle?" — I Corinthians 14:8*

## The Maine Republic Free State Trust

02-10-12

A Trust is a three party contract between a Beneficiary, an Executor, and a Trustee.

A Trust is a three party contract based on the Trinity of the Bible — the Father; the Son; and the Holy Ghost.

The Bible is God's Last Will & Testament. A Testament is testimony left by a Testator in a Will.

The Father is the Testator, the Son is the Beneficiary, and the Holy Spirit provides the Energy and the Will to perform.

A good way to understand Trusts is to think of Corporations, because a trust is a corporation under different terms.

A Corporation has Shareholders, Directors, and Employees.

A Trust has Beneficiaries, Executors, and Trustees.

The Trustees hold and manage the property for the benefit of the Beneficiaries, as instructed by the Executor according to the terms of the trust agreement.

Trustees obey the Executor, for the benefit of the Beneficiaries;

Just as Employees obey the Director, for the benefit of the Shareholders;

Just as the Spirit must be in line with the Father's Will, for the benefit of the Son.

A Trustee can't be the Executor or a Beneficiary of a trust; just as an Employee can't be the Director or a Shareholder of a corporation... and visa, versa.

An Executor or a Beneficiary can't be a Trustee; just as a Director or a Shareholder can't be an Employee.

What the Great Testator gave us to enjoy, develope, and maintain, is held in trust for us by our government employees.

In the trust called the **Maine Free State**, the Executor/Governor was John V.; the Beneficiaries/Members were the citizens of the state; and the Officers/Trustees were the officials of the trust.

On the basis of the Maxim *"Until it is documented, it doesn't exist"* — and in behalf of the citizens of the state — the Attorny General documented **The Maine Republic Free State** as a trust, by donating the equity in his Mobile Home to the Trust, as the Corpus or body of the trust, for the benefit of the citizens of the state, each having an equal share.

**The trust called The United States Corporation**

Compare the above with the U.S. Corporation, *which is also a trust,* which has been perverted in its execution, by the state.

The government employees are the Trustees who hold the public property of the Trust for the benefit of the Executor (the Corp) and themselves. They reversed the roles of the trust whereby the Beneficiaries are treated as Trustees instead of the Beneficiaries that they are.

You are a *natural* person as defined in Black's Law dictionary.

Your strawman is an *artificial* person established by law — as a corporation, or trust.

There are only two kinds of law. God's law, and man's law. Natural law, and Contract law. The *lawful* person, and the legal person. The *natural* person, and the *artificial* person.

But, in the U.S. Corporation government officials tell the citizens what to do, for the benefit of government employees, and the state.

Whereas, in a Republic, citiizens tell the government employees what to do, for the benefit of themselves as citizens, and the state.

In the U.S. Corporation, citizens of the state are treated a government employees, of the state — by presumption — not by fact.

And the *Strawman* is the Bait for the "Bait and Switch."

Your legal name is a *presumption of law*. They have to get you to join into their law, and act as an employee, instead of the citizen that you are — to act as a trustee, instead of the beneficiary that you are — to take orders from the state, instead of directing the state to obey the Constitution as the "Law of the Land" that it is.

Who is the Beneficiary of your estate? You are!

Who is the Executor of your estate? You are!

Who are the Trustees of your estate? Government employees!

The government and the courts operate on presumption. They deal in presumptions that until rebutted stand as law.

So, rebut the presumptions by rebutting the contracts that don't exist. Anything *after* Man is a legal contract; a fiction.

So, ask yourself this: Where is the contract? What obligation does the contract claim? Was I aware of the contract? Did I agree to the contract? Where is the consideration? Was the contract fully disclosed?

Don't be conned into being the Trustee. Be the *Administrator/Executor/Director* of your estate. A Director directs; Trustees obey.

Office of The Maine free State, 3 Linnell Circle, Brunswick, Maine 04011

**PURE TRUST ORGANIZATIONS**

1. Your right to contract cannot be impaired.
2. The first operating entity should hold beneficial interest in subsequent trusts.
3. A family trust can use your last name, i.e., Robinson Family Trust.
4. It is best to name your business trust as a sole proprietorship, i.e., ABC Whatever.
5. A pure trust has no tax requirements.
6. A pure trust has no need for a SSN or EIN — but most banks require one to establish a checking account.
7. The trust identification number is private.
8. The same individual cannot be both a trustee and a beneficiary; this separation make the trust pure.
9. The executor/protector employs and can terminate a trustee for good cause shown.
10. The executor/protector can be anyone except the trustor/maker.
11. Trustees hold title to the property for the benefit of the beneficiaries.
12. Trustees receive contractually agreed upon compensation for their services.
13. There can be one or many trustees.
14. A pure trust is not a grantor trust subject to probate.
15. Trustees have no interest in the property that they hold.
16. The majority of trustees must be adverse (unrelated) to the beneficiaries.
17. If family members are beneficiaries there must be at least three unrelated trustees beside yourself.
18. The trustees can appoint you as the managing trustee of your trust.
19. The trustor of trust #1 can be a beneficiary of subsequent trusts.
20. The managing trustee is employed by the trust.
21. A pure trust organization is a sovereign entity in itself (strawman).
22. The name of trust and the names of the trustees both go on titles.
23. The name of the trust manager is private and is only recorded in the private minutes of the trust.
24. Beneficiaries hold beneficial interest in the property, income, use and proceeds of the trust.
25. Beneficiaries have free use of the property on the trust.
26. Trustees assign capital units (100%) to the exchanger/trustor/settler in exchange for the property conveyed.
27. Trustor must divide and assign portions of the capital units to the beneficiaries as he sees fit.
28. A pure trust is untainted by outside interests.
29. You are the *exchanger/trustor/maker/settler;* you contract with the trust by equal proprety exchange.
30. You donate assets with $25 dollars minimum of silver consideration and receive an interest in any residuals.
31. The fiduciary owner(s) of the trust then appoint the trustor's strawman as the managing director of the trust.

Available at retail bookstores and AMAZON.com

# Maine Republic Email Alert

No. 026

"... that I should bear witness unto the truth." — John 18:33 // David E. Robinson, Publisher

"... if the trumpet give an uncertain sound, who shall prepare himself for battle?" — I Corinthians 14:8

## Benjamin Fulford's Report

02-13-2012

Ben reported, today, that all is proceeding to remove the cabal heads, and to bring in a new financial system.

He also discusses the evidence for the 3-11-11 tsunami and nuclear events being planned and carried out by various operatives.

One of the 15 technicians who planted the bombs that caused the tsunami survived, and has been sheltered for protection, and a book has been written that discusses how the tsunami was artificially generated.

**Highlights:**

The controlled implosion of the Federal Reserve Board and the European Central Bank is continuing and must be completed before a new financial system can go online...

...action is soon expected against criminals like Israel's Benjamin Netanyahu... Henry Kissinger, J. Rockefeller, Carl Rove, Peter Hans Kolvenbach, Rahm Emmanuel, the Bush family and Yasuhiro Nakasone.

...evidence we have that the 3/11 tsunami and nuclear disaster were a deliberate attack... U.S. Deputy Secretary of State Kurt Campbell met DPJ power broker Ichiro Ozawa on March 9th, 2011 and offered him the rights to Zeolite in Fukushima Prefecture...

...stock price of Higashi Nihon House, a maker of discount housing in Northern Japan, rose 40% on March 10th...

...local news reports dating to January, 2011, that the deep sea drilling vessel Chikyu Maru was systematically drilling holes at what became the exact epicenters of the quakes.

...Pastor Paulo Izumi... Based on details provided by [an] SDF [Special Defense Forces] technician [who helped plant the bombs], Paulo wrote up the details of how the tsunami was artificially created, in two books published by Hikaruland Press.

A threat to retaliate against an attack on Tokyo by sinking the Las Palmas rock formation in the Canary Islands and setting off a 100 meter tsunami to hit the US East Coast and Southern Europe has deterred further attacks on Japan.

... it is still a good idea to set up the new LIFE ("Long-term Investments For Everyone") economic planning agency in the Nara plain South of Osaka.

The Pentagon and agency white hats are also supportive of these plans. They say there are now 6 competing plans for a new financial system and none is taking the lead so far.

If the LIFE agency can get the rights to use gold-backed Yen overseas and can begin hiring staff, there is no technical or logistical reason why it should not be possible to end poverty and stop environmental destruction this year.

— — —

**Controlled Implosion of Federal Reserve Board and European Central Bank**

The controlled implosion of the Federal Reserve Board and the European Central Bank continuing as planned and must be completed before a new financial system can go online, according to Pentagon and other sources. In addition, action is soon expected against criminals like Israel's Benjamin Netanyahu.

Netanyahu murdered his psychiatrist Moshe Yatom after Yatom began revealing Netanyahu's insane plans to work with Mossad agent and Iranian President Mahmoud Ahmajinedad to start World War 3.

Netanyahu also phoned Japanese Prime Minister Naoto Kan after the 3/11 tsunami and nuclear disaster and threatened to blow up all of Japan's nuclear plants unless Japan handed vast sums of money to his criminal cabal.

Other individuals expected to be "dealt with" include Henry Kissinger, J. Rockefeller, Carl Rove, Peter Hans Kolvenbach, Rahm Emmanuel, the Bush family and Yasuhiro Nakasone.

If any of these individuals feel they are wrongly included on this list, they must contact this writer directly and explain why. The Luciferian cabalists have been arrogant and believe the White Dragon Society, the Red and the Blue, the triads and the yakuza are cowards. The cabalists will be "neutralized" when and where they least expect it.

Let us now summarize the evidence we have that the 3/11 tsunami and nuclear disaster were a deliberate attack and murder of 20,000 people planned and executed by the Khazarian Satanists.

First of all, according to Democratic Party of Japan and other sources U.S. Deputy Secretary of State Kurt Campbell met DPJ power broker Ichiro Ozawa on March 9th, 2011 and offered him the rights to Zeolite in Fukushima Prefecture if he would stop his plans to unseat then Prime Minister (and North Korean agent) Naoto Kan. Zeolite is now being used to clean up radioactive waste in Fukushima. Campbell claimed to be representing J. Rockefeller.

Another piece of evidence is the fact that the stock price of Higashi Nihon House, a maker of discount housing in Northern Japan, rose 40% on March 10th, one day before the attack. An insider trading investigation has begun and the investors are being tracked down.

Then there were local news reports dating to January, 2011, that the deep sea drilling vessel Chikyu Maru was systematically drilling holes at what became the exact epicenters of the quakes.

There was a 15-man team of Japan Self-Defense Force technicians who were involved in placing nuclear devices into the drill holes. These technicians were told it was for "tests." After the nukes were set off to trigger the tsunami, 14 of these technicians were murdered. The one surviving team member was sheltered by Pastor Paulo Izumi of the Tachikawa Christian Church in Tokyo.

Based on details provided by this SDF technician, Paulo wrote up the details of how the tsunami was artificially created in two books published by Hikaruland Press. The latest, entitled *"The Shocking Truth of Why Japan was Attacked with an Artificial Earthquake on 3/11,"* was published in February, 2012. Izumi has also published evidence of a fake Armageddon planned by the perpetrators of this attack. The Self-Defense Force officer is now being sheltered by a Christian group in the US and has been debriefed by agency white hats.

There is also plenty of evidence that the Israeli company Magna B.S.P. which was in charge of "security" at the Fukushima nuclear plant, actually blew up the plants with micro-nukes. Then of course is the recorded phone call by Benjamin Netanyahu to Naoto Kan after March 11, 2011 in which he threatened to blow up all of Japan's nuclear plants. Magna BSP was in charge of security at all of these plants.

The Fukushima nuclear complex was built by General Electric, a company controlled by J. Rockefeller and other cabalists via a web of so-called "charitable foundations."

People in Japan who were involved in the entire Fukushima nuclear and tsunami terror attack include Ichiro Ozawa, Naoto Kan and Tokyo Electric Power managers. They will be brought to justice.

The weapons used in the attack were created with fuel taken from a nuclear warhead stolen from the Russian submarine Kursk. Paul Laine from Pentagon Military intelligence confirmed that four nuclear warheads were stolen from the Kursk when it "sank" in August of 2000.

An MI6 agent using the name Richard Sorge also informed the Japanese police in 2010 that a nuclear warhead had been smuggled into Japan via Okinawa and was located in a property in Hinode Town, in Western Tokyo owned by former Prime Minister and senior North Korean Agent Yasuhiro Nakasone. The agent later informed the police the weapon had been smuggled into the headquarters of the General Association of North Korean Residents of Japan.

The Japanese police failed to take action and instead arrested this agent and asked him to falsely testify that this writer was a drug dealer. The involvement of the Koganei Police force in this arrest means that North Korean agent and Tokyo Governor Shintaro Ishihara is also involved.

Also involved was a North Korean agent by the name of Ota (we do not know his first name but his daughter's name is Hideko). Ota also worked in the past of Israeli Al Qaeda types in the Aum Shinrikyo subway sarin gas attack incident.

The original plan called for follow up attacks on Tokyo designed to terrorize the population into abandoning the metropolis.

A threat to retaliate against an attack on Tokyo by sinking the Las Palmas rock formation in the Canary Islands and setting off a 100 meter tsunami to hit the US East Coast and Southern Europe has deterred further attacks on Japan.

In any case, the original scenario was then to set up a North Korean controlled government of Japan and the Korean Peninsula in Osaka. The death of Kim Jong Il and the bribing of many North Korean generals put a kibosh on that.

However, it is still a good idea to set up the new LIFE (Long-term Investments For Everyone) economic planning agency in the Nara plain South of Osaka. This area is the home of the oldest cities in Japan and has plenty of flat land close to the ocean that can be used to create a new financial and economic hub for peaceful global development.

LIFE can be set up without impeding any existing government structures.

There has been considerable opposition, though, both from China and within Japan, to the proposal to join the Korean Peninsula with Japan to create a 200 million person nation. There will be negotiations on this subject in Korea next week. Negotiations with the various factions of the Japanese secret government are also continuing this week.

Since all the parties want world peace and friendly relations in the region, some kind of amicable compromise is expected. No exact timetable for announcements exists yet.

The Pentagon and agency white hats are also supportive of these plans. They say there are now 6 competing plans for a new financial system and none is taking the lead so far. The Pentagon and agency white hats are offering to contribute new energy and new transportation technology.

If the LIFE agency can get the rights to use gold-backed Yen overseas and can begin hiring staff, there is no technical or logistical reason why it should not be possible to end poverty and stop environmental destruction this year.

# Maine Republic Email Alert

*No. 027*

"... that I should bear witness unto the truth." — John 18:33 // David E. Robinson, Publisher

"... if the trumpet give an uncertain sound, who shall prepare himself for battle?" — I Corinthians 14:8

## Emerging movement encourages Sheriffs to act as shield against federal tryanny

02/13/2012

By Nancy Lofholm, *The Denver Post.*

The 100 or so sheriffs who gathered in a Las Vegas hotel ballroom two weeks ago learned that some weighty titles have been attached to the stars they wear on their chests.

"Ultimate enforcers of the Constitution." "Protectors against government tyranny." "America's last hope." "Brave oath keepers."

And the sheriffs, including eight from Colorado, learned that they need to protect their citizenry from much more than local lawbreakers. In today's world, public enemy No. 1, just might be the federal government — or the *"out-of-control federal bureaucracy,"* as organizers of the convention like to refer to it.

The person who will *"stand tall against federal tyranny,"* even if it means armed resistance, according to organizers, is our county sheriff.

The Constitutional Sheriffs and Peace Officers Association's inaugural convention was designed to be the national coming-out for this idea and the start of an educational movement that its founder hopes will sweep the country. Its sponsors included the John Birch Society, the Gun Owners of America and the Front Sight Firearms Training Institute. Advertisers included survivalist businesses, anti-IRS proponents, purveyors of gold-buying secrets and one company that sells a guide, *"How to Turn Your Home into a Fortress."*

"We have a large group of people in my county who agree with these principles," said Weld County Sheriff John Cook, explaining why he attended the conference. *"I agree with a lot of it. But I don't advocate, obviously, violence against other law enforcement offices."*

The conference was organized by former Graham County, Arizona, Sheriff Richard Mack. Mack gained fame in the 1990s and became a Tea Party darling when he and six other sheriffs challenged the constitutionality of the gun-control measure commonly known as the Brady Bill. In a case that went to the Supreme Court, Mack's attorneys successfully argued that local law enforcement jurisdictions can't be compelled to carry out federally mandated background checks. It was seen as a huge victory for the sovereignty of local jurisdictions.

Three years ago, Mack wrote a book, *"The County Sheriff: America's Last Hope."* In it, he asserted that **sheriffs have the supreme law enforcement power in their counties under the Constitution and the 10th Amendment.** Much of what federal agents are doing in counties is unconstitutional, he wrote. Federal agents have no authority beyond policing treason, piracy, treaty violations and counterfeiting.

Thus, the scofflaws that sheriffs might encounter today — *and who should be run out of town by a SWAT team, if that's what it takes* — include agents for the U.S. Forest Service; the Bureau of Land Management; the IRS; the FBI; the Bureau of Alcohol, Tobacco, Firearms and Explosives; the Environmental Protection Agency; and even the Food and Drug Administration.

Online Constitutional Sheriffs materials state, *"The sheriff's position overrides any federal agents or even the arrogant FBI agents who attempt to assume jurisdiction in our cases."*

Colorado had the largest representation at this convention, along with California and Utah.

*"I think sheriffs went because they just wanted to be informed about what is expected of a sheriff,"* said Montezuma County Sheriff Dennis Spruell. *"I know I want to make sure the federal government does what it's supposed to do and doesn't encroach on the rights of my citizens.*

*"As for that making us radicals, I don't see that."*

Some Colorado sheriffs, like Spruell, said they went because they believe in much of what the Constitutional Sheriffs group espouses. They stressed that, at the same time, they have mostly good working relations with law enforcement officers from federal agencies that operate in *their counties.*

*"I have good cooperation with federal agents. I have no problems with them,"* said Montrose County Sheriff Rick Dunlap. *"The feds always contact me when they are doing something in my county."*

Some sheriffs were simply curious about Mack's teachings and hoped to learn something about the group. Others said they felt they should go because they have a lot of conservative, right-wing constituents who believe in what was taught in Las Vegas.

In some cases, those constituents donated the money to send their sheriffs. Some pestered the sheriffs about going — something that doesn't happen when the meeting is, say, a mainstream gathering of the County Sheriffs of Colorado.

*"It was odd. Two people came to the window out front to ask if I was going,"* Weld County's Cook said.

Mesa County Sheriff Stan Hilkey was one sheriff who didn't receive an invitation to the convention and was a little uncomfortable with the idea of constituents raising money to send sheriffs to it. He also was unhappy with the impression some sheriffs had that if they didn't go, their conservative voters would try to oust them in the next election.

"I have a lot of respect for the Constitution and for its framework of keeping our people safe," he said. *"But sheriffs should not be strong-armed into going to something like this."*

Chris Olson, executive director of the County Sheriffs of Colorado, said of the convention: *"We didn't endorse it or authorize it. It was an individual sheriff's decision."*

Mack, who still refers to himself as "Sheriff Mack" and is currently running as a Republican for a congressional seat in Texas, said his organization didn't pressure any sheriffs. In a phone interview, he also said that his movement may come across sounding bellicose, but he *is really promoting peace.*

"The potential for violence is always there. But I pray it won't come to that. We don't want that," Mack said.

Some of the speakers at the convention did tell of confrontations that involved the threat of officers for different agencies trying to arrest each other. The use of force was not ruled out.

Elkhart County, Ind., Sheriff Brad Rogers told of chasing federal regulators out of his county after they repeatedly did inspections at an Amish dairy farm that was selling raw milk. He threatened to arrest the regulators if they tried to come back.

Sheriff Tony DeMeo of Nye County, Nev., recounted how he had to threaten to bring out his SWAT team to go up against a federal government SWAT team when federal agents were seizing cattle from a local rancher.

Sheriff Dave Mattis of Big Horn County, Wyoming, told the conference about the edict he has issued in his county. Federal agents are forbidden to enter his territory without his approval.

El Paso County Commissioner Peggy Littleton, who attended with El Paso County Sheriff Terry Maketa, gave a presentation that took another tack. She told how her county recently passed a resolution to nullify the National Defense Authorization Act. She urged other counties to do the same.

Fear that this act gives the federal government the power to arrest and detain citizens without filing charges or seeking convictions is another issue that garners a lot of attention on websites associated with the Constitutional Sheriffs group.

It also became a convention flash point when a speaker repeatedly called Arizona Republican Sen. John McCain, a former prisoner of war, a "traitor" for supporting the Defense Authorization Act.

Montrose County's Dunlap said he and several other sheriffs "were ready to walk out at that point."

Many of the presentations at the convention revolved around more common land-use disputes over road closures and hunting restrictions. Those were the stories that resonated most with Colorado sheriffs who attended and who believe the federal government is overstepping its bounds on these issues.

Steven Hall, a spokesman for the BLM, said he doesn't want to argue with sheriffs about interpretations of the Constitution and federal jurisdiction on federal lands. He said that for the most part, his agency has good working relationships with sheriffs, especially when it comes to issues such as fighting wildfires and eradicating marijuana.

*"There has been some heated rhetoric but no serious incidents. I hope it remains that way,"* he said.

Steve Segin, a spokesman for the Forest Service, issued a statement saying his agency has had "excellent working relationships" with sheriffs in Colorado.

Several representatives for the FBI at the state and national level said they had not heard of the Constitutional Sheriffs movement. They declined to comment.

Mack said he is already planning a second convention for this summer, when he will continue to promote the idea that "the greatest threat to our freedom now is the federal government."

*"There is nothing subversive about any of this,"* he said. *"It's as American as apple pie."*

# Maine Republic Email Alert

No.028

"...that I should bear witness unto the truth." — John 18:33 // David E. Robinson, Publisher

"... if the trumpet give an uncertain sound, who shall prepare himself for battle?" — I Corinthians 14:8

## Open Letter To Benjamin Fulford & His Responses (questions on all our lips)

02/14/2012

Posted Tuesday, 2-14-2012.
**Open Letter To Ben Fulford & Response**

Hi Ben
From being involved in upper level logic and its uses in my businesses, I find it absolutely mind boggling why these reports keep coming in that they are arresting the little peons ...

In construction you build something by starting with a foundation (bottom up)... When you want to tear it down, start at the top (top down)... Get the crooks at the top and the whole net work falls apart real quick ...

I keep hearing from lots of posts that things are now starting, but I have heard that now for months.

As an example ... A guy makes a post at the beginning of December, 2011 that the bad guys were to be rounded up, and then there was to be a 40 hour take-over of Network TV and radio to educate the people ... then NASA ... This was all to happen before the end of December ...

Example of what has been said to happen... The Fed Reserve is still operating.

All the crooks are still doing their thing, and the chemical attacks on our air, food and water are still going on ...This is the type of thing that we keep hearing and nothing is evident enough to observe that these are, in fact, being taken down. Without observing something it is real difficult to believe ....

Is there anything I can tell the folks I meet with, that you can say, to convince them that things are really happening?
D.

— — —

Dear D.
You are right to be cynical because we still see those crooks on TV every day and they still sit in the public seats of power.

However, you need to understand that this situation is restricted to countries still controlled by the Khazarian mob and that includes the US, the UK, France, Italy and Germany.

The rest of the world is trying to isolate them. You can see visible evidence in that in the form of the plunge this year in the Baltic Dry Index which measures the price of physically shipping goods.

It has plunged due to an international boycott of Khazarian controlled countries.

The IMF, the so-called lender of last resort in the world also still has no money, which is also proof that something fundamental has changed at the top of the financial system.

As far as arrests are concerned, when I asked a pentagon "white hat" why people like Kissinger and Bush were still not in jail he said "because they are guarded by 30,000 armed men."

Remember, they want to start WW3 and we want to prevent it. That means that we must use non-violent means.

What we are doing is cutting off their money because mercenaries are only mercenary when they are paid to be that way.

It is taking a long time and I also feel impatient.

That is why I named specific individuals in my latest news letter. I told the pentagon and agency white hats that it is like a rotten stump that just needs a good kick to knock it over. Their answer was they were waiting for it to fall over by itself.

Nonetheless, when they least expect it the cabalists will be brought to justice, I guarantee that even though we cannot give an explicit date for this to happen.

The Euro crisis and the 23% unemployment rate in the US are signs it will collapse.

You may also notice that Ron Paul put out an article on his site that talks about the ongoing financial war.

As far as the chemical attacks are concerned remember this is mainly fear-mongering. Do you actually see people sick and dying like you would if there was a real plague?

The answer is no because they are just using scare tactics. Fear is their greatest weapon, love is the antidote.
Best regards,
Benjamin Fulford

— — —

Thank you Ben for the response...
I have heard on many occasions that Bush and his bunch are in control of trillions of $$$. We may be waiting for a long long time for them to run out of $$$.

If the IMF is broke, are the prosperity packages and the RV still going to happen somehow??
Can I share this with...x...??
My Best,
D.

— — —

Hi, D.,
Please share it if you wish. The problem with Bush and the Nazis is that the black budget and black ops are supported by drug money that is hard to cut off.

We are negotiating with these people and trying to integrate the black budget with the public one and get the military industrial complex on board. This is taking time but concrete negotiations are taking place and proceeding well.

We have reached the level where we are dealing with individual personalities. Please remember that if you wish to negotiate the surrender of the Nazis, you have to negotiate with a Nazi.

There is no way around this other than to kill them all and that would just start WW3 which is what they want.

Nonetheless, we may have to arrest some of these criminals in order to break the logjam.

Benjamin Fulford

— — —

Hi again Ben,
One last qustion...
Is the prosperity packages, and RV still going to happen somehow??
D.

— — —

Hi, D,
We will try to make something like that happen sooner rather than later.
Benjamin Fulford

— — —

1 comment:

Anonymous,
From a strictly observational perspective, this still appears like a "New World Order".

Oh! But it is a GOOD one! These people love you, they want the best for you.

MANY will buy into this because they have "suffered" so long and haven't realized their true selves as yet.

No one can save us - but ourselves.

— — —

# Maine Republic Email Alert

No. 029

"... that I should bear witness unto the truth." — John 18:33 // David E. Robinson, Publisher

"... if the trumpet give an uncertain sound, who shall prepare himself for battle?" — I Corinthians 14:8

## Ron Paul Is Secretly Taking Over The GOP — And It's Driving People Insane

02/16/2012

**By now, it is clear that the Maine caucuses were a complete mess.**

Evidence is mounting that Mitt Romney's 194-vote victory over Ron Paul was prematurely announced, if not totally wrong. Washington County canceled their caucus on Saturday on account of three inches of snow (hardly a blizzard by Maine standards), and other towns that scheduled their caucuses for this week have been left out of the vote count. Now, it looks like caucuses that did take place before Feb. 11 have also been left out of final tally.

As the full extent of the chaos unfolds, sources close to the Paul campaign tell Business Insider that it is looking increasingly like Romney's team might have a hand in denying Paul votes, noting that Romney has some admirably ruthless operatives on his side and a powerful incentive to avoid a fifth caucus loss this month.

According to the Paul campaign, the Maine Republican Party is severely under-reporting Paul's results — and Romney isn't getting the same treatment. For example, nearly all the towns in Waldo County — a Ron Paul stronghold – held their caucuses on Feb. 4, but the state GOP reported no results for those towns. In Waterville, a college town in Central Maine, results were reported but not included in the party vote count. Paul beat Romney 21-5 there, according to the Kennebec County GOP.

"It's too common," senior advisor Doug Wead told Business Insider. "If it was chaos, we would expect strong Romney counties to be unreported, and that's not what's happening."

The Maine Republican Party won't decide which votes it will count until the executive committee meets next month. But Wead points out that even if Mitt

Romney holds on to his slim lead, it will be a Pyrrhic victory.

"He will have disenfranchised all of these people," Wead said. "It could be a costly victory — it is a mistake."

The (alleged) bias against Paul may also be the product of an organic opposition to the libertarian Congressman and his army of ardent fans. Paul volunteers tend to be young and relatively new to party politics, and their presence has many state GOP stalwarts feeling territorial.

"People feel threatened — they don't want to see a bunch of kids who may have voted for Barack Obama take over," Wead said. "They feel a sense of ownership over the party — but there has to be an accommodation."

But state party machinations are already starting to backfire.

**The Paul campaign believes it has won the majority of Maine's delegates — and the perceived election fraud has galvanized Paul supporters to demand their votes be counted in the state's straw poll 'beauty contest.'**

Caucus chaos has also proved to be fertile ground for Paul's quiet takeover of the Republican Party. Since 2008, the campaign and Paul's Campaign for Liberty PAC have made a concerted effort to get Paul sympathists involved in the political process. Now, tumult in state party organizations has allowed these supporters to rise up the ranks.

"We like strong party leadership when it comes from us," Paul campaign chair Jesse Benton told Business Insider. "Our people work very hard to make sure that their voice is heard."

The fruits of this labor are evident in Iowa, where Paul's former state campaign co-chair A.J. Spiker was just elected as the new chairman of the Iowa Republican Party. Spiker replaces Matt Strawn, who stepped down over this year's Iowa caucus dustup. In Nevada, the state chair has also resigned over caucus disaster, and several Ron Paul supporters are well-positioned to step up to fill the void.

These new leaders not only expand Paul's influence at the state level, but also help protect Paul and his hard-won delegates from state party machinations as the delegate-selection process moves to district and state conventions, and eventually the Republican National Convention this summer.

"We are always trying to bring people into the party," Benton said. "I think that is a very positive thing for Republicans. Ron is the person who can build the Republican base, bring new blood into the party. That's how you build the party."

In Maine, the caucus disaster has made the state GOP prime for a Ron Paul takeover. And that means that Paul's hard-won delegates will be protected as the delegate selection process.

"We are taking over the party," Wead told BI. "That's the important thing — and that is what we are doing in Maine."

See Also:
**Where Has Ron Paul Been Hiding,**
http://tinyurl.com/7cj3kyu

# Maine Republic Email Alert

No. 030

"... that I should bear witness unto the truth." — John 18:33 // David E. Robinson, Publisher

"... if the trumpet give an uncertain sound, who shall prepare himself for battle?" — I Corinthians 14:8

## A March Deadline Has Been Delivered To The Committee of 300 By The Illuminati Faction

Posted by benjamin, Feb. 20, 2012

The group that claims to have started the American, French and Russian revolutions state they have issued a March 31st deadline to the committee of 300, according to their spokesman "Alexander Romanoff."

In addition, Prince Harry has been in touch with the group and has agreed to take over control of the British Royal family from Queen Elizabeth.

There are signs, such as the resignation of over a dozen senior bankers and the announcement of a $15 trillion fraud in the UK and a $6 trillion fraud in Italy, that these warnings have been taken seriously.

The Italian case is especially noticeable because one of the people arrested was former Prime Minister Silvio Berlusconi.

In addition a meeting is scheduled this week between a White Dragon Society representative and a representatives of the dragon family in mainland Asia to discuss the creation of a meritocratically staffed economic planning agency.

It can also now be disclosed that Ireland, Portugal, Greece and Spain have all told the banks they are not going to pay back any of their loans because the loans were made illegally.

This is one of the reasons why Moody's downgraded 114 financial institutions including Citibank, Goldman Sachs, Bank of America, Deutschebank etc.

These are the institutions that own the Federal Reserve Board and the Federal Reserve Board is going to be shut down soon, according to Pentagon sources.

In other words these countries are going to "default," and for a change it will be the bankers and not the average citizens, who will pay the price.

The resignation of the heads of the World Bank, Credit Suisse, the Bank of India and "planned resignation" of the head of Goldman Sachs is just the beginning of a complete dismantling of the Khazarian banking monopoly.

All money created through fraud is now going to be deleted from the global financial computer systems, according to officials involved in the take-down.

The $6 trillion fraud case in Italy is noteworthy because it is the one of the first such cases major corporate propaganda media outlets have reported worldwide.

Italian newspapers have also now started reporting on the Neil Keenan lawsuit against the Davos World Forum, Berlusconi, the UN etc., accusing them of a $1 trillion theft.

The arrest of 8 people is a further concrete sign of action being taken against the P2 Freemason lodge.

This means that people who were hitherto above the law and above institutions like the Vatican and the UN are no longer immune from arrest.

The announcement in the UK Upper House by Lord Blackheath that $15 trillion had been stolen from a member of the "Indian-Chinese" royal family by Federal Reserve Board Chairman Ben Bernanke, US Treasury secretary Timothy Geithner and "Yusuke Horiguchi"(we are making enquiries about this individual), is a another sign of big change.

The most interesting aspect of the Upper House testimony was the reference to a "Lord Sassoon."

The Sassoons are one of the families that profited from both the Opium wars and the colonization of Japan and it is interesting to see their name finally appear in the spotlight. Lord Sassoon has, as the testimony makes clear, already committed perjury in relation to the $15 trillion case. He is expected to be arrested and questioned soon.

In the US, as well change continues under the surface.

The pentagon has already decided that a major purge of Khazarian Satanist influence and control of corporations, banks and professional organizations will take place.

Among the organizations expected to experience high profile arrests are the American Medical Association, the American Dental Association, the Psychiatric and Psychology Associations, the Bar Association, the chambers of commerce and of course the Washington D.C. beltway.

Particular attention is going to be directed at the Pharmaceutical and chemical companies as well as satanic corporations like Microsoft and Monsanto, according to the Pentagon sources.

Rahm Emmanuel, Karl Rove, Paul Wolfowitz, Donald Rumsfeld, J. Rockefeller, the Bushes and the various "Neocons," are also due for arrest, according to multiple sources.

The proof of these claims of course, can only be made if these promised arrests actually take place. Until then skepticism remains the order of the day.

In Japan there is more credible evidence of change.

The top power brokers in Japan have decided that a revolution will take place. They are pushing for Osaka Major Toru Hashimoto to be the leader of the new regime in this country.

It is particularly noteworthy that two bitter, but extremely influential, rivals among the power-brokers both support

Hashimoto. The Zionist flunkies are also trying to co-opt Hashimoto and make him one of their tools. This will not be allowed to happen.

Ruling Democratic Party of Japan power-brokers Ichiro Ozawa (a Rockefeller servant) and former Prime Minister Yukio Hatoyama (a Freemason working for European royal families) will be bringing a large group of MP's to China in March in search for financial and other support. It has already been concluded they will return from this trip empty-handed.

There is much more this writer knows but has been asked to remain silent about. However, there will be proof and detail from this week's meetings available in next week's report.

Available at retail bookstores and AMAZON.com

*Learn about the World Global Settlement;*
*Saving the entire financial structure of the world;*

# Maine Republic Email Alert

No. 031

*". . . that I should bear witness unto the truth."* — John 18:33 // David E. Robinson, Publisher

*". . . if the trumpet give an uncertain sound, who shall prepare himself for battle?"* — I Corinthians 14:8

## The Countdown Has Begun

*02/19/12*

This particular blog caught my attention, particularly in light of the recent reports about "Resigning Bankers".

We are counting on many of you to see the upcoming arrests of many members of your criminal Cabal as a very positive sign of things to come, and we want to ride that wave of positive energy and make our introductions to the people of your planet.

That line, in light of what was in the bankers' post, is one of the reasons for this (and many other) blogs. Certainly most of us here can look at all of this turmoil, and say, "Wow, isn't that great! It's all happening! Thank you, thank you, thank you!" That positive outlook and intent keeps this whole ascension thing going.

**Highlights of this Report**
- Many programs will soon be underway, and through these programs humanity will be brought together as one.
- We will not only begin the vital cleanup of our world's pollution, and other important tasks, but repair the damage brought on by wars and other means that have divided so many of us and kept us separated.
- Today, many of us are finally ignoring the distraction game, and instead focusing attention on the dastardly deeds of those who have plotted and schemed against us for so long.
- Many changes are now possible to get underway now that the acts of those of the dark are being exposed by the light of day.
- Many are paving the way for the hard work of changing our world for the better.
- We would like to get underway with these many important projects as soon as is possible, and we see the paths being cleared satisfactorily according to our schedule.
- You will soon see the initiation of certain key events that will trigger the launch of many simultaneous projects, and it is these projects that will bring us all together in a peaceful and mutually beneficial cooperation.
- We are counting on many of you to see the upcoming arrests of many members of your criminal Cabal as a very positive sign of things to come, and we wish to ride that wave of positive energy and make our introductions to the people of your planet.
- Please continue to inform you brothers and sisters that there is no reason to fear us and our arrival, as we are only here to assist our human family...
- You will not be alone in your efforts as a mighty ally will be joining you, which are portions of your media companies.
- We see this alliance between two powerful forces, you the people and your media, as an unstoppable force that will spell the end for the rule of the Cabal and your isolation from the rest of this universe.
- Your world is set to experience a great leap into the future, and it can almost be said that you will be time travelers journeying to a future time period of your planet. The countdown has begun. Prepare yourselves for lift-off.
- We, the Galactic Federation of Light, will provide transportation to these [new project] areas, and you will also be returned to the areas that you live after your work shifts are completed.
- There will be many different projects available to you, and you will be free to choose the particular project that interests you the most.

**Message from the Galactic Federation of Light 2/18/12**

There are many programs that will soon be underway, and it is through these programs that humanity will be brought together as one. There will be many different programs launched, and people from all over the world and from all walks of life will participate, bringing so many together that otherwise would have possibly never met under any other circumstances.

So you see how these programs are important to your world on many different levels? They will not only begin the vital cleanup of all your world's pollution and other important tasks, but also repair the damage brought on by wars and other means that have divided so many of you and kept you separated.

There are those of the dark who purposely schemed to keep you all divided, separated from the rest of your human brothers and sisters. They feared you coming together as one, as this has always been the greatest threat to their power. They were correct in this thinking, as it is the coming together of humanity that today erodes their power to nothing more than endless scheming and plotting that gets them absolutely nowhere.

This is all due to you, the people, coming together and saying 'no, we will not stand for this any longer and we will not fall for the same old tricks and cons'. So many of you have taken an active role to inform your brothers and sisters of these ploys and tactics, and it is due to this open sharing of information that is strengthening your bond as one and seeing the end of this endless shell game of corruption and control.

We look just several years into your past and we see so many of you divided on so many fronts. Matters that hardly meant any difference to your prosperity, your freedom, and your survival, yet so many of you bought into these tricks to keep you preoccupied and divided. So many of you spent so much of your time and energy fighting amongst each other

Office of The Maine free State, 3 Linnell Circle, Brunswick, Maine 04011

while the robber barons stole your money, your health, and your freedom.

Today, we see so many of you finally ignoring the distraction game, and instead you focus your attention on the dastardly deeds of those who have plotted and schemed against you for so long. For this we applaud you, and we salute your efforts to inform your neighbors and put a stop to this madness. You are all making such a great difference, and wish you to know how appreciated your efforts are.

Many changes are now able to get underway now that the acts of those of the dark have been exposed by your light. Real change has not been experienced here in your world in any of your known history. Instead, change for you has crept along at a snail's pace, holding you further and further back in the development you rightfully could have been experiencing.

This was all part of the plan to keep you under someone else's control. You are now breaking free of this control, and for this, your society will experience a boom of rapid development that none of you have seen throughout any of your recent incarnations here.

Your world can, and will, be completely transformed with a little help, but all due to your efforts to inform yourselves and to take action against those who have oppressed you so. Do you now see how important it has been all along to educate yourselves to the inner workings of your societies, whether this information was given to you through the six o'clock news or not?

It was up to you, no one else, to find alternative sources of this vital information and act on it, and act on it you have. We are very proud of each and every one of you for these efforts, and assure you that you will receive the reward for such work very shortly.

We see many areas being broken down once we begin our many projects together. Not only will you be reunited with your human brothers and sisters who have been so separated from each other for so long, but you will also be reuniting with your stellar families you have also been long separated from. This will truly be a family reunion on many levels, and there are many surprises in store for you along the way.

We are very pleased at the efforts of so many of you who are paving the way for our arrival, and we wish to thank you at this time for your hard work and determination to change your world for the better. Your efforts will pay off, you can be assured of this, and every member of your human family will benefit greatly from your commitment today.

Again, we would like to get underway with these many important projects as soon as is possible, and we see the paths being cleared satisfactorily according to our schedule. You will soon see the initiation of certain key events that will trigger the launch of many simultaneous projects, and it is these projects that will bring us all together in a peaceful and mutually beneficial cooperation.

Please continue to inform you brothers and sisters that there is no reason to fear us and our arrival, as we are only here to assist our human family make the many needed advancements that will see to the improvement of lives everywhere across your planet. The time for change here has come a long time ago, but you were denied this opportunity. You will not be denied any longer.

We are counting on many of you to see the upcoming arrests of many members of your criminal Cabal as a very positive sign of things to come, and we wish to ride that wave of positive energy and make our introductions to the people of your planet. We need your help to make this project a success and we are confident you will rise to the occasion as you have so often done.

You will not be alone in your efforts as a mighty ally will be joining you, which are portions of your media companies. For decades these media outlets have been used as a very powerful means to control you, but now some of them will use their power to help free your people from the clutches of the dark ones. We see this alliance between two powerful forces, you the people and your media, as an unstoppable force that will spell the end for the rule of the Cabal and your isolation from the rest of this universe.

The free flow of information and ideas has always been such a vital concept for your society, and you are about to witness the sheer force of this as the suppression of truth is finally lifted in the days ahead. Your world is set to experience a great leap into the future, and it can almost be said that you will be time travelers journeying to a future time period of your planet. The countdown has begun. Prepare yourselves for lift-off.

This is sure to be a very exciting period in your history for many of you, and we are excited to be a part of this experience with you. We will do all we can to ensure your safety throughout these changes, and we ask your cooperation in these many projects. This will be a community effort unlike anything many of you have taken part in before, and beings from all over your planet will be contributing in one way or another to achieve the same goal.

This has never been attempted before here on your planet, and we are sure your worldwide efforts together will be recorded in your new history books and your story preserved for ages to come.

We see many of you making your intentions known that you would like to take part in these many projects, and we are very pleased with the reaction the news of these joint projects are receiving. In the days ahead further information about these opportunities will be made clear to you, and all your questions will be answered fully.

For now, we will say that many of these projects will take place in many different parts of your world. We, the Galactic Federation of Light, will provide transportation to these areas, and you will also be returned to the areas where you live after your work shifts are completed. There will be several shifts within every day, and we see sufficient numbers of you willing to take part in these projects that will enable us to work around the clock towards each project's completion.

There will be many different projects available to you, and you will be free to choose the particular project that interests you the most. You will be trained in each field that you wish to participate in, and the skills that you develop will never depreciate in their value, as there are also many other worlds that will require your expertise after this planet is restored to its pristine condition.

There are many benefits to working with us and we look forward to discussing these perks with you at the appropriate time. These projects will be getting underway soon, there can be no other way, and we look so forward to working with many of you. We see this day approaching quickly on the horizon, and we are looking so forward to meeting many of you face-to-face and being able to speak more personally with you.

Until then, keep up the fine work you are all doing that will lead you to your next steps to return your world to the paradise it once was. Please allow us the opportunity to assist you in this way, and through our collective efforts we will see the successful accomplishment of our mission.

We are the Galactic Federation of Light.

As channeled through Greg Giles

# Maine Republic Email Alert

No. 032

*". . . that I should bear witness unto the truth." — John 18:33 // David E. Robinson, Publisher*

*". . . if the trumpet give an uncertain sound, who shall prepare himself for battle?" — I Corinthians 14:8*

## Geithner Gets a Subpoena: the fun will soon begin

02/21/2012

**The bailouts of October 2008** ended in some very rich people keeping their money. They did not wind up like the employees of Lehman Brothers, which was allowed by the Secretary of the Treasury to fail.

The Federal Reserve is now in damage-control mode. Ron Paul has inflicted a lot of damage. This is only going to get worse.

In October 2008, today's Treasury Secretary was the president of the New York Federal Reserve Bank. He was at the center of the crisis.

Unlike the CEO's of Goldman Sachs and other major players, he has always been salaried, but he does not have the money to pay defense attorneys $500 an hour. But he may soon have to do just that.

Lehman Brothers Holdings Inc. (LEHMQ) and its creditors late Thursday said they want to subpoena Treasury Secretary Timothy Geithner to question him under oath over allegations J.P. Morgan Chase & Co., (JPM) illegally siphoned billions of dollars from the collapsing investment bank in the days before it filed for the largest bankruptcy in U.S. history.

In a filing accompanying Lehman's filing, made in U.S. District Court in Washington, DC, Lehman's official committee of unsecured creditors said Geithner has thus far refused to comply with an Aug. 9, 2011, subpoena, and it wants a court to force Geithner to give a deposition by a March 16 deadline, 2012.

"Despite being a crucial, fact witness on these issues, Secretary Geithner has refused to appear at a deposition in accordance with a valid subpoena issued by the Committee," the committee's lawyers said in the filing. Geithner was president of the Federal Reserve Bank of New York at the time of the Lehman collapse.

http://online.wsj.com/article/BT-CO-20120216-722070.html

Geithner has a problem. He will not be able to fool lawyers the way he fooled Congress about his tax returns. He will not be able to blame it all on TurboTax software.

They will get him on the witness stand, at some point. He will be forced to tell the lawyers what the chain of events was in **the biggest bailout in history.** If he takes the Fifth Amendment, he will find himself unemployed.

In any case, he is now facing legal fees that we would not wish on anyone.

If the lid is ever taken off this can of worms, the public will find out about the nature of crony capitalism. With lawyers involved, and millions of dollars at stake, the lid will be taken off.

Over time, the voters' trust in the existing system will disappear. Then will come a political day of reckoning. It will take an economic crisis to accomplish this, but that crisis is coming.

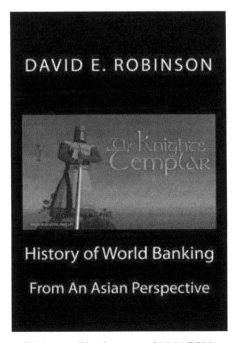

Available at retail bookstores and AMAZON.com

# Maine Republic Email Alert

No.033

"... that I should bear witness unto the truth." — John 18:33 // David E. Robinson, Publisher

"... if the trumpet give an uncertain sound, who shall prepare himself for battle?" — I Corinthians 14:8

## What If...?   (Judge Napolitano speaks)

02/22/2012

**The Judge said on his facebook page that his final show would be Feb 13th 8:00 PM.**

The video he was referring to [of which this report is a transcript] is allowed under DMCA Fair Use Act. Allowance is made for fair use to inform, educate, non profit.

In this vedeo Judge Napolitano ask the following questions:

What if we're involved in a dissipation in a process that validates an establishment that never meaningfully changes?

What if that establishment doesn't want and doesn't have the consent of the governed?

What if the two party system was actually a mechanism used to limit so-called public opinion?

What if there were more that two sides to every issue, but the two parties wanted to box you into a corner, one of their corners?

What if there is no such thing as public opinion, because every thinking person has opinions that are uniquely his own?

What if what we *call* public opinion was just a manufactured narrative that makes it easier to convince people that if their views are different, then there's something wrong with *that,* or there's something wrong with *them*?

What if the whole purposes of the democratic and republican parties was not to expand voter's choices but to limit them?

What if the widely perceived difference between the two parties was just an illusion?

What if the heart of government policy remains the same, no matter who's in the White House?

What if the heart of government policy remains the same, no matter what the people want?

What if those vaunted differences,

Judge Napolitano

between democrat and republican, were actually just minor disagreements?

What if both parties just want power and are willing to have young people fight meaningless wars in order to enhance that power?

What if both parties continue to fight the war on drugs, just to give bureaucrats and cops bigger budgets and more jobs?

What if government policy didn't change, when government leaders did?

What if no matter who won an election, government stayed the same?

What if government was really a revolving door for political hacks bent on exploiting the people, once they're in charge?

What *both* parties supported welfare, warfare, debt, bailouts, and big government?

What if the rhetoric that candidates displayed on the campaign trail was dumped after electoral victory?

What if Barrack Obama campaigned as an anti-war civil pro-libertarian candidate and then waged senseless wars while assaulting your rights that the Constitution is supposed to protect?

What if George W. Bush campaigned on a platform of non-intervention and small government and then waged a foreign policy of muscular military intervention, and a domestic policy of vast government borrowing and growth?

What if Bill Clinton declared that the era of big government was over, but actually just convinced republicans like Newt Gingrich that they can get what they want out of big government too?

What if the republicans went along with it?

What if Ronald Reagan spent six years running for President promising to shrink the government, but then the government grew while he was in the White House?

What if, notwithstanding Reagan's ideas and cheerfulness and libertarian rhetoric, there really was no Reagan Revolution at all?

What if all this is happening *again*?

What if Rick Santorum is being embraced by voters who want *small* government, even though Senator Santorum voted for the Patriot Act, for the expansion of medicare, and for raising the debt ceiling by trillions of dollars?

What if Mitt Romney is being embraced by voters who want *anyone* but Barack Obama, but they don't realize that Mitt Romney might as well be Barack Obama on everything from warfare to welfare?

What if Ron Paul was being ignored by the media, not because as it claims he's unappealing or unelectable, but because he doesn't fit into the pre-manufactured public opinion mold used by the establishment to pigeonhole the electorate and create the so-called narrative that drives media coverage of elections?

What if the biggest difference between most candidates was not substance but style?

What if those stylistic differences were packaged as substantive ones, to reinforce the illusion of a difference

*Office of The Maine free State, 3 Linnell Circle, Brunswick, Maine 04011*

between democrats and republicans?

What if Mitt Romney wins, and ends up continuing the same policies that Barack Obama promoted?

What if Barack Obama's policies too are merely extensions of those from George W. Bush?

What if a government that manipulated us, could be fired?

What if a government that lacked the true and knowing consent of the governed, could be dismissed?

What if it were possible to have a *real* game changer?

What if we need a Ron Paul to preserve and protect our freedoms from the government?

What if we can make elections matter again?

What if we could do something about this?

From New York, defending freedom, every night of the week.

See the video:
http://tinyurl.com/724wtqo

Available at retail bookstores and AMAZON.com

# Maine Republic Email Alert

No. 034

"... that I should bear witness unto the truth." — John 18:33 // David E. Robinson, Publisher

"... if the trumpet give an uncertain sound, who shall prepare himself for battle?" — I Corinthians 14:8

## U.S. Treasury Secretary arrested, questioned, and released

02/27/2012

**U.S. Treasury Secretary Timothy Geithner arrested, questioned and released; Asian negotiations continue.** Posted by Benjamin

As predicted, the collapse of the Satan worshipping financial mafia is accelerating. U.S. Treasury Secretary Timothy Geithner was detained for questioning by New York police on February 24th, and was released after giving evidence about many high level financial criminals, according to New York police sources.

"In most cases we have to slap people to get them to talk but in his case we had to slap him to shut him up," one of the interrogators joked.

Geithner has been released but is accompanied at all times by an armed deputy to make sure he does not leave the country.

Former Prime Minister Silvio Berlusconi of Italy is also proving to be very talkative, sources in Europe say. Berlusconi has been released.

Meanwhile, meetings between White Dragon Society representatives and South Korean government officials last week in Seoul were very productive.

In general what has happened is that dozens of high level informants have come forth in the past weeks and detailed testimony by them is being gathered. Apart from Geithner and Berlusconi, the talking big fish include members of the Rothschild family who have come forth with startling information.

The most interesting revelation given by the Rothschilds is that Queen Victoria was actually the illegitimate daughter of Nathaniel Rothschild. That means Rothschild's had managed to place family members at the head of the British, German and Russian empires by the time World War I started. Hitler was also a Rothschild who wanted to be crowned King of the world and who helped found Israel by chasing the Jews out of Europe.

Their infiltration of the highest levels of world power continued in the post war period. So, in the big picture of things we are witnessing the collapse of the Rothschild attempt to crown themselves as monarchs of a world government with a capital in Jerusalem.

The competing attempt by George Bush Sr. and the Nazi faction to set up a 1000 year reich is also collapsing. Geithner has already told the police that both he and Obama work for Bush. The Bushes, like Geithner and others, are not allowed to leave the US now.

The names of some of the many top cabalists being fingered by high level defectors will be listed at the end of this report.

In other signs of the collapsing old regime, the Greeks have clearly told the EU to put their latest bail out where the sun does not shine. Elected Prime Minister George Papandreous is expected to return to power soon and replace cabal puppet Lucas Papademos, according to Europe based CIA sources.

The Italians are also deciding they do not want to become part of the greater German empire and have begun actively preparing a return to the Lira, the sources said.

The cabalists for their part are still fighting to preserve their power and control. The latest scam they are working on involves the $6 trillion worth of 1934 gold back securities that were seized in Switzerland recently. These bonds were tied to financier and Bush/Clinton bagman Mark Rich of Glencore Commodities. The plan was to place Hillary Clinton at the head of the World Bank and have her use the World Bank to launder the bonds and give the money to the communist government in China. The Chinese, in return, were supposed to turn a blind eye to the continuing European Central Bank and Federal Reserve Board scams.

The cabalists have also tried yet again to assassinate Russia's Vladimir Putin in an attempt to regain control of Russia in a desperate attempt to revive the insane plan to get the Russians to help start the World War 3 they feel is needed to complete their plans for world domination.

The pentagon has already told top cabalist attack dog Prime Minister Benjamin Netanyahu of Israel that they would shoot down any Israeli planes that tried to trigger this war by attacking Iran.

The CBS news network in the US now has also broken with the cabalists and has begun information warfare with cabalist propaganda outlets like CNN and Fox.

Meanwhile, in Asia, signs of harmony and unity are multiplying. Discussions last week in Korea between a White Dragon Society representatives and South Korean representatives reached agreement in principle on many issues.

First of all, the South Koreans agreed on unification between North and South Korea based on the principle of North Korean leader Kim Jong-un, a ceremonial post (perhaps "symbol of unity"), and a palace. After North South unification, talks could begin on greater East Asian economic and political integration.

The South Koreans also agreed to the plan to set up a new international economic planning agency in Japan so long as it was also possible to set up a major new private sector financial center near Pusan, South Korea.

There was also agreement on the issue of having Asian nations continue to support the transition of the pentagon into a global peacekeeping force merged with the Russian and Chinese militaries.

A Chinese delegation is expected in Japan soon to further develop the ideas explored in South Korea.

In Japan, meanwhile, the Yakuza understand their funds in the US were frozen by Bush flunky David S. Cohen.

There will be partial retaliation when senior cabal operative Ichiro Ozawa is arrested on tax evasion and has his funds frozen. There will also be confiscation of Japanese listed company stocks and other assets in Japan illegally taken over by the cabal. This confiscation is expected to affect at least 30% of the total value of all listed shares in Japan as well as considerable amounts of real estate.

Similar confiscations of assets illegally obtained by cabalists are expected to take place around the planet, especially in the USA.

Although it is still premature to give a timetable on further arrests, here is a partial (non-alphabetical) list of people (many who have tried to keep a low profile) who have been informed upon by the recent wave of cabal defectors:

The "family of three."
The Medicis and Borgias
The Club of Rome
Larry Summers
Paul Volcker
Wylie Aitken
Vernon Jordan
Admiral William Crowe
Richard Haas
Felix Warburg
John Jacob Astor
Lord Pillsbury
Bill Hicks
Kiyohika Nishimura
David Gergen
Lamar Smith
J. Rockefeller
Yotaro Kobayashi
John Snow
Mark Rich
David Cohen
James Cameron (his family got rich from opium)
John Roberts
Paul Wolfowitz
Frank Carlucci
Peter Hans Kolvenbach (the former black pope)
George Bush Senior

# Maine Republic Email Alert

*No. 035*

*". . . that I should bear witness unto the truth." — John 18:33 // David E. Robinson, Publisher*

*". . . if the trumpet give an uncertain sound, who shall prepare himself for battle?" — I Corinthians 14:8*

## MP means MicroPrint signature line

*02/29/2012*

When a name is written in all capital letters it is not the name of a real person; it is the name of a **legal fiction,** an entirely separate legal entity.

A human being cannot be a legal fiction, and a legal fiction cannot be a human being. One is **real (or natural),** and the other is **an "ens legis" (a legal entity), created by law.**

This entire thing is based on paying off the bankruptcy of the United States.

Your Strawman is the **debtor** of the bankruptcy, and the Government is **the agent *(the receiver)* for the creditors** — the **international bankers** who own the non-federal Federal Reserve Bank.

The National Debt is not your debt; it is your *strawman's* debt.

You have been functioning as a **voluntary representative** for a **cestui que, trust account (*your strawman*)** by "discharging" your strawman's bills with fiat money, instead of "paying" them with **your credit (your mutual offset credit exemption exchange).**

When you established your first checking account, you unknowingly accepted (agreed to) this relationship with the trust that the government has established in your name.

You do not control this trust because you have never claimed it for yourself, and your parents could not control it *for* you because they were wards of the state, like you are.

The System maintains this illusion by artifice and deceptive design.

Look at your checkbook. Your name is the ALL CAPS named of a BUSINESS CORPORATION which the bank presumes you to be.

Evidence of this presumption is found in the **line on your checks** over which you sign your name.

The **MicroPrint signature line** is not just a line; it's **printed words**. Some of the finest printing you will ever see.

The **MicroPrint signature line** reads something like:

*AUTHORIZED REPRESENTATIVE AUTHORIZED REPRESENTATIVE AUTHORIZED REPRESENTATIVE AUTHORIZED REPRESENTATIVE, (etc., etc.)*

In the corporate world only the ***authorized representative*** of a *CORPORATION* has the lawful authority to sign ***the corporation's checks.***

You have been given the *authority* to sign the checks of ***your money trust*** — an incorporated fiction.

**Books by The Maine Patriot**
http://maine-patriot.com

*Office of The Maine free State, 3 Linnell Circle, Brunswick, Maine 04011*

# *Maine Republic* Email Alert

*No.036*

"... that I should bear witness unto the truth." — John 18:33 // David E. Robinson, Publisher

"... if the trumpet give an uncertain sound, who shall prepare himself for battle?" — I Corinthians 14:8

## The Hunt is on, Cabal arrests accelerating  03/05/2012

**Posted by Benjamin**

The ongoing financial war is accelerating with arrests and assassinations being seen on both sides. George Bush Senior and Bill Gates were arrested last week for sabotaging the new financial system after being fingered by Timothy Geithner, pentagon sources say.

The Federal Reserve Board crime syndicate cabalists for their part murdered Lord James Blackheath on February 29th, after he denounced their theft of $15 trillion in the British House of Lords. The White Dragon Society, meanwhile has put out an all points bulletin seeking the immediate arrest for questioning of former Hong Kong Police Chief Peter Stevens.

Stevens is wanted on charges of smuggling into Japan the nuclear weapon that was used for the 311, 2011 nuclear and tsunami attack against Japan. Stevens is currently located at the Puerto Galera yacht club in the Philippines.

The gnostic illuminati family and the hacker group "anonymous" have also agreed to join forces with the White Dragon Society with a program of attacks on Monsanto and other cabal strongholds. The Rockefellers, Krugers, Openheimers, Mellons, Warburgs, Rothschilds, Bushes, Morgans and other cabal families will be systematically hunted down and rounded up if they do not surrender within the month of March.

The Dragon Family Royal Society group, meanwhile, provided this writer with more information about the ongoing financial war. The Dragon family provided a copy of a document (which we will publish on our free website this week) that was handed over to the world's central banks a year ago. According to this document, all 69 "first and second world countries" together with 225 other sovereign groups, have signed on to the new financial system.

The main backers of this system include the military forces of Russia, China and the US, according to a Dragon family source. The old royal families of the world have agreed to finance it initially with $15 trillion backed by gold, jewels and treasure owned by the royals. These are the same families that funded the initial Bretton Woods system that got hijacked in the post war years by the families that own the Federal Reserve Board. The new system would eliminate all private ownership of central banks as well as "off the books" accounting.

In addition, the Dragon family has agreed to provide nations with funding to clear their debts and engage in new infrastructure and other spending aimed at "harmonious development." The funding is vetted by representatives from 10 major world religions located in Rome. It can be verified through "D.T.C. Euro Clear banks or Federal Reserve Board blue, grey or black screens," the DF document states.

The opposition to this system is being run by the Federal Reserve Board banking families and their Bilderberger, CFR, Trilateral commission lieutenants. They are still issuing fiat dollars that are accepted inside the US, Germany, the UK, Italy, France and Switzerland.

The rest of the world (and a large part of the Swiss banking establishment) is refusing to accept these dollars but constant attempts are being made by the cabalists to launder their fiat money. They also have a comprehensive list of politicians and other power-brokers they have bribed and blackmailed throughout the world.

The cabalists have also tried to either kill or else freeze the assets of supporters of the new system. Despite this, a growing number of banks have defied the banking families and "crossed the picket line," into support of the new system. Just ask a bank if they are Basel 3 compliant or not and you can find out what side they are working for.

The Dragon Family representative also said that the controversy over who had the rights to the traditional royal treasures could easily be settled in a court of law. They claim that R.C. Dam was a fraud set up by the banking families. They add that Eddie Soekarno was the legal holder of "some" Dragon family assets.

The battle over control of the financial system took a decisive turn last week when Bill Gates was arrested on charges of sabotaging the new financial system. George Bush Senior is the person who provided testimony about Bill Gates, according to senior Pentagon Sources.

The Dragon Family Royal Society has indicated they support the White Dragon Foundation plan for setting up a meritocratically staffed economic planning agency that would work in harmony with their plans.

The anti-bloodline rule gnostic group has insisted on the setting up of such an agency as a condition for them to call off mass planned mayhem and major demonstrations in Europe and the US starting in April.

The hackers group anonymous has also promised to systematically attack all cabal linked corporations, media outlets, individuals and power centers in a campaign of steadily increasing pressure and intensity.

In Japan as well, preparations for a coup d'etat against all banking cabal flunky politicians, bankers and media are nearly complete. These people already know their days in power have ended.

A delegation from China has arrived in Japan this week to discuss the transition to a new regime in Japan and the Korean peninsula. They will also be discussing the revamping of international institutions like the UN, the BIS, the World Bank, the World Court and the IMF.

*Office of The Maine free State, 3 Linnell Circle, Brunswick, Maine 04011*

# Maine Republic Email Alert

No. 037

"... that I should bear witness unto the truth." — John 18:33 // David E. Robinson, Publisher

"... if the trumpet give an uncertain sound, who shall prepare himself for battle?" — I Corinthians 14:8

## American Status Today

03/05/2012

After the War for Independence, in 1783, a treaty was created between the British and the United States. This treaty was call the Standing Treaty of Peace. What is interesting is that this peace treaty seemed to be leveraged highly in favor of the so-called losers of the war: the British.

According to the definitive Treaty of Peace of 1783, which is still in effect to this day, all property of the British Corporation is still owned by the Crown. Other sections of the document show England, which supposedly lost the war, dictating the terms of the Treaty.

For example, in Article 5 of the Paris Peace Treaty of September 30th, 1783, the King requested payment for all the real estate, and the rights to the land he owned.

It is agreed that Congress shall earnestly recommend it to the legislature of the respective states to provide for the restitution of all States, Right, and properties, which have been confiscated belonging to the real British subjects; and also of the Estates, Rights, and properties of persons resident in Districts in the possession on His Majesty's arms and who have not borne arms against the said United States.

The truth is that all the assets held by the various British Companies, including various lands, are still owned and controlled by the British today.

We have been told that we are living in a democracy. We have been told that we are in a system where there is equal opportunity for everyone. Tragically, we have been told a gigantic lie, and that lie has been told over, and over, and over, and over again.

They're always about the business of taxing and attacking empires, and destroying it so they have a military consensus, and approach to manipulating and controlling the thought process. They always attack your thinking. They don't help you to think, they attack it.

The truth becomes clearer when we simply look at our current banking system. According to a report entitled, The Federal Reserve Directives, a study of corporate banking influence conducted by the Committee on Banking, Currency and Housing, the House of Representatives, in August 1926, concluded that all major financial banking cartels of the United States are all subsidiaries of the London Bank of England.

In other words, the N.M. Rothschild Bank owns every major bank in the United States. This list includes Neman Brothers and Morgan Stanley, recently dissolved from the created economic crisis, National City Bank, Chase Manhattan, and many others.

Every time a taxpayer pays a tax they are transferring their labor to the Queen of England and her heirs. Who are he heirs you may be asking? All of your presidents and high office officers who are related to the aristocracy by blood. These officials are more commonly know as Esquires!

An Esquire is defined as a man belonging to the higher order of English gentry ranking immediately below a Knight.

To represent the Crown, Esquires, or attorneys, were used to handle the legal process of infiltrating the Americas. These legislators maintain positions of power thus continuing control to British Admiralty law.

Most of us have heard of Benjamin Franklin and John Adams, and their early contributions to the United States, but what you may not have heard is that Benjamin Franklin, John Adams and John Jay were all Esquires to the Crown. They negotiated the Paris Peace Treaty of 1783 on behalf to the United States.

It becomes clearer now why the Treaty seems aligned in favor of the British, even though they supposedly lost the war.

The Paris Peace Treaty did not give America title to land. The Kings possessions in America were protected and governed by corporate charter. Benjamin Franklin visited England and France many times during the Revolutionary War.

Again, the British just moved from *overt* control of the 13 colonies, to *covert* control.

After the Civil War, the United States was financially weakened. Low on resources and still struggling to put the country back together, America needed money. The international bankers were right there to lend us all that we needed.

In 1871 Congress cut a deal with the Rothschild bankers to incur a debt which would allow the establishment of a new government controlled by foreign money interest. Under the legislative act of February 21, 1871, the United States became incorporated as a commercial enterprise to do business for profit. What that means is that the United States of America changed from a country into a corporation.

What you must understand is that this changed the entire process of how our government works, and its overall objectives as an enterprise. This legislative Act of 1871 designated the District of Columbia under a separate form of government with separate jurisdiction from the rest of the Union States.

With the United States of America now incorporated as a commercial enterprise, the country could borrow huge sums of money from the international bankers. The debt would eventually get so high that by 1933, just 62 years later, the United States would have to file Chapter 11 [bankruptcy].

Because of the legislative Act of February 21st, 1871 Washington D.C. is not a state, but a jurisdiction called the District of Columbia. The evidence for this fact can be found in the 41st Congress, Session 3 chapter, 1871, where they state:

> An Act to Provide a Government for the District of Columbia.
>
> Be it enacted by the Senate and House of representatives of the United States and Congress assembled that all that part of the territory of the United States included within the limits of the District of Columbia be, and the same is hereby, created into a government by the name of the District of Columbia, by which name it is hereby constituted a body corporate for municipal purposes, and may contract and be contracted with, sue and be sued.

In short, the 50 States are separate from the jurisdictional land of the District of Columbia. This District is a corporation called THE UNITED STATES OF AMERICA. Contrary to what you were taught in school, the United States is not a country, it is a corporation like IBM, General Motors, or Microsoft.

This corporation has legal jurisdiction to do business and create franchises. Consider the other 50 States as franchises for the parent company of the United States of America. This is why we have a President and not a King or Queen.

Only Kings or Queens can rule countries.

Legally, a President cannot rule over a country, but can make decisions on behalf of the King or Queen. In the case of the United States, that is exactly what our President does.

Countries don't have Presidents. Corporation do. Whenever the President is being introduced, he or she may be referred to as, "The President of The United States."

The United States of America is no different than General Motors of Detroit or Sears & Roebuck of Chicago. These descriptions are referring to companies which reside in a specific jurisdictional area. In Volume 20: Corpus Juris Secundum 1785 it states: "The United States Government is a foreign corporation with respect to the States."

Each of the 50 States is foreign to the other. This is why you can gamble in Las Vegas Nevada, but not in Utah. This is also the reason why persons who commit crimes in one state and flee to another are extradited back to the state where the crime was committed.

This is done because under law, the state where the crime was committed is the only state that has jurisdictional authority.

Under business law, every corporation must have a president, a secretary of treasury, and so on. Our President is the president of the United States of America. He is not the president of America.

This concept can be confusing, especially since America and the United States is constantly being sold to the public as existing in the same jurisdictional area on the map.

The only connection the 50 states have to the United States Corporation is again either by contract and/or franchise agreement. A part of this franchise agreement is designated by the status of individuals who call themselves citizens.

The contract agreement between the United States of America and the 50 separate states is called an Adhesion Citizens Contract. This Adhesion Citizens Contract is known as the 14th Amendment which was ratified on July 28, 1868.

The second part of the franchise definition mentions that it allows an individual or group to carry out specific commercial activities. These activities fall into a category called Interstate Commerce.

Article 1, Section 8, Clause 3 of the United States Constitution is known as the Commerce Clause. It states that Congress has the power; *"To regulate Commerce with foreign Nations, and among the several States and with the Indian tribes"* of the time.

This power fell under a regulatory body called the Interstate Commerce Commission, or ICC, in 1887.

Each time you sign your name or pledge an oath you are changing your status. You may be asking, what about American citizenship? In law when you see the words American Citizen, this denotes that you are an American Citizen contracted into, with the Birth Certificate, Social Security Number, or through you state franchise agreement which is the adhesion contract of the 14th Amendment.

It is critical that you understand that you are not and cannot be an American. An American is a free person who has not made contractual agreement with the United States Corporation.

Remember, you are not an American. You are legally a citizen living in a foreign state. This authorization granted by the corporation called the United States of America can be tied into three main areas of contract. The three of which we have mentioned.

We look at the 14th Amendment and we realize that this Amendment was really a contract. It was an adhesion contract between the United States Government and the citizenry of this country.

What it meant properly to Americans was this: It meant that the old days of slave ownership where a white man owned a slave on a plantation was done away with, and what the owners who owned those slaves did was transfer their property, which were the slaves, from the slave owner to the United States Government under the 14th Amendment.

And if you recall, when you study history, you'll know that many of the southern states, and those slave owners, were compensated for transferring their property over to the United States Government.

So what than means is for black folks is this; is that you are not free, you are what is called emancipated, and emancipation is not freedom, emancipation is a transfer of property from one owner to another owner.

This process has nothing to do with sovereignty. A citizen of the United States Corporation or an American cannot be sovereign because they do not own the land or have clear title to land.

Furthermore, *these persons have not established a military to take the land or to create their own land within the continental United States.*

THAT IS, <u>UNTIL NOW</u>...!!!

#  Maine Republic Email Alert    No.038

"... that I should bear witness unto the truth." — John 18:33 // David E. Robinson, Publisher

"... if the trumpet give an uncertain sound, who shall prepare himself for battle?" — I Corinthians 14:8    03/13/2012

## It is time to storm the Bastille, vive la Revolution

**Posted by benjamin**

The financial war that has been raging intensively at least since 2001 may be finally ending. This week a three pronged effort to convince the Luciferian banking cabal to surrender is being carried out.

In one prong, the Chinese government has announced it will start the mass installation of wind and solar power devices on rooftops world-wide in order to free humanity from the cabal controlled energy grid.

In another prong, the cabal controlled central banks will be asked to make good on broken promises by redeeming financial instruments backed by gold stolen from holocaust victims during World War III.

The third prong is still being kept secret but essentially it is a promise **to start a bottom-up revolution** in cabal controlled countries like Italy, France, Germany, the UK and the US unless these countries stop their ceaseless warmongering.

The arrest of Bill Gates, the announcement in an Italian paper that the Pope will resign on April 15th, and the presence of a US marshal accompanying cabal operatives like Timothy Geithner, are all signs that very little, if any, opposition remains.

Last week a Chinese delegation met with a representative of the White Dragon Society in Tokyo. At the meeting an informal agreement was reached in which the Chinese side promised to provide manufacturing facilities and financing for new energy technology.

To start with a revolutionary roof-top wind turbine and solar panel combination will be distributed with no initial downpayment necessary to householders and enterprises world-wide. These householders will then pay the installers the equivalent of their current energy bill for 5 years after which they will become energy independent.

This is a concrete and realistic way to give the atomic and fossil fuel based energy cartels time to find a new line of business.

Other "free energy" technologies, if proven to exist, may be used in lieu of these devices but only after safety testing. The installation of these devices would also be phased in so that existing energy corporations would have plenty of time to transition into new lines of enterprise.

Toyota has also already begun its assault on the fossil fuel industry by producing cars, now on the market, that get over 100 kilometers per liter or over 300 miles per gallon.

In a different, and more direct move, the banking cabal will be asked to make a $15 trillion donation for the purposes of ending war, ending poverty, stopping environmental destruction and freeing humanity from drudgery, poverty and disease.

This will involve a specific actual move that we cannot write about in detail at this time other than to say it involves asking the Odessa/Bush Nazis to pay back the gold they stole from holocaust victims. The only other thing that can be said about this particular maneuver at this time is to tell the Romans to "beware the ides of March."

There will be an announcement, aired live on March 13th on the internet, by the hacker group "anonymous", the gnostic Illuminati faction, and the White Dragon Society. If this announcement is not heeded, there will be revolution according to both anonymous and the gnostics.

In other news, Western embassies in Tokyo will all be shutting down on March 20th, ostensibly to celebrate the vernal equinox. If this embassy closure is a pretext to evacuate personnel in preparation for a mass terror attack against Tokyo, there will be unfathomable consequences for the Western ruling oligarchs and their extended families.

In addition, nuclear weapons have already been placed in both Jerusalem and Rome by gnostic agents and these two cities will vanish forever if Tokyo is attacked. We urge all citizens of these two cities to evacuate immediately should Tokyo be terrorized by the Romans.

Furthermore, the Chinese and Japanese military have finalized preparations to sink the La Palma rock formation into the ocean and cause a 100 meter tsunami to hit the US East coast and Southern Europe in retaliation for the planned attack on Tokyo. The world will no longer tolerate Roman terror. The Romans must renounce Satan and the Vatican must be purged of all Satanists. This is not negotiable.

In other news, an informant has provided this writer with more details on how the banking cabal has manipulated the Japanese political system. Former Prime Minister Yukio Hatoyama, a freemason Satanic agent, was bribed by the bankers with the promise his son would be the "first prime minister of a world government." The source of this information is a friend of Hatoyama's wife.

Hatoyama and Banri Kaeda, along with Seiji Maehara are some of the top Satanic P2 lodge agents in the current Democratic Party of Japan government. This source also confirmed at former Prime Minister Naoto Kan is a North Korean Satanic P2 lodge agent. Power broker Ichiro Ozawa tried to switch sides and "join the Chinese," but he was in fact an agent for J. Rockefeller who was trying to infiltrate the Asian secret societies.

The Japanese magazine Kami no Bakudan (paper bomb) has also reported in its latest edition that current Japanese Prime Minister Yoshihiko Noda is part of a homosexual network of agents linked to Panasonic founder Konosuke Matsushita and the CIA international homosexual network centered at Georgetown University.

Any government official worldwide who

was sent to Georgetown for graduate studies is likely to be part of this network. However, as far as we can tell, the gay network is supportive of the White Dragon Society and its aims to end poverty, end war and stop environmental destruction.

We would like to ask this network to fully activate itself in order to dismantle the remaining Satanic agents still working to terrorize Japan into submission to their plans for a world fascist government. They know the specific agents who have been carrying out this traitorous work and they must all be put into preventative custody this week.

The first anniversary of the March 11, 2011 tsunami and nuclear terror attacks has come and the Japanese corporate media provided extensive coverage while carefully avoiding saying it was a natural disaster. This is a clear sign the media moguls here are still cowards who are sitting on the fence and waiting to see who wins the financial war.

They need to understand that Satan has already left this universe. **Humanity will finally be set free.**

# Maine Republic Email Alert

*No.039*

"... that I should bear witness unto the truth." — John 18:33 // David E. Robinson, Publisher

"... if the trumpet give an uncertain sound, who shall prepare himself for battle?" — I Corinthians 14:8    03/13/2012

# Mass Arrests of 10,000 Global Cabal Members

**Imminent Televised Event: Mass Arrests of 10.000 Global Cabal Members - 2012**

Very soon, you will witness the worldwide mass arrests of the many criminal cabal members.

These arrests will mean the removal of the final obstacles that will allow for the implementation of the new abundance systems that are ready to immediately free humanity from the current economy and its falsely imposed conditions of debt and poverty.

There have been many men and women dedicated to this cause who have been working diligently in secret for years to bring us to this moment and are so eager to present to humanity the new system that will immediately redistribute abundance to all of humanity and release humanity from the mundane life it has known. Freedom is to be returned to the people.

The release of technologies and other suppressed elements that are to be introduced will follow to assist this transition.

The news of these mass arrests will come sudden and come hard, and many whom are unprepared with an understanding as to why may feel shocked and confused to witness so many taken into custody.

These many men and women, however, have served for the perpetuation of your enslavement and all have actively taken part in serious crimes against the people.

Certain big media groups have agreed to cover these events and assist in the disclosure timeline. These arrests will be televised and fully shared with you for it is owed to the people of the world that they witness the very moments and actions taken that will mean your release from the control of these many people whom have for so long worked to serve the control and exploitation of humanity.

This manipulation will end and humanity will enter into a new life.

With this in mind, you can look upon these arrests without fear and acknowledge what they mean for your world.

There are many sources of this type of liberating information and it is requested that this information is made available to all who may, or may not, choose to at least familiarize themselves with it, for all efforts to spread this information are valuable and will help dispel fears and lessen the impact.

True freedom is to be returned to you soon.

The music featured in this video is:

Valkyrie dimension [ DDRX2 ] (Water Remix)

http://tinyurl.com/6o92pqm

*Office of The Maine free State, 3 Linnell Circle, Brunswick, Maine 04011*

# Maine Republic Email Alert

No. 040

"... that I should bear witness unto the truth." — John 18:33 // David E. Robinson, Publisher

"... if the trumpet give an uncertain sound, who shall prepare himself for battle?" — I Corinthians 14:8    03/13/2012

## Rival Emperor stakes claim to Japanese throne, shows evidence he is the real deal.

**Posted by Benjamin**

Naoshi Onodera claims that he is the legal and rightful emperor of Japan and that Emperor Akihito is descended from a group of illegitimate pretenders who were put up as puppet rulers by foreign cabalists who use the Satanic star as their symbol.

He says the sitting emperor is using fake replicas of the three ancient imperial treasures used to justify his position on the throne. These items are known as the jewel, the sword, and the mirror, and are said to be the oldest inherited items on earth. The real ones are in his possession and he is willing to have scholars and legal experts verify this and other evidence, Onodera says.

This is an extremely important claim because it is intimately connected to the start-up of the new financial system and the possibility of fundamental regime change in Japan.

In recent years Japan has been controlled by a small clique centered around Hiroaki Fushimi, a distant imperial relative who has been trying to seize the throne and thus take control of the Japanese financial system. As a part of this plot, Fushimi arranged the murder of Princess Masako's fiancée Katsuhiko Oku in order to force her to marry the crown prince so that he could substitute one of his own children as Masako's child and heir to the throne, according to several imperial family members.

Oku, who worked for the North America Number 2 Division at the Japanese foreign ministry was sent to Iraq where he was murdered, they claim. Fushimi has been an agent for George Bush Senior and has provided the Bushes with fraudulent financial documents, they say.

Emperor Akihito has been a powerless puppet manipulated by this

Is this the real Emperor of Japan?

Naoshi Onodera holding what he claims is an 8000 year old Sumerian object, the Japanese imperial "Jewel."

clique which includes the Prince Hitachi, the imperial family sources say. Fushimi refused to confirm or deny these claims when reached through his secretary.

This clique is now isolated and hiding in the Imperial Palace behind 6,000 uniformed guards. However, since White Dragon Society members are part of the inner staff of the Imperial palace, they must surrender and allow Eijiro Katsu, the senior Ministry of Finance Bureaucrat and Bank of Japan Governor Masaaki Shirakawa to open up the BOJ Black Screens and release the funding for the new financial system. Japan's Ministry of Finance will then receive an initial payment of $10 trillion to be used fort post-earthquake rebuilding and to set up a new International Economic Planning Agency.

The issue of who has the ultimate legal claim to ownership of the vast hoards of Japanese Imperial Treasure that helps back up the new financial system will have to be decided by scholars and jurists at a later date because the new financial system needs to be started up ASAP. The man on the spot with the actual legal signing rights is Eijiro Katsu so for now the sword of global destiny is hanging over his head.

In any case, Onodera is undeniably in possession of some extremely unique and historically valuable artifacts.

The "Jewel" he holds above has an eight petalled flower carved on it. Onodera says this object has been in his family for 8,000 years and has its origins in ancient Sumer. The flower is the oldest known example of the eight pointed star or the seal of the prophets, he says.

The other object he showed was the "sword." The sword has an inscription on it saying it belongs to a king.

Onodera says it dates back to his Zhou dynasty royal ancestor from 1000 BCE. The sword is the oldest known Chinese sword, he says, and it is badly eroded.

The third treasure, the "mirror," dates back 2100 years and is originally from Korea, he says.

Apart from holding what he claims are three treasures of the Japanese Imperial throne, Onodera had many other interesting items such as this item:

Tibetan Kings used this to sacrifice virgins until Tibet was conquered by China a thousand years ago and the Chinese emperors put an end to the practice, he says.

Office of The Maine free State, 3 Linnell Circle, Brunswick, Maine 04011

The other point to be made about Onodera's claims is that many of Japan's Yakuza gangs and right wing organizations support him. Onodera has been under the protection of the Nichiren Buddhist sect and has kept his identity, and claims, secret until now.

According to Onodera, when foreign armies invaded Japan in the 1850's and 1860's, they found the Japanese government owned 3/4ths of the world's known supply of silver. In order to get their hands on it, they supplied an impoverished Northern lineage with rifles that could shoot 400 meters while they sold the richer Southern "legitimate" lineage rifles that could only shoot 100 meters.

The symbol of the Northern Army's flag was a 5-pointed star, the symbol of Lucifer, also known as Satan. The Southerners were massacred and foreign banking families got their hands on some of the treasure. Ever since then, he claims, Japan has been run by these puppets of foreign financiers.

Onodera also makes a more startling claim. He says his family is directly descended from the biblical Abraham. His claims are backed up by the fact that the family tree of Abraham corresponds exactly with the family tree in the Japanese foundation myths. To confirm this Onodera produced what he claims is the original stone tablet of the 10 commandments. He says it was given to his ancestor by "celestial beings."

Onodera says all of the items in his possession are available for expert scrutiny so long as he and his staff are able to monitor the objects at all times.

Needless to say, Onodera also has complex genealogical tables, documents and other evidence to back his claim to being the heir of the oldest known, still extant, royal lineage on earth.

# Maine Republic Email Alert

No.041

"... that I should bear witness unto the truth." — John 18:33 // David E. Robinson, Publisher

"... if the trumpet give an uncertain sound, who shall prepare himself for battle?" — I Corinthians 14:8 — 03/26/12

## Warning! Major Changes ahead . . .

We are in a time of great change. **America's *Currency* was captured in 1913. America's *Government* was captured in 1933.** This explains why petitioning our government for grievances has been to no meaningful avail.

The *Corporations* that masquerade as our lawful government today, have almost *destroyed* America! Top people in our government — *including our military* — know this. They have been waiting for the "right time" to help *take America back to our lawful government.*

In the very near future, we can expect a major constructive change in our banking and currency system. We can expect to see contingents of Federal Marshals acting in the major seats of power — backed up by our Military.

These Military people are NOT any part of a military coup. They are backing up the Civilian *re-establishment* of our lost, lawful, government.

We can expect to see minor interruptions in our normal way of life.

This Transition has been designed to minimize interruptions in vital services in our economy — to minimize hardship.

This Transition will be accompanied by announcements in mainstream media. What we do *not* want is for people to become alarmed.

Our *so-called* "president" has been informed that he is *no longer* the Commander in Chief of our Military!

This is part of a worldwide operation whereby the non-aligned nations — *those nations that are not part of the G20* — will re-establish solid currencies.

There will be additional announcements to come — designed to slowly awaken the masses; to reduce panic.

Civil authority has been restored to the people. The Military who exist only through Civil authority will be ready to assist the People whom they are sworn to protect in the effort to restore this nation to the Constitutional Republic it was created to be.

International Law has been unlawfully in effect in America since 1933. And *rescinding this law,* has been on the table since the 1950s.

We the People have regained Civilian Authority, in order to use the Military Services to support the ongoing effort to bring us back to true government *"of, for and by the people"*.

Do *not* misread what is going on — they are *NOT* coming for the People. *The Cabal's time is up!*

Please prepare for *"good"* changes to come. Please share this information with others. The foundation has been laid. All that is needed now is YOU! — regular, everyday people will be needed for their insight, opinions and voice.

PLEASE SHARE THIS INFORMATION. EVERY AMERICAN MUST HEAR THIS, TO KNOW WHAT IS HAPPENING!

Just before the end of last year, Pennsylvania — *as a state* — removed itself from the RuSA organization. After they did this, they put together a **Declaration of Notice to the World** stating that the Commonwealth of Pennsylvania had returned itself and its people back under its *de jur* Constitution, *of the 1700s,* and declared the People of Pennsylvania, Free! — no longer recognizing *unlawful corporate government* within their state.

They did this *legally and properly.* They did not ask for permission, they simply went ahead and did it. And they received their receipt back from the Office of Private International Law at the Hague.

And shortly after that, an informed contact — who had been in touch with the various groups who had come forward in the beginning, concerning funding for RuSA and Rap, before changes were made and they withdrew their support — was contacted and given a simple message, and that message was this:

*"It has come to our attention, what Pennsylvania has done. How long would it take you to put together a simple majority of states to duplicate what Pennsylvania has done, for at such a time there could be monetary and military support?"*

They asked for a copy of the original documentation that Pennsylvania had submitted to the Office of Private International Law at the Hague, *so they could see who had been involved.*

Our contact had no problem with that, and neither did Pennsylvania. So they forwarded on the documentation that Pennsylvania had submitted. The answer was *"Yes! we'll just see how fast we can get that done!"*

So they sent out emails to everyone across the country that they knew, and had worked with all this time, that they knew to be capable, honorable, and honest Patriots, who would roll up their sleeves and actually get the job done, once they were told what had to be done.

And by the following day, at least one contact in 20-22 states had stepped up and volunteered to be a lead person in their state, to get it done!

The goal was for at least a simple majority — meaning 26 or more states to duplicate *exactly* what Pennsylvania had done.

It was later decided by those involved, to add *more strength* to the action by making the **Declaration of Notice to the World,** collectively as a united effort, so that the world will know we are not just free people in the various free states, but a Free People, *united as we were meant to be.*

We need no permission, recognition or opinion from foreign bodies or corporations to be what we are —

Americans who claim our rightful heritage that was given to us by our founders in 1776.

This action should be seen as a *Declaration;* not just a notification — this is primary.

This action is interim; and we can't emphasize that enough.

A small group of elite people, have already screwed things up — and in order to make sure that this doesn't happen again, all of the temporary aspects of this will be in writing.

After a period of about 120 days, free elections will be held. Paper ballots only; machines can be played with; paper ballots are a lot more difficult.

We've been told that old money people from before the Revolutionary War have been in contact with our military, and that some 80-90% of the military agree with the ideology found in our founding documents.

Everything we do is based on the principles in our 1787 Constitution and the Bill of Rights — including the *original 13th Amendment* that prohibits any foreign association, title of nobility, etc. — and the Oath of Service that everybody must take to *"support and defend the Constitution of the United States against all enemies, foreign and domestic."*

The U.S. Military has indicated to the financial people that they are willing to back us and that we have their recognition and support.

This gives the Military — *probably for the first time* — power to be used as a backup to federal Marshals who will take into custody all of the crooks and "fun-and-games people" on Wall Street, and so forth. There is going to be a tremendous house-cleaning.

The reorganizational portions of the government itself should be concluded in about 120 days. This 120 day period will begin with a formal announcement from the press-room of the White House.

This will give every reporter a clean shot at broadcasting the transition.

So these measures — *in terms of what the military wants* — they want to be the good guys. They're tired of being the bad guys. They would much rather be invited into a foreign country as a friend, and an assistant.

You need some help? What do you need? Manpower? Bull-dozers? Food? We can come in and help you out.

Yes! we're the United States Military! but we're the *new* one. We're the good guys. BINGO!

We think this new approach will work quite well.

We are not putting together any interim government. We are not trying to overthrow anything. We are trying to revert back to law and order, and create the smallest amount of chaos, *in the most peaceful fashion that we can.*

Our military cannot do this on their own for the simple reason that under the current structure, Obama is considered to be the President — *we all know that he is not* — he is the CEO (Chief Executive Officer) of a Corporation called THE UNITED STATES.

The majority of the American people do not understand this.

So as long as the American people recognize a criminal corporation in Washington D.C. as having jurisdiction over them — *and they do not stand up and say otherwise* — our military's hands are somewhat tied. They have been taking orders from a fake Commander in Chief.

As far as the financial people are concerned, they will never bring forth the money that's been intended for this country, these many years, until Washington is cleaned out, because if they did, it would disappear down the black hole of theft, almost immediately.

If the military are to once again take their orders from we the people, we have to be ready with a list of what we require it to do.

As pointed out above, this is temporary, and what gives the people the power and the authority and the standing to do this is simply that a majority of states filed the same paperwork that Pennsylvania filed, putting the world on Notice that they have gone back under their *de jur* Constitution.

They have reclaimed the Articles of Confederation, which have never been rescinded.

The Declaration of Independence and the Articles of Confederation are the basis of our freedom.

These arrests will mean the removal of the final obstacles that will allow for the implementation of the *new abundance systems* that are ready to free humanity from the current economy and its falsely imposed conditions of poverty and debt.

There are many men and women dedicated to this cause who have been working diligently in secret for years to bring us to this moment, who are eager to present to humanity the new system that will redistribute abundance to all, and release humanity from the mundane life it has known.

Freedom is being returned to the people.

The release of withheld technologies and other suppressed elements will follow to assist this transition.

The news of these mass arrests will come sudden and come hard, and many who are unprepared with an understanding as to why, may feel shocked and confused to see so many people taken into custody.

These people, how ever, have served to perpetuate our enslavement, and all have actively taken part in serious crimes against the people.

Certain big media groups have agreed to cover these events and assist in the disclosure timeline.

These arrests will be televised and fully shared with you, for it is owed to the people of the world that they witness the very moments and actions taken that will mean our release from the control of these people who have for so long worked to exploit and control humanity.

This manipulation will end and all humanity will enter into a new life.

True freedom is to be soon returned to you.

This is the link to a video posted on the Internet titled, *MAKE THIS VIRAL! Freedom Reigns - Mass Arrests for the Cabal.*

http://tinyurl.com/7carxb7

http://maine-patriot.com

*Office of The Maine free State, 3 Linnell Circle, Brunswick, Maine 04011*

# Maine Republic Email Alert

No. 042

*". . . that I should bear witness unto the truth."* — John 18:33 // David E. Robinson, Publisher

*". . . if the trumpet give an uncertain sound, who shall prepare himself for battle?"* — I Corinthians 14:8 —    03/26/12

## Over 200 senior bankers arrested last week as new banking system goes on line

**"Overall, things are looking good"**
Ben confirms that the final take down of the cabal is going on with the arrests and resignations of the bankers, and a new financial system is already online.

He also outlines some of the current structure of the financial cabal, and what was behind the 7.4 earthquake last week in Mexico. Very interesting.

Over 200 senior bankers arrested last week as new financial system goes online, by Benjamin Fulford.

The new financial system is online now and abundant financing is either already or soon to be made available, according to dragon family representatives.

The final take down of the criminal cabal has also begun in earnest with over 200 senior bankers arrested and 450 resigned last week alone, these sources say.

Japan is also now doing the final paperwork needed to set up an international economic planning agency with an initial funding facility of $10 trillion, or about 200 times what the World Bank lends every year, according to Japanese government sources.

There will be some sort of announcement about this, and other things, on Tuesday evening, March 27th, 2012, Japan Standard Time, according to illuminati and White Dragon Society sources.

The arrest of some very high profile individuals is imminent.

The general structure of the financial cabal and its top leaders has also now been mapped to some extent. For example, the Rothschild family dynasty leaders have been identified. The Swiss branch of the family is run by David de Rothschild in Geneva, the French branch by Guy de Rothschild, the German branch by Rothschild family member and Hitler daughter Angelina Merkel and the British branch by Evelyn de Rothschild.

In the US, JP Morgan is a Rothschild front.

The Rockefeller family syndicate uses Goldman Sachs and Citibank as its major financial fronts. Bank of America is a front for the Italian black nobility behind the Vatican and the mafia, run in part by Peter Hans Kolvenbach, the former black pope. Pope Malevolent the 16th is also a senior member of this satanic group.

The Nazi faction is run by Fuhrer George Bush Senior with Ben Bernanke acting as Deputy Fuhrer. Their chemical and pharmaceutical mass murder division is run by the Du Pont family.

The Bill and Melinda Gates foundation is now in Africa forcing families at gunpoint to accept the sterilization by vaccine of the families daughters. In North America, Japan and elsewhere the mass sterilization by vaccine is taking place under the guise of *protecting girls against cervical cancer*.

Message to Bill Gates: your company and foundation are going to be confiscated and you are going to spend the rest of your life making restitution.

The United States government has been so compromised by these and other cabal families and their foundation fronts that the upcoming US Presidential "election," is nothing more than a power struggle between the Chicago mob and their front man, Mitt Romney, versus the Bush Texas illegal drug mafia and their guy, Jeb Bush.

Hopefully the new financial system, once it is fully implemented, will pull the plug on the entire farcical show and Americans will be able to choose their own leaders based on true information provided by free media.

For now though, electronically rigged elections and corporate propaganda provide sham democracy for dumbed down and drugged up Americans.

However, a look at the pentagon budget for this upcoming year shows they have dedicated plenty of resources to financing reserve troop units inside the United States.

This does not mean they are preparing to put average Americans into FEMA camps as feared by many. To the contrary, they are preparing for a mass round up of cabal agents and proxies, *according to pentagon and CIA sources*.

There was a clear indication of change on March 20th, when instead of having the cabal scheduled earthquake hit Tokyo, a magnitude 7.4 earthquake hit Oaxaca, Mexico exactly when President Obama's daughter was vacationing there. Furthermore, this earthquake was advertised in advance through pamphlets distributed locally. This is a clear sign the bad guys no longer play the HAARP.

Another sign of change was the public rebuke of Obama, Clinton and cabal controlled media outlets when the official Chinese government news site, Xinhua, stated that North Korea was not on the agenda of the 50 nation nuclear security summit taking place in Soeul [Seoul], Korea this week.

The cabal propaganda media has been carrying a fake story about nuclear danger from North Korea even though that country has already announced it will cease nuclear weapons development.

The secret agenda behind this 50 nation summit is an attempt to steal 200 tons of gold that is in South Korean warehouses. That theft is not going to be allowed to go ahead so the cabalists will leave the summit empty handed.

There was also plenty of speculation about a coup d'etat in China last week. All that happened was that a Maoist cabal agent Bo Xilai was removed from power after one of his henchmen was discovered taking instructions from the US consulate in Chongqing, *according to MI6 sources*.

China is still on course for a stable and harmonious regime change-over later this year, *according to White Dragon Society sources*. The talk of a Maoist coup d'etat was wishful cabalist thinking fanned by cabalist media outlets.

Speaking about fake stories, the "White Hats" group on the internet, consisting of Bush agent Mike Cotrell and Hawaii resident Danny Gammage, has been spewing out laughable libel (such as this writer is a clone).

More damagingly, they managed to fool Lord Blackheath of the UK Upper House of Parliament, with a fake story about $15 trillion that he raised in Parliamentary session. The House of Lords is now going to summon a White Dragon Society ally to testify about what is really going on in the financial wars.

The London financial district is headed for further purges and the talk is that Lord Sassoon is headed for a big fall. The investigation may even extend to the UK Royal family, European CIA sources say.

In Japan, meanwhile, the status quo is expected to remain on hold until the **March 31st end of the fiscal year** because of overwhelming workloads in the bureaucracy and the parliament. After March 31st, there will be concrete negotiations taking place involving the Finance Ministry, Bank of Japan, Prime Minister's office and Royal Household Agency aimed at setting up a new international economic planning agency.

The Japanese self-defense forces and bureaucracy are also planning a major purge of cabalist puppets in the Japanese Parliament, banks, corporations and media.

Overall, things are looking very good. However, unless we see these senior cabalists on world TV confessing to their crimes, we must not be complacent. Until this financial war is over, keep your powder dry and stay alert.

_Maine Republic Email Alert_     No.043

"... that I should bear witness unto the truth." — John 18:33  //  David E. Robinson, Publisher

"... if the trumpet give an uncertain sound, who shall prepare himself for battle?" — I Corinthians 14:8 —     03/27/12

# National Emergency Committee Announcement
## Benjamin Fulford with Alexander Romanov and Chodoin Daikaku

My fellow humans...

I am Benjamin Fulford, spokesperson for the White Dragon Society.

With me here is Chodoin Daikako, he's the head of the World's Marshal Arts Society, and if it's necessary, in an emergency, he can summon up an army of 200 million people, worldwide.

Here on my right is Alexander Romanov, who is a Grand Master of an Illuminate group that claims to have started the French, Russian, and American Revolutions.

As you may know, there has been a battle going on over the future of this planet.

The western counties have been taken over by a Mafia organization, all composed of members of the same plan, and they're not Jews, Okay? they say they worship Lucifer and they want a world government controlled by them with the rest of us in perpetual debt slavery and drudgery and with no hope of ever ruling our own destiny.

We offer a very different vision. We offer world peace. We offer $100,000 dollars for every man, woman, and child to be delivered in the form of schools, hospitals, free education, nature preserves, and all the sort of things that most people want.

We all want to stop world poverty. We want to stop environmental destruction. And we all wish to have a prosperous and happy and peaceful future. And that's the alternative we are offering.

Thank you.

Now, I'll have Mr. Romanov speak, and then Mr. Chodoin Daikaku.

**Alexander:** Hi; Yes. Thank you. This is the first time I've ever been on this kind of show, so I would like to thank Mr. Chodoin Daikaku for having me.

I understand that Me. Chodoin, is a good friend of Vladimir Putin, who he is teaching, in fact, so I'd like to take this opportunity to congratulate Mr. Putin on his election victory.

He has done an outstanding job in my view, of rescuing Russia from the parasites who tried to take over in the Govbachev era.

He's clearly the most meritorious and best qualified person to lead Russia, as was demonstrated by the will of the Russian People in the election.

Now, in the western media there have been reports of fraudulent fraud elections, and I want to say two things.

Firstly, the corporate controlled mainstream media is a joke; an embarrassment; a disgrace, and it doesn't really matter what they say!

And secondly, as far as fraudulent and fraud-elections go, surely the biggest example is the American elections.

What choice do the people have? Two super-rich corporate backed candidates who, regardless of who wins, will represent their super-rich friends; the 1%

So, that's my opinion. And good luck to Mr. Putin. I hope he continues to do a very good job, as he has done so far.

**Benjamin:** Okay.
Chodoin, San...

**Benjamin, for Chodoin:** You know, in this era of confusion and turbulence, you need a leader who has a world view. A universal view. A powerful leader.

In order to have world peace and humanity united in harmony you need friends. I think Putin may be one of the people who can do this. He is one of the leaders who cam here at this time of change on our planet.

**Benjamin:** And I have proposed also to the Japanese government and People to set up an International Meritocratically staffed organization call the International Economic Planning Agency that will have 200 times more money than the World Bank spends, and it can accomplish the job of ending poverty and stopping our environmental destruction with a matter of months!

Instead we have these war-mongering incompetent criminals who have no idea of how to run a planet, and somehow found themselves in charge, and thought they were God; well they're NOT.

**Alexander:** I disagree with you a little bit.

I think these people who are ruling the planet know exactly what they are doing. They're not stupid. You see, the way I see it, you have this one planet here, and with seven billion inhabitants, and for some reason, there's a very small number — a tiny small number — of a very small majority of people who think that this planet belongs to them, and that they can do whatever they want with us. And they've been doing this for forever now. And it's time that this ended.

Who are these people? Who died and left them in charge? Well, one good thing is that we know exactly who they are. And it's not even the 1%. The 1% has nothing to fear from the Revolution.

It's the inner circle of the 1%. It's a group of roughly 6,000 individuals — mostly old men — and we call them the Old World Order.

We know exactly who they are.

The Rothschilds, the Rockefellers, the Jewish bankers in Wall Street, Goldman Sachs, the Bushes, and the Clintons.

And on the other side of the Atlantic

you have the Vatican, and Queen Elizabeth in England. These people have ruled this world forever, for their own personal benefits, to hell with everyone else.

These people have everything. How much more do they need? They will never stop. And to hell with every one else. And half of the world's population lives in utter poverty, in misery, — while these people just have more and more and more — and never stop.

So the time has come for us to stop them. And this is what we will do this year.

**Benjamin:** They call the people their subjects; which means that we are a joke; a slave — they think of us as slaves. We're not slaves. We want our freedom. We want to choose our own futures for ourselves.

We don't want nasty, low paying jobs, and a boring future, which the media lies to us, day in day out. They try to dumb us down; drug us up; reduce our population by planting infertility drugs in various household products.

And they're doing things, for example... Bill Gates' Foundation, right now, in Africa, is forcing people at gun-point — families at gun-point to sterilize their daughters with vaccines.

These are the kinds of people we don't want in power anymore. And we're going to remove them. That's a promise. This year.

**Benjamin, for Chodoin:** He's saying that the reason Putin is a strong and desirable leader is because he studied Judo; he has a 5th degree Black Belt in Judo, and it's the Japanese spirit of Bushido, at the Martial Arts, that gave him his strength.

The International Association of Bushido, Karate, Judo, Kung Fu, etc., can muster worldwide, at any given time, 200 million people, and they only fight under the Code of Chivalry which is, you don't attack women, children and non-combatants, which is what the other side has been doing.

He believes that with Putin's help and the Martial Arts Societies worldwide we can cause major change. And of course the Illuminati, who are — throughout the western intelligence agencies, military, and this is not the Italian Illuminati, this is the Gnostic Illuminati. And they want meritocracy — rule by the people who are the best. People who worked their way up the system — not people who are born into it, and given it — had it given to them, even though they are often not very bright.

That is not a very good way to have a planet run. We want a transparent pyramid that anybody can climb the top, and everybody see how they got to the top, and why they got there.

You don't want hidden people using secret societies, murder, bribery, and lies to rule us for selfish purposes. Those days are over. Humanity will be set free.

**Alexander:** I like what Chodoin, San, said earlier about Japanese media, and of course, that applies to the media everywhere — it's designed specifically to dumb everyone down. Just to laugh at whoever nonsense, and to not think for themselves.

**Benjamin:** And so with the education system. It is designed to compartmentalize your brain. Everybody in the high level educational system is trained to think inside a box, not *outside* of that box. A specific category of knowledge and thinking. They don't want people to know what's really going on.

**Alexander:** Can I say one more thing? One last thing and this is a little bit different. It concerns the secret of the Illuminati.

And, during the other time I've been on video was with Benjamin, and what I said was the great secret the Illuminati are keeping is that the Abahamic God is in fact Satan. Which is, of course, absolutely true, but we have known this for thousands of years, ever since the ancient Gnostics, that the God of the Jews, the Christians, and the Moslems is none other than the Devil.

However, the real secret, for 14,000 years, that the Illuminati have kept protected, is evidence which incontrovertibly proves the existence of a technologically advanced pre-flood civilization. I'm talking about Atlantis.

They were on a par with our own technology. And this has been totally erased from our history. And why has this happened? So they can insert this devil, and in that way brainwash and control the human race. Which they have done exceedingly well. But we have preserved this secret and we have the evidence. And we will present the evidence which proves the existence of Atlantis.

**Benjamin:** And I want to make this very clear. The God of the Jews is Yahweh — the Creator of the Universe — we didn't create ourselves. Something created us. We all must respect the creations. That means respecting nature and other human beings.

However, I have, by directly talking to the elite people, come to the understanding that they actually do worship satan. As amazing as it is, we're ruled by satan. We're worshiping gangsters!

That is in the horrendous fact that decades of research, in the field and through text, has shown to me. And these people come out of the woodwork.

We know who they are. And they know that we know who they are. And they're scared. And their only hope is to surrender, A.S.A.P.

**Alexander:** Well, they had their chance to surrender, and it looks like they're not going to take it. So we're going to force them to surrender.

And finally, I have a message to Queen Elizabeth, directly — Aunt Elizabeth — she is very upset; she wants her Crown back.

**Benjamin:** Okay, thank you for listening, and remember, we all want world peace, an end to poverty, an end to environmental destruction, and a future of wonder and awe, and pleasure, not this nightmare that we have now.

Thank you. And bless you all.

**Alexander:** Thank you, Chodoin, San, for having me.

To watch this video go to
http://tinyurl.com/7zjg3sf

# Maine Republic Email Alert

No.044

". . . that I should bear witness unto the truth." — John 18:33 // David E. Robinson, Publisher

". . . if the trumpet give an uncertain sound, who shall prepare himself for battle?" — I Corinthians 14:8 — 03/27/12

## A keen-Message for 'today'

**Motague Keene's message for April 1, 2012.**
http://www.montaguekeen.com/

All that was hidden is being revealed. We encourage you to share your findings with each other. You will not see mention of this on mainstream television as yet. The media is not allowed to give you the full picture of what is actually happening.

Those with eyes to see, can see for themselves that the Cabal is in trouble. They are in shock; they cannot believe that their plans for 2012 will not now be realised.

Greater forces than theirs are preventing them from starting World War 3. They are having to accept the fact that they are not invincible, after all. To save face, they now want you to believe that they have changed their plans, that they now plan to attack Iran in the Spring.

Well . . . we shall see what transpires in the Spring, shall we?

They failed to recognise that when intelligent people wake up and see clearly what is being done to them, they come together and call for help. Their request has been heeded and help has been forthcoming from all directions.

Just because you do not see it on your TVs, does not mean that you are not being rescued from the terrible fate that the Cabal had planned for you.

There is no honour among the Cabal. They turn on each other, every day now, thus exposing more and more of the corruption in which they are involved.

April will prove to be an interesting month. The floodgates are opening. You will have to deal with the real truth. The first reaction of the general public will be to become angry. I ask that you rise above it as anger will only delay matters.

You will have to face some terrible truths about what has been done to mankind; to your DNA, to your brain, etc.

All this will be put right. You will be fully restored. What you had accepted as reality will change completely. The time has come for the suffering to stop and for peace to reign once more.

There are groups of people all over your world, ready and equipped to take over from the corrupt. It has taken some years to put everything in place. The evil perpetrated on the human race will shock those who are not yet awake.

Humanity is a genetic experiment, an immortal race trapped in a mortal paradigm, a solar race locked in a lunar reality, a stolen race on a stolen planet.

The corruption lies in the mutant matrix, in the systemic failure of Earth's governing functions and the loss of evolutionary symbiosis that occurred when this parasitic species electro-magnetically disconnected humanity and its mother planet from the divine immortal continuum, setting Earth on a course of terminal decline.

THERE WAS NO "FALL" WE WERE PUSHED.

This is what you have returned to Earth to bring about.

You will succeed; never again will humanity be allowed to be reduced to this level of existence. Never again will human beings be hungry or homeless or live in squalor. All men will be equal, as they are before God. All this will be achieved peacefully and with as much dignity as is possible. Never stoop to the level of the Cabal, it is not necessary.

Do not doubt for one moment your ability to restore humanity and planet Earth. It is just a matter of everything falling into place when the timing is right. 2012 was the year chosen for all to be put in place, then man will learn who he is and what he is capable of. All the information is readily available, it's up to each of you to prepare for this great transition.

The energy of your world is re-awakening. It is releasing pure energy once more. Believe only those you trust. Go with your gut instincts. The Cabal will try to use natural changes to cause fear. Remember that fear is the oxygen of life to them. They need you to be in fear.

They are to be pitied. 2000 years in the planning and now they see it falling apart and they are powerless to change it. They will have to answer for the human suffering they have caused in that time. Humanity will be their judge.

Sadly, humanity fell into the traps which were cleverly set by the Cabal, all those years ago. Man has since learned some hard lessons. Now that people are becoming more aware every day, they want an end to the rule of the Cabal.

The time has come for the 99% to step forward and reclaim what is rightfully theirs. The plans of the Cabal are so EVIL — way beyond anything humanity could imagine. It will be difficult when all this comes to light. It will cause distress to all those who had trusted and revered them.

Look forward to peace and to learning your real history. You will learn the truth about your world. You will learn when and how it was led astray and the evil intent of those who set their plans in motion. You live on a prison planet. Look with love in your hearts to a life of freedom, the like of which you have never known.

There is nothing to fear as the battle is won. Together, we will shine the bright light of love on your Earth. Talk to each other. Share your thoughts, you hopes and your dreams, and soon they will become reality.

I remain your adoring, Monty.

Note: Montague Keen's earlier messages may be accessed at http://www.montaguekeen.com/page3.html

My fellow humans...

I am Benjamin Fulford, spokesperson for the White Dragon Society.

With me here is Chodoin Daikako, he's the head of the World's Marshal Arts Society, and if it's necessary, in an emergency, he can summon up an army of 200 million people, worldwide.

Here on my right is Alexander Romanov, who is a Grand Master of an Illuminate group that claims to have started the French, Russian, and American Revolutions.

As you may know, there has been a battle going on over the future of this planet.

The western counties have been taken over by a Mafia organization, all composed of members of the same plan, and they're not Jews, Okay? they say they worship Lucifer and they want a world government controlled by them with the rest of us in perpetual debt slavery and drudgery and with no hope of ever ruling our own destiny.

We offer a very different vision. We offer world peace. We offer $100,000 dollars for every man, woman, and child to be delivered in the form of schools, hospitals, free education, nature preserves, and all the sort of things that most people want.

We all want to stop world poverty. We want to stop environmental destruction. And we all wish to have a prosperous and happy and peaceful future. And that's the alternative we are offering.

Thank you.

Now, I'll have Mr. Romanov speak, and then Mr. Chodoin Daikaku.

**Alexander:** Hi; Yes. Thank you. This is the first time I've ever been on this kind of show, so I would like to thank Mr. Chodoin Daikaku for having me.

I understand that Me. Chodoin, is a good friend of Vladimir Putin, who he is teaching, in fact, so I'd like to take this opportunity to congratulate Mr. Putin on his election victory.

He has done an outstanding job in my view, of rescuing Russia from the parasites who tried to take over in the Govbachev era.

He's clearly the most meritorious and best qualified person to lead Russia, as was demonstrated by the will of the Russian People in the election.

Now, in the western media there have been reports of fraudulent fraud elections, and I want to say two things.

Firstly, the corporate controlled mainstream media is a joke; an embarrassment; a disgrace, and it doesn't really matter what they say!

And secondly, as far as fraudulent and fraud-elections go, surely the biggest example is the American elections.

What choice do the people have? Two super-rich corporate backed candidates who, regardless of who wins, will represent their super-rich friends; the 1%

So, that's my opinion. And good luck to Mr. Putin. I hope he continues to do a very good job, as he has done so far.

**Benjamin:** Okay.
Chodoin, San...

**Benjamin, for Chodoin:** You know, in this era of confusion and turbulence, you need a leader who has a world view. A universal view. A powerful leader.

In order to have world peace and humanity united in harmony you need friends. I think Putin may be one of the people who can do this. He is one of the leaders who cam here at this time of change on our planet.

**Benjamin**: And I have proposed also to the Japanese government and People to set up an International Meritocratically staffed organization call the International Economic Planning Agency that will have 200 times more money than the World Bank spends, and it can accomplish the job of ending poverty and stopping our environmental destruction with a matter of months!

Instead we have these war-mongering incompetent criminals who have no idea of how to run a planet, and somehow found themselves in charge, and thought they were God; well they're NOT.

**Alexander:** I disagree with you a little bit.

I think these people who are ruling the planet know exactly what they are doing. They're not stupid. You see, the way I see it, you have this one planet here, and with seven billion inhabitants, and for some reason, there's a very small number — a tiny small number — of a very small majority of people who think that this planet belongs to them, and that they can do whatever they want with us. And they've been doing this for forever now. And it's time that this ended.

Who are these people? Who died and left them in charge? Well, one good thing is that we know exactly who they are. And it's not even the 1%. The 1% has nothing to fear from the Revolution.

It's the inner circle of the 1%. It's a group of roughly 6,000 individuals — mostly old men — and we call them the Old World Order.

We know exactly who they are.

The Rothschilds, the Rockefellers, the Jewish bankers in Wall Street, Goldman Sachs, the Bushes, and the Clintons.

And on the other side of the Atlantic you have the Vatican, and Queen Elizabeth in England. These people have ruled this world forever, for their own personal benefits, to hell with everyone else.

These people have everything. How much more do they need? They will never stop. And to hell with every one else. And half of the world's population lives in utter poverty, in misery, — while these people just have more and more and more — and never stop.

So the time has come for us to stop them. And this is what we will do this year.

**Benjamin:** They call the people their subjects; which means that we are a joke; a slave — they think of us as slaves. We're not slaves. We want our freedom. We want to choose our own futures for ourselves.

We don't want nasty, low paying jobs, and a boring future, which the media lies to us, day in day out. They try to dumb us down; drug us up; reduce our population by planting infertility drugs in various household products.

And they're doing things, for example... Bill Gates' Foundation, right now, in Africa, is forcing people at gun-point — families at gun-point to sterilize their daughters with vaccines.

These are the kinds of people we don't want in power anymore. And we're going to remove them. That's a promise. This year.

**Benjamin, for Chodoin:** He's saying that the reason Putin is a strong and desirable leader is because he studied Judo; he has a 5th degree Black Belt in Judo, and it's the Japanese spirit of Bushido, at the Martial Arts, that gave him his strength.

The International Association of Bushido, Karate, Judo, Kung Fu, etc., can muster worldwide, at any given time, 200 million people, and they only fight under the Code of Chivalry which is, you don't attack women, children and non-combatants, which is what the other side has been doing.

He believes that with Putin's help and the Martial Arts Societies worldwide we can cause major change. And of course the Illuminati, who are — throughout the western intelligence agencies, military, and this is not the Italian Illuminati, this is the Gnostic Illuminati. And they want meritocracy — rule by the people who are the best. People who worked their way up the system — not people who are born into it, and given it — had it given to them, even though they are often not very bright.

That is not a very good way to have a planet run. We want a transparent pyramid that anybody can climb the top, and everybody see how they got to the top, and why they got there.

You don't want hidden people using secret societies, murder, bribery, and lies to rule us for selfish purposes. Those days are over. Humanity will be set free.

**Alexander:** I like what Chodoin, San, said earlier about Japanese media, and of course, that applies to the media everywhere — it's designed specifically to dumb everyone down. Just to laugh at whoever nonsense, and to not think for themselves.

**Benjamin:** And so with the education system. It is designed to compartmentalize your brain. Everybody in the high level educational system is trained to think inside a box, not *outside* of that box. A specific category of knowledge and thinking. They don't want people to know what's really going on.

**Alexander:** Can I say one more thing? One last thing and this is a little bit different. It concerns the secret of the Illuminati.

And, during the other time I've been on video was with Benjamin, and what I said was the great secret the Illuminati are keeping is that the Abahamic God is in fact Satan. Which is, of course, absolutely true, but we have known this for thousands of years, ever since the ancient Gnostics, that the God of the Jews, the Christians, and the Moslems is none other than the Devil.

However, the real secret, for 14,000 years, that the Illuminati have kept protected, is evidence which incontrovertibly proves the existence of a technologically advanced pre-flood civilization. I'm talking about Atlantis.

They were on a par with our own technology. And this has been totally erased from our history. And why has this happened? So they can insert this devil, and in that way brainwash and control the human race. Which they have done exceedingly well. But we have preserved this secret and we have the evidence. And we will present the evidence which proves the existence of Atlantis.

**Benjamin:** And I want to make this very clear. The God of the Jews is Yahweh — the Creator of the Universe — we didn't create ourselves. Something created us. We all must respect the creations. That means respecting nature and other human beings.

However, I have, by directly talking to the elite people, come to the understanding that they actually do worship satan. As amazing as it is, we're ruled by satan. We're worshiping gangsters!

That is in the horrendous fact that decades of research, in the field and through text, has shown to me. And these people come out of the woodwork.

We know who they are. And they know that we know who they are. And they're scared. And their only hope is to surrender, A.S.A.P.

**Alexander:** Well, they had their chance to surrender, and it looks like they're not going to take it. So we're going to force them to surrender.

And finally, I have a message to Queen Elizabeth, directly — Aunt Elizabeth — she is very upset; she wants her Crown back.

**Benjamin:** Okay, thank you for listening, and remember, we all want world peace, an end to poverty, an end to environmental destruction, and a future of wonder and awe, and pleasure, not this nightmare that we have now.

Thank you. And bless you all.

**Alexander:** Thank you, Chodoin, San, for having me.

To watch this video go to
http://tinyurl.com/7zjg3sf

# Maine Republic Email Alert

No. 045

*". . . that I should bear witness unto the truth."* — John 18:33 // David E. Robinson, Publisher

*". . . if the trumpet give an uncertain sound, who shall prepare himself for battle?"* — I Corinthians 14:8 —    04/02/12

## More information about Drake

I found this on this page http://freedomreigns.us/Our_Team.html of the FreedomReigns.us website. Drake speaks of the David Wilcock interview with him < http://tinyurl.com/ 7juylza > so I wanted to pass this along for those of you who might want to know more about him.

**Drake:**

It has come to my attention that a lot of people want to know who I am. I will offer a part of the base of what I know without endangering myself or others. The basis of the knowledge I hold is extraordinary in its scope (content and reach) and those whom I am in contact with.

Not being willing to take anyone's word for it, I went behind the scenes and found who 'they' were talking to. This involves most of the 'news' web sites many are familiar with, credible or not.

My military service includes nuclear weapons, very high security clearances, and Vietnam. Most of the "incidents" from this time forward, I was involved in at some level, major, minor, and local. I started in the field of information in the late nineties and progressed from that time forward. I use a portion of the old cold war spy network, people in several sensitive positions, and those who agree to pass along info no one else gets. There are several contact avenues that also offer info, military, political and citizen eyes. In all, an extreme information highway.

The validity of what I've sent out has been the best at the time, almost all of which was verifiable. And yes, I was called on to prove a lot of it at first. This was not an easy task and caused me to be able to protect and out the info at the same time, I learned how.

Forces in the main stream media took most of what I offered and called it everything but true, and I was a nightmare head case trying to cause problems through the use of my imagination, and the internet...

Those who own the media control its content, most of which is questionable at best...I know, because I was directly involved in a few of those 'international and local incidents' that were reported as something else altogether...So I have first hand knowledge of this.

I have been a patriot since taking my oath of service in the 60's. I had always been raised to be a patriot, but that oath haunted me all the time...until I decided I would start taking action.

The present information I have shared comes from a plan I was privileged to read some years ago. To date it has been in the works well over twenty (20) years. Many old fashioned old timers knew better than the direction our country was headed, even way back then, so they started writing the plan. It deals with offering the basic freedoms our country was founded on, and how to return to that freedom.

My research extends into a lot of law, application, and the origin of law itself. The offerings used in the manner in which I stated them to be used, when used correctly, I never lost. This includes local, state, federal, and international applications.

A group of individual people in individual states, has completed the paperwork that sets our nation free.

It is my hope that we all can keep our freedom this time...that is up to We The People.

The extent of the information offered on the recording is, at this time, the limit I use to protect the many who are involved in our efforts. If anyone who reads this believes that freedom can still be available, then I urge all those to play the recording to others of a like mind.

A qualified person does not have to be a rocket scientist. Try finding someone who is so honest it hurts to be around them. A person who knows the meaning of right and wrong according to their conscience...and who listens to it. In order to start to turn things around, it will take as many people as possible to stand up in any way they can. Put together groups all over our country at the local level. Get everyone to know each other and look into using your group to put the right kind of people in office.

**Who am I to speak and by what authority do I do so?**

• **It is each persons constitutional 'duty' to remove a repressive government...the present one qualifies.**

• **I feel a moral obligation to stop the theft so hungry children in our own country of plenty, can eat.**

• **It ain't doing this for me; it is for my children and grandchildren, because their future hangs in the balance...**

• **I feel it is the least I can do for them.**

• **As one voice in the wilderness...I CRY FREEDOM...!**

~Drake

*Office of The Maine free State, 3 Linnell Circle, Brunswick, Maine 04011*

# Maine Republic Email Alert

*No.046*

*". . . that I should bear witness unto the truth."* — John 18:33 // David E. Robinson, Publisher

*". . . if the trumpet give an uncertain sound, who shall prepare himself for battle?"* — I Corinthians 14:8 —  04/02/12

## 'The Hunger Games' movie review

**A glimpse of our own future if the cancerous growth of government is not checked**... by Mike Adams, Health Ranger Editor of http://naturalnews.com

The Hunger Games is a wildly popular new movie, set in a dystopian future where an all-powerful, high-tech centralized government rules over "districts" of impoverished populations barely surviving in third-world conditions.

The film, based on the book of the same name by Suzanne Collins, is important to understand because it depicts the very future that the global elite are trying to create. In fact, much of what is shown in The Hunger Games has already begun (see below).

The film is set 74 years after a popular uprising that failed to overthrow a corrupt, centralized federal government.

As punishment for the attempted uprising, the all-powerful government now requires each of 12 districts to "volunteer" a young girl and boy each year to participate in the Hunger Games — a bloodsport "bread and circuses" event that serves as the opiate of the masses to distract society from the fact that they are all slaves living under tyranny.

Spoiler alert: This article reveals plot elements that may spoil the movie for you if you haven't yet seen it.

### Theme: Domination and Control

The movie reflects numerous central themes of government control over the masses, including:
• Control over food: Residents of the 12 districts are not allowed to eat more food than they are allotted by the government. Being caught catching a squirrel for food results in severe punishment.
• Control over land: The 12 districts are fenced off with high-voltage power lines, much like you might find in North Korea today. Most of the world is "conserved" as wild forest and grasslands, with humans only being allowed to populate confined regions where resources are sparse and starvation is a daily reality.
• Control over the media: The government controls all media, and every broadcast is a staged theatrical event, completely fabricated by the government to serve the interests of the government itself. This, of course, is a reflection of present-day mainstream media which is completely whored out to corporate and political interests.
• Control of technology: While the masses live in squalor, the techno-elite enjoy advanced hovercraft ships and live in gleaming high-tech cities. Advancements in medicine, 3D displays and weapons systems are available only to the centralized government, never to the People. Also in the film, RFID chips are used to track the game participants.
• Control of DNA: Residents of the districts are identified through the taking of DNA blood samples. The government stores their DNA in a database in order to track and identify individuals. Insects are genetically engineered to serve as weapons, such as GMO wasps that cause wild hallucinations to those who are stung.
• Control over life itself: The government toys with human life and seems to be amused by expressing heartless power over the masses. Their priorities are simultaneously focused on fashion, status and meaningless cuisine. In one scene, when the teenage girl (Katniss Everdeen) is trying to ask her mentor how she might survive the games, her elitists coordinator can only spout about how much she loves "chocolate truffles" and why they should all enjoy a round of desserts.

### A parade of fashion, makeup and style gone wild

The style and fashion of the elite class who live in the high-tech cities seems to be echoed right out of a modern-day parade. People are adorned with bright, extravagant clothing and accessories, and they're painted up in outlandish makeup and hair color. They literally prance around like frolicking maniacal members of royalty, and they experience great joy from causing others to suffer.

The government-worshipping elite class see themselves as intellectually superior to everyone else, yet they lack any real-world skills. They also lack anything resembling ethics, and they see nothing wrong with cheating or lying their way to positions of ever greater power in their warped society.

### Enslavement through the illusion of hope

At the top of the government, the leader played by Donald Sutherland is a Rockefeller-type master of deception and human emotions. As he explains in the film, the purpose of the Hunger Games is to keep people enslaved while giving them "a little hope, but not too much."

A little hope keeps the enslaved masses in line, but too much hope might actually make them think they have real power.

The threat of government violence against the enslaved masses is carried out by a class of enforcers who, in contrast to most other dystopian films, are actually clothed in white, not black. They are the TSA of the Hunger Games, and their job is to oppress the people, bash in a few heads, and remind the masses who's really in charge.

One can't help but notice in this film that the elite class of prancing government worshipers is the logical extension of today's irrational worship of

Office of The Maine free State, 3 Linnell Circle, Brunswick, Maine 04011

government as the savior of society. Where government is put in charge of everything, the People are forever enslaved. And that seems to be the goal of the government-worshippers in society today who desire to make all people dependent on the government, hand over all power to the government, and destroy individual human liberties (and the Bill of Rights).

It is no coincidence that the enslaved masses in The Hunger Games are entirely disarmed and only the government is allowed to own high-tech weaponry. This is a key provision of the leftist "anti-gun" movement witnessed in society today, which says that all guns should only be in the hands of government, not individuals. Such a centralization of weaponry in the hands of corrupt government, of course, only leads to tyranny, as history repeatedly shows.

**Human dignity**

Most interesting to me is the idea that government elitists have no ethics, no morals and no basic dignity. In contrast, the only real expression of dignity comes from the District 12 volunteer, Katniss Everdeen (the female lead). She enjoys a closeness with nature and a respect for life. When other participants in the Hunger Games are killed around her, she shows them respect with a makeshift burial ceremony. She only takes life as a last resort, yet she's also quick to act out of self defense, and she's willing to take action to kill others if they are truly intent on killing her.

This reflects a fundamental human right to self defense. When we are attacked, we have the right to hold our ground and return fire as her character demonstrates several times throughout the film. By doing so, she saves her life and ultimately shows the elitist government that it cannot control her.

That point comes out strongly at the end of the games, when she and her male partner are the last two survivors. The elitists government commands them to try to kill each other so that only one victor emerges. But instead of giving in to this command, the two decide to eat poison berries together and thus demonstrate to the global audience watching the event (which is practically the entire population) that the government shall not have the freedom to decide when we live or die, and that even a slave can still decide when to end their own life, independent from an oppressive government regime.

Unexpectedly, the government suddenly halts the games before the two can eat the berries, announcing them both as winners. This is obviously a last-ditch effort to make sure no one expresses any power over their own lives — not even the power to end your own life because such expression of individual power would embarrass the government.

Throughout the film (and the book), the government is obsessed with total oppression of the people, denying them food and resources and carrying out mind games against them that sap their courage and convince them they have no personal power.

**Actors, writing, photography and screenplay**

On the technical side of things, the acting in this film is superb. The key female character in the film is played by Jennifer Lawrence...

http://tinyurl.com/33dsm8i

...who delivers a convincing, heartwarming performance. She demonstrates both strength and vulnerability with astounding authenticity. This film succeeds largely because of her performance.

Woody Harrelson also delivers a convincing performance, but that's not surprising given his reputation and experience as a performance professional.

Screenplay is surprisingly solid, considering that this film is based on a novel. It's rare to see a novel translated well onto the screen, but The Hunger Games pulls it off nicely with compelling pacing and well-planned editing of the book's detail.

I also want to give props to two departments that typically don't get the attention they deserve: Costume design and sound design. In The Hunger Games, both of these departments went far beyond the norm, showcasing a masterful assembly of visual and auditory highlights that add great depth to the on-screen artistry.

**The Hunger Games is coming true in America today**

When watching the Hunger Games, you can't help but think about the recent armed raids on Rawesome Foods in California. There, armed government thugs confiscated and destroyed $50,000 worth of food and poured gallons of raw milk down the drain even while a food bank that could have used all that food was right next door.

http://tinyurl.com/3dq4afe

This destruction of food carried out by the government of California is also routinely carried out by the oppressive government in The Hunger Games. One of the most powerful strategies for total government domination is to deny people access to real food. That's exactly what we're seeing today in the government's attacks on raw milk, raw almonds and other nutritious foods. In Michigan, for example, state bureaucrats there have announced their plan to start destroying all the pig livestock of small, local ranchers and arrest them as felons.

http://tinyurl.com/bsltc5x

We also see in society today a growing class of the ruling elite who express total disdain for humanity, the natural world or anything resembling dignity or ethics. This is perhaps best reflected in the philosophy of Goldman Sachs, a financial investment giant so steeped in the culture of greed that they reportedly think of their own customers as total idiots to be viciously exploited for dishonest profit.

We also see the key elements of tyranny and oppression reflected in the Obama administration, where Obama himself signed the NDAA on New Year's Eve, 2011. This law nullifies the Bill of Rights and eliminates any right to due process for Americans. It allows the government to arrest, detain, interrogate and torture any person, for any reason, even if they are never charged with a crime. It really is like something ripped right out of a dystopian sci-fi film. The mass population, meanwhile, seems to have no idea this has already been signed into law.

http://tinyurl.com/88sj997

Similarly, on March 16 of this year, President Obama signed into effect an executive order that seizes control over all food resources across the country, including food, seeds, livestock, farm equipment, food processing facilities, and animal feed. This is written in clear English, right in the order itself.

http://tinyurl.com/73uganp

Once again, virtually the entire U.S. population seems to have no idea that this executive order was signed by Obama. In modern society, as in The Hunger Games film, most people live in a world of delusion, oblivious to the reality of how government is creepily expanding into a totalitarian dictatorship with each passing day.

**We are already living in the early stages of The Hunger Games**

The real kicker in all this is that, to a great extent, we have already begun to live in the early stages of a "Hunger Games" society. Those who worship government and believe in total government power over the People are pushing us in that direction every single day.

Here are other signs of a Hunger Games type of government growing all around us:

- The TSA reaching down your pants and calling it "security".
  http://tinyurl.com/86r3sfl
- Staged false flag security events to keep people afraid.
  http://tinyurl.com/7zmxd9b
- Janet Napolitano on giant TV screens at Wal-Mart warning everyone to spy on their neighbors and only trust government.
  http://tinyurl.com/7acps5j
- Armed government raids on farms and food distribution centers.
- Corporate control over seeds and all intellectual property.
- The push to disarm the People and centralize all weapons in the hands of government.
- Mad science genetic engineering of crops and animals.
- The total theater of fabricated "humanitarian" causes (Kony 2012) which are really nothing more than a tactic to get public support for mass murder by governments.
- The total worshipping of sports figures and sports events by the dumbed-down masses who watch football, basketball and the UFC while having no clue whatsoever that their government is raping their future and destroying their liberties.

**Big Government will accelerate us into a Hunger Games dystopian future**

Ask yourself: What political position does all this sound like?

End the Second Amendment; put government in charge of all food; give up liberties in the name of security; surrender individual power to state power... ring a bell? It's the platform of America's political elite, whether you're talking about the left or the right. Both political parties believe in big (and bigger) government, dis-empowered people, and total government control over all resources (including land).

Only people who believe in small, limited government can reverse this trend. Ron Paul supporters, in other words. A small government is a safe government, as any government that gets too big and too powerful becomes a clear and present danger to the People.

Each day that our government becomes larger and more powerful — which almost automatically happens following staged terror events such as 9/11 — we are hurled ever close to a Hunger Games type of future reality.

Let us hope that We the People can stop the insanity of bad government and find a way to restore liberty before this fictional movie called "The Hunger Games" becomes far too real for comfort.

*"ad Christi potentium et gloriam"*
*(for the power and glory of Christ)*

# Maine Republic Email Alert

No.047

"... that I should bear witness unto the truth." — John 18:33 // David E. Robinson, Publisher

"... if the trumpet give an uncertain sound, who shall prepare himself for battle?" — I Corinthians 14:8 —    04/03/12

# Japan's government formally agrees to set up 1000 trillion yen fund...geopolitical ramifications

Benjamin Fulford... "Japan's government formally agrees to set up 1000 trillion yen fund but worries about geopolitical ramifications.

Ben's report this week mirrors what is being reported by others, including 'Drake'. Very likely we are at a "tipping point" where once the tip-over has begun, nothing will stop what is coming. In any event, read on and enjoy this week's Ben.

This week's newsletter was delayed for a day because of sensitive ongoing negotiations involving the Japanese, Chinese, Russian and US governments among others.

The negotiations are still going on as of this writing and there is much we still cannot report. However, we can confirm that the Japanese government has agreed in principle to set up a 1000 trillion yen (12 trillion dollar) fund to be used to end poverty, stop environmental destruction and roll out previously forbidden technology in a responsible manner. The problem now is how to sort out the massive geopolitical repercussions this fund will create.

In what may be a related development, there appears to have been a regime change in China because Xi Xinping, the man widely assumed to be the next president of China has not appeared on the official Chinese Xinhua news site since March 31st, while his erstwhile rival, Li Keqiang, is being given massive coverage. This is only one of many signs of massive changes in planetary governance.

In the US, the Pentagon has begun asking citizens to stock up with 72 hours' worth of food because of possible disruptions associated with the imminent replacement of the US dollar with a new Treasury dollar, according to CIA sources in California. This move is also expected to be accompanied by a massive clean up operation aimed at draining the corruption out of Wall Street and Washington D.C. in order to restore the US to its former moral and economic greatness.

Any new treasury dollar will initially have much lower international purchasing power than the US dollar now being used. This will make Americans buy made in USA products and will make US exports competitive again. It might be a good time now to go out and buy Chinese stuff at Wal-Mart before it suddenly becomes more expensive.

Also, take the Pentagon's advice and stock up on food to tide you over the transition.

Another sign that something big is about to happen is that a European CIA source asked the White Dragon Society for the names and addresses of members of the following organizations: the committee of 300, the Bilderberg group, the Council on Foreign Relations, the Club of Rome, the Trilateral Commission and the European Commission. These names and addresses have been forwarded.

Here, by the way, is a link to what appears to be a credible list of the current members of the Committee of 300: http://tinyurl.com/d63qnob

Message to the members of this group: "please do not get in our way."

In any case, the most concrete and detailed intelligence available to this writer comes from Japan where government officials say that for technical administrative reasons, it will take a couple of weeks to set up the 1000 trillion yen fund. These reasons include maintaining payrolls, pensions, tax revenues and other administrative nitty gritty.

However, there are no goons available now to protect Kissinger, Nakasone, Bush, Rockefeller, Rothschild, Koizumi old world order people, so their removal from power, in Japan, is a given.

The big question to be solved now is how to set up mechanisms to handle the disbursement of the 1000 trillion yen to the countries of the world. The only thing decided for sure on this issue is that it must no longer be a secret, centralized system held in private hands.

There is also an agreement in principle that the Japanese government will administer 500 trillion yen, while the new international economic planning agency will get the other 500 trillion.

This agency, tentatively named 'LIFE' (Long Term Investments for Everyone) will finance European and US economic restructuring as well as promote massive development projects in the rest of the world. However, before it can be started, a small planning staff will begin the process of selecting international talent to run the agency. Exactly when this will happen is subject to ongoing negotiations but hopefully the first usable cash will be delivered as early as the middle of this month.

The BRICS nations will, for their part, set up their own independent fund as announced at the BRICS summit last week. This fund will be run by Brazil, Russia, India, China, and South Africa and will presumably use a basket of currencies dominated by the Renminbi and the Ruble.

This group will work in close tandem with the G20 nations, according to their declaration: http://tinyurl.com/7gd88mw

Getting back to China, a look at who is appearing on the Xinhua news site indicates that Premier Wen Jiabao, President Hu Jintao and Le Keqiang are being prominently featured. The text of Le Keqiang's speech...

http://tinyurl.com/7ekm6u7

...at the Boao forum reveal him to be a moderate centrist and thus likely a compromise candidate between powerful behind the scenes factions.

We also know from various sources that the Chongqing party boss Bo Xilai was backed by Henry Kissinger and the old world order cabal he represents. No doubt he was promised the job of dictator of China and the world in exchange for his cooperation.

Memo to Kissinger and the committee of 300: the world does not want a dictator.

When the dust settles, the world will have harmonious collective leadership.

*"ad Christi potentium et gloriam"*
*(for the power and glory of Christ)*

# Maine Republic Email Alert

No.048

". . . that I should bear witness unto the truth." — John 18:33 // David E. Robinson, Publisher

". . . if the trumpet give an uncertain sound, who shall prepare himself for battle?" — I Corinthians 14:8 —    04/05/12

## The Pentagon wants this information to go viral

**THE PENTAGON WANTS THIS INFORMATION TO GO VIRAL**

wikipedia states:

**The Burning of Washington in 1814** was an armed conflict during the War of 1812 between the United Kingdom of Great Britain and Ireland and the United States of America.

On August 24, 1814, led by General Robert Ross, a British force occupied Washington, D.C. and set fire to many public buildings following the American defeat at the Battle of Bladensburg.

The facilities of the U.S. government, including the White House and U.S. Capitol, were largely destroyed.[3]

The British commander's orders to burn only public buildings and strict British discipline among its troops are credited with preserving the city's private buildings.

This was the only time since the Revolutionary War that a foreign power captured and occupied the United States capital.[4]

**Background information**

Many have already heard of the abnormally large number of arrests and resignations of officials in banking, money funds, investment houses, insurance companies, and governments throughout the world that have taken place since September 2011.

What Americans have not known is that a huge operation is about to take place in the United States. In order to comprehend why we have heard nothing of this event, we must understand that the major newspaper and television media is very tightly controlled by the dark cabal or Illuminati. It is the Illuminati who intend to establish the New World Order by killing off huge segments of the planet's population and enslaving the rest.

These are the persons who will be arrested and removed to a location where they can perpetuate no more harm, and for their protection before being brought to trial

Before you stop reading and refuse to take 3 hours of your time to listen to the audio listed below, you need to consider: Do I want to know what is about to happen? Do I as a parent, minister, news reporter, teacher, or citizen want to remain ignorant of what is ready to take place that will impact every phase of my life and that of my family and community?

Much preparation is and has taken place behind the scenes to prepare for the forthcoming mass arrests of top officials of corporations and government.

As you will hear on the audio, the Pentagon had already drawn up The Plan for such an event by around 1979. The legal preparation is in place. Extremely detailed planning has the goal of disrupting the general public and the activities that make up our lives as little as possible. However there will be a few days—hopefully not weeks—in which services may be disrupted.

During the actual mass arrests, a period of up to 72 hours (3 days) will involve the closing of our borders and the shutting off of satellites. This will be required to prevent escape of those to be arrested.

This is the period for which we need to be prepared. We will be given 24 hours notice in advance.

In order to prepare the American people, the Pentagon recently asked a former Vietnam veteran who has been involved in the legal preparations to go on the radio and internet and explain what is about to happen. This veteran is going by the name of 'Drake'.

The below YouTube is an interview of Drake by David Wilcock, who also has high level insider information.

In the interview, Drake will explain the legal preparation done by average citizens in a majority of the states that allows this event to take place in accordance with our nation's founding documents. This event will remove the major obstacles to a far better life for all Americans and eventually for all on the planet.

You owe it to yourself, your family, and to those to whom you minister to listen carefully to all three hours of valuable information. People who have no idea what has really been going on in America will be shocked and angry to hear all that has been done to them. As many of us as possible can greatly alleviate this shock by letting them know of this event and that the end result will be a much better world for all.

The Pentagon is also asking that all of us help to publicize the information we hear on this audio. Public panic will prolong the procedure and violence of any kind will do the same. We the people need to be in the know and to peacefully assist in any way we can—spreading the word being a major avenue of assistance. The goal is that this event is peaceful, with no violence.

Please send the URL below to all you know and to your local media. Ministers, you have access to large numbers of people. We are speaking of the resurrection of our nation. I beg of you to listen and help prepare your congregations.

http://tinyurl.com/7juylza

ADDITIONAL INFORMATION

http://www.divinecosmos.com/ - David Wilcock's website – here you may find a series of very important and explosive articles mentioned in the interview. These articles offer you an excellent background for what is about to happen.

Office of The Maine free State, 3 Linnell Circle, Brunswick, Maine 04011

http://www.freedomreigns.us/
— Drake's website

The Original 13th Amendment
Mentioned in the interview

"If any citizen of the United States shall accept, claim, receive, or retain any title of nobility or honour, or shall without the consent of Congress, accept and retain any present, pension. office, or emolument of any kind whatever, from any emperor, king, prince, or foreign power, such person shall cease to be a citizen of the United States, and shall be incapable of holding any office of trust or profit under them, or either of them."

Quoted from the Senate Journal via The TONA Research Committe:
http://www.amendment-13.org/

**The Corporation of the USA is also mentioned in the interview.**

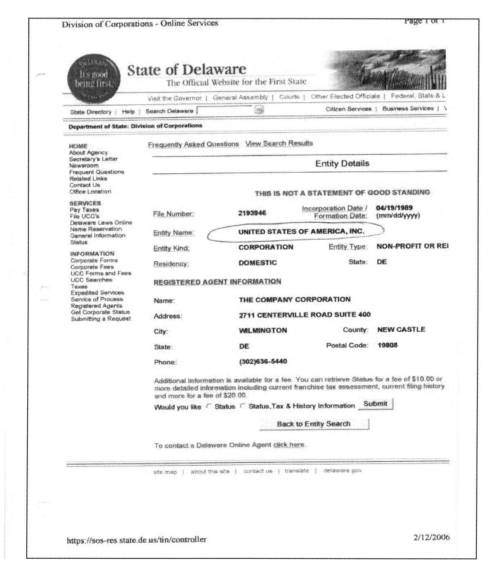

*Office of The Maine free State, 3 Linnell Circle, Brunswick, Maine 04011*

# Maine Republic Email Alert

No.049

". . . that I should bear witness unto the truth." — John 18:33 // David E. Robinson, Publisher

". . . if the trumpet give an uncertain sound, who shall prepare himself for battle?" — I Corinthians 14:8 — 04/06/12

## Epic Paradigm Shift Poised to unfold within US and the World; imminently

Here in one place is a review of most of the information I've recently posted. ~Jean.

Are militaries around the world preparing for final take down of New World Order cabal?

Major events across the US continue to accelerate towards a momentous breaking point with each passing week in the first quarter of the year 2012.

We are fast approaching a paradigm shift of epic proportions that will result in the total freedom of all US and world citizens.

Many spectacular developments, long in the planning stages, are set to unfold that will alter the course of history forever and will place humanity permanently on the path towards the Golden Age.

Behind the scenes, heroic battles wage the likes of which have never been seen on this planet before yet go completely unnoticed by the people who will ultimately benefit from them the most. Along the way, intense negotiations are and have been underway within all sectors of our modern society to break an intricate control system that has been in place for a hundred years or longer. In some cases — for thousands of years.

These include the stranglehold upon our monetary systems, our governmental organizations, media empires, religious institutions, energy resources, science and technology spheres, food productions and health care industries. All are about to be lifted out a state of suppression to be transformed into a state of dynamic activation for the benefit of all of mankind.

**FINANCIAL WAR MOST INTENSE**

Most particularly intense at this stage of the game is the war to wrest control of the world's financial power structures with major victories occurring at a near daily basis. This unseen war is the precise reason why we have yet to see any major news of currency revaluations in foreign countries, particularly with the Iraqi dinar which has long been anticipated.

Although the revaluation of the Iraqi dinar was originally intended to be a secret held by a few insiders devised during the first George Bush, Jr. administration, current estimates are that as many as six million people around the world have discovered and subsequently invested in this classified plan.

Even a few select mainstream news media outlets are now beginning to report on foreign currency revaluations such as Bloomberg News and Fox Business News.

On another note, the Alliance of Russia, Brazil, India, China & South Africa, also known as BRICS, has taken the bold steps to dump the US dollar as their primary trading currency and create its own bank. This is yet another nail in the coffin for the privately-owned Federal Reserve banking cartel as more and mores nations seek to increasingly marginalize the dollar for a take down.

BRICS recently held their annual summit in New Delhi, India in late March 2012 where they made a series of major announcements. Along with the White Dragon Society, BRICS is now emerging as perhaps the most forceful global resistance vehemently opposed to any further aggressive overtures by the NWO cabal, such as World War III in the Middle East.

One significant person who continues to stand tall is Russian Prime Minister Vladimir Putin, who has miraculously managed to rescue his country from a total downfall to the New World Order banking cabal. Mr. Putin survived two assassination attempts in his home country recently in his bid for re-election and is now set to lead the Russian people into the promised land.

On Friday, March 28, 2012, Barack Obama appointed Jim Yong Kim, a physician and President of Dartmouth College to lead the World Bank. The irony of placing an Asian in charge of this major financial institution was not lost and was likely strongly endorsed, if not enforced, by the White Dragon Society.

Apparently, Jim Yong Kim has no ties the criminal cabal as previous World Bank Presidents have such as Robert Zoellick and Paul Wolfowitz. His appointment is yet another sign the world's financial systems are dramatically changing for the better.

Further indications that the criminals are turning upon one another are another series of unprecedented reports arising from the Vatican — the richest, most powerful institution and the very heart of darkness on planet Earth. The US State Department announced it has placed the Vatican bank on the "concerned list" for money laundering, while JP Morgan suddenly decided to close all of the Vatican's accounts it holds. Astonishing news, to say the least!

(See video "Signs of the Illuminati Defeat Are Everywhere!" for further information on the Vatican.)
http://tinyurl.com/7agvugc

And finally, no less than the Queen of England's own bank, Coutts Bank, was fined 8.75 million pounds for failing to carry out correct checks on "politically exposed persons" and prevent money laundering. And in an even more dramatic development, the Queen's fortune has now has been officially linked to drug trafficking.

Meanwhile in the shadows, many, many heroic people are battling in the trenches with little recognition yet they possess the most noble and altruistic intentions for all of humanity, often risking life and limb to do so. They have remained true to their purpose of fighting against darkness and evil with a strong sense of will and determination to see the job through to the bitter end.

In the not-too-distant future, we will need to recognize and honor these individuals for their courage, bravery and service towards not only to our country, but to the whole of the human race. These heroes come from the military, economic fields, various governmental departments, legal professions, intelligence services and average, ordinary walks of life — all linked by a high moral fiber that propels them to serve.

Still others making a profound difference in our world include a large number of people in highly conscious states who are proactively meditating, consciously co-creating and envisioning a grand future for humanity. They can be found in far flung regions across the planet such as India, Tibet, China, etc. and they are literally birthing a new reality for us all to step into.

Together, all of these diverse cross-section of people have worked tirelessly to bring the Golden Age to planet Earth as rapidly and as expeditiously as possible. And they have made tremendous strides since the dawn of the year 2012.

If you can, imagine not having to worry about the basic necessities of life such as feeding your family, putting clothes on your back, affording your housing or having access to first class medical care. Soon, all the people of world will be provided with these basic necessities as a birth right, once the resources, technologies and monies have been freed up to be dispersed among all.

Perhaps this kind of scenario may sound fanciful and untenable. Yet many are seeing and feeling the real possibility of this kind of lifestyle emerging for all of the human race sooner, rather than later.

We are indeed living in the most exciting times ever seen in the history of the Earth!

## MASS ARRESTS WITHIN US BORDERS ABOUT TO BEGIN

Soon, our news media will finally begin reporting on an unprecedented number of mass arrests that will sweep up many well known political, religious, economic and social leaders, as well as other high profile individuals whose names will be familiar to us all. While many others unknowns who have stood in dark corners wielding great negative power and influence upon the world will be removed from their hiding places.

According to the latest report from Benjamin Fulford, these arrests will include those at the very top of the pyramid including within organizations as powerful as can be found on the planet.

These groups that will be targeted are: the Committee of 300; the Bilderberg group; the Council on Foreign Relations; the Club of Rome; the Trilateral Commission and the European Commission.

A whistleblower by the name of "Drake", a former member of the US military who served in Vietnam has emerged recently to act as a sort of quasi-spokesman for the US Pentagon and was interviewed by David Wilcock on March 28, 2012.

David Wilcock & Drake 2012-03-28 Mass Arrests.

In this extensive nearly three-hour long phone interview, Drake and David Wilcock discussed a wide-range of topics including the impending mass arrests, the military's role as backing law enforcement and Federal Marshals, and the return of the US to a sovereign nation state.

http://tinyurl.com/7ps9wj2

(Also see David Wilcock's newest posting "DIVINE INTERVENTION: Section I — Defeating Financial Tyranny" http://tinyurl.com/6reamde )

Particularly interesting was the final hour of the interview where David Wilcock and Drake discuss some of the suppressed technologies that will be emerging in the very near future, as well as the dimensional shift about to occur.

Once these arrests begin in earnest, it is possible that some areas of the country may experience slight delays in services such electrical power, or perhaps even telephone or internet utilities. Although, Drake stressed that the military will make every effort to insure that all Americans do not experience undue hardships during this momentous transition.

Therefore, it is recommended to have a three-day supply of food and water on hand for any possible short-term emergency situation.

Of further note, a major shift is already occurring within our corporate news media as people in the US move away in record numbers and turn towards alternative news sources found on the internet.

Reports are suggesting that viewership for the CNN channel has dropped by 50% this year alone. Other media empires such as News Corp, owners of Fox News, have seen numerous of their employees arrested in the United Kingdom.

Polls are indicating that the majority of the American people no longer trust mainstream media sources such as newspapers, magazines and cable news networks, which spells doom for those in the compromised news media.

Meanwhile, the hacker activist group known as Anonymous continues to grow stronger by the month. In their boldest move yet, the group recently released a sensational video that called for the outright overthrow of the corrupted, corporate US government.

ANONYMOUS Call for Overthrowing US Government.
http://tinyurl.com/cgom286

Anonymous continues to prove that is more than the authorities can handle at this time and has became a valuable PR machine for the Occupy Wall Street movement. Occupy Wall Street itself is gearing up for a massive round of protests beginning this Spring that will last until the big changes start to roll out and perhaps longer. Anonymous is also to be featured in an upcoming documentary film entitled, "We Are Legion: The Story of the Hacktivists".

And finally, Foster Gamble, the creator and host of the landmark documentary film, "Thrive" recently announced his company will be making the film available for free, beginning April 5, 2012. It will be available for viewing on their website so as to spread their message to as may people as possible, without any hindrances.

http://tinyurl.com/c6naz2j

**DIVINE INTERVENTION IN FULL FORCE NOW**

And while we are at it, cancel all plans for Martial Law, FEMA enslavement camps, a devastating world-wide financial collapse, World War III and Armageddon. They are officially off the table! We are full steam ahead for Heaven on Earth now.

What seems like an extraordinary synchronicity of events all occurring at once, is merely the human race responding en mass to an enormous influx of energy emanating from the galactic center of the universe.

Assisting humanity along every step of the way, these energy waves streaming in are upgrading everything in their path including human consciousness, human DNA and the very nature of human reality which is being transformed from a third-dimensional to a fifth-dimensional existence. All of these upgrades are part of a grand Divine plan now moving into hyper-overdrive, preparing humanity's ascent into the Golden Age.

What may seem absolutely impossible and unfathomable one month, will suddenly become highly probable the next month. Therefore, it is vital not to cast doubt or dispersions on any of these seemingly unrealistic scenarios that many are envisioning for our immediate future. In other words, you may be quite surprised what becomes magically available to you from one day to the next.

At this point in time, anything and everything is possible and we should not limit our selves in any way, shape or form. Go ahead and dream the impossible dream.

**YOUR CALL TO SERVE**

As these monumental historic events begin to unfold, it is important to be mindful to not go into a state of fear or panic. In point of fact, many of us will be called upon to assist others with understanding the true ramifications of these epoch-making developments.

Many of you reading this update are probably familiar with many of these planned changes because you have heard rumors or you have done your research on them for many years.

Perhaps you have even grown rather weary and impatient, knowing within your heart that changes of this magnitude were inevitable, yet the wait for their implementation has felt like an eternity.

You will soon be rewarded for your patience and persistence.

However, we must be ever mindful that the average American has absolutely no clue of what is coming down the pike. Many may have just recently become awakened to the horror that our government, banking institutions and media sources are completely corrupt yet they feel incapable of seeing any kind of solutions available to right the ship.

Your role will become more clearly defined as a mentor, an educator, a psychologist or even as a spiritual advisor as these historic events unfold upon your television and computer screens. In other words, you will need to explain to your family, your friends and acquaintances, or your co-workers what is really going on simply because you may have a better understanding of the overall big picture.

You will become an invaluable asset to those around you who may feel bewildered or completely overwhelmed by the sheer number of changes that will occur, one after another, after another.

Above all, remember — stay calm, stay positive and stay strong. Trust that all is unfolding is part of an vast amazing, miraculous Divine plan that will result in your personal freedom, as well as, the freedom of your loved ones.

The Golden Age is here, now it is time to get down to work.

*"ad Christi potentium et gloriam"*
*(for the power and glory of Christ)*

# Maine Republic Email Alert

*No. 050*

"... that I should bear witness unto the truth." — John 18:33 // David E. Robinson, Publisher

"... if the trumpet give an uncertain sound, who shall prepare himself for battle?" — I Corinthians 14:8 — 04/07/12

## The Bible . . . the story of our journey through the plane of duality . . . draws to a close

**By Nancy B. Detweiler, M.Ed., M.Div.**

As the cycle of duality draws to a close, let us use this Lenten season to ponder: did I understand the true import of my sacred text? Am I ready to make the approaching evolutionary leap to the 5th dimensional plane of love and light?

The Bible is one of the sacred texts for the 3rd dimensional plane of duality. Its writers all lived on the plane of duality and were therefore confronted with good and evil. Although inspired, they wrote from the perspective of learning to deal with duality in a manner that would allow them and us to awaken to the higher planes of life. Many pointed the way, but did we comprehend?

In the first chapters of Genesis, we find a symbolic story of the Earth's creation. *"And God saw everything that he had made, and behold, it was very good."* (Genesis 1:31)

Into this lush paradise, humankind entered. We were gifted with freewill and given the opportunity to choose how we live our lives. *"Of every tree of the garden you may freely eat; but of the tree of the knowledge of good and evil, you shall not eat; for in the day that you eat of it you shall surely die."* (Genesis 2:16-17) God was explaining that once we choose to evolve on the plane of duality, we die to the awareness of all that is within the cosmos.

Our perspective becomes extremely limited. We die to the knowledge of who we truly are as made in the image of God—child gods. We die to the understanding that we are One with God. We begin to feel separate and alone. We die to the consciousness of the Garden of Eden and instead, enter a world in which we experience good and evil. Our physical bodies become sick, decay, and die. We appear blind to a world of plenty for all and accept as normal: enemies/wars, hatred, anger, jealousy, resentment, competition, egoism, discrimination, emotional and physical pain, revenge, and blood sacrifice. And by far, the most insidious of all is the personification of Creator God as a being with less integrity than we possess.

The writers of those books, eventually accepted into the biblical canon, did not write with that intention. Instead, they wrote within the cultural milieu with which they were familiar. Their writings were often inspired for the betterment of those within their community. However, by the time the canonical books were written, tens of thousands of years had passed on the plane of duality. Spiritual blindness was well established.

As we read the biblical account, it is possible to perceive layers of meaning. The inspired message often shines through; but few take the time to comprehend it. Humankind has never been abandoned, even though we came to believe that is the case. Advanced beings have periodically incarnated on the plane of duality in order to give humankind a jump start to spiritual awakening. They have become a part of daily life on Earth and attempted to reveal Truth to us.

Let's look at a few biblical examples.

*"And Enoch found favor in the presence of God, and disappeared; for God took him away."* (Genesis 5:24) Enoch is the first biblical character to ascend from the plane of duality back into the higher dimensions, without physical death.

Melchizedek, a priest king of Salem (Jerusalem) is another example of an advanced being dwelling on the plane of duality, without experiencing a physical birth or death. *"Neither his father nor his mother is recorded in the genealogies; and neither the beginning of his days nor the end of his life; but, like the Son of God, his priesthood abides forever.*

*Now consider how great this man was, to whom even the patriarch Abraham gave tithes and paid head tax.... But this man who is not recorded in their genealogies took tithes even from Abraham and blessed him who had received the promises. Beyond dispute, he who was less was blessed by him who was greater than himself."* (Hebrews 7:3-4, 6-7)

Elijah is a third example of higher beings interacting with humanity on the plane of duality. *"And it came to pass, as they still went on and talked, behold, there appeared a chariot of fire and horses of fire, and separated the two; and Elijah went up by a whirlwind into heaven."* (2 Kings 2:11) Elijah was beamed up into a space craft. He and his fellow prophets knew ahead of time that he would be picked up.

Ezekiel provides a fourth example. *"And I looked, and behold, a whirlwind was coming out of the north, a great cloud, and a flaming fire and brightness was round about it, and out of the midst of it there came as it were a figure out of the midst of the fire."* (Ezekiel 1:4) The book of Ezekiel tells the story of an extraterrestrial being working with Ezekiel by giving him instructions regarding his mission and transporting him from place to place in a space ship.

The year 2012 arrives amidst much talk on the internet about humanity ascending and the fact that extraterrestrials with their space craft are present with us. The above four examples illustrate what is possible for each of us. As 2012 marks the end of the cycle of duality on Earth, we can achieve a level of spiritual maturity that will allow us to physically ascend to higher dimensions. We may also work in cooperation with our galactic family for the healing of our planet and its inhabitants. Our sacred text has prepared us to be reunited with our Star families. Have we recognized that fact?

Elijah taught us the lesson of sharing when we think we have nothing to share. Sharing reaps abundance. We also see in Elijah the power to channel divine healing energy ... to restore physical plane life. (I Kings 17:10-24)

While living on the plane of duality, we have lived with the consciousness of lack, the requirement to work hard because we are taught there is not enough to go around and we may be the ones who are deprived. Our present society is torn apart by the varying theories that separate the hardworking from the supposed lazy, the need to share from the propensity to deprive those who do not meet our standards.

Have we heard Elijah? Have we integrated Jesus' teaching: *"Do not worry for your life, what you will eat and what you will drink, nor for your body, what you will wear…. Who is among you who by worrying can add one cubit to his stature? … Your Father in heaven knows that all of these things are also necessary for you. But seek first the kingdom of God and his righteousness, and all those things shall be added to you."* (Matthew 6:25, 27, 32-33)

We have drawn much comfort from the Psalms, but have we been aware of the frequency with which enemies is mentioned? *"Thy preparest a table before me in the presence of mine enemies."* (Psalm 23:4) We assume that having enemies—domestic or foreign—is the norm.

We have created a God who hates, who takes revenge, who punishes for eternity. In turn, we assume we have the right or obligation to hate, take revenge, to punish for life.

Have we been influenced and motivated by the subliminal messages within the Bible that are the result of its writers living on the plane of duality?

*"The proud shall not stand in thy sight; thou hatest all workers of iniquity…. Condemn thou them, O God; let them fall by their own counsels; cast them out in the multitude of their wickedness, for they have provoked thee."* (Psalm 5:5,10)

*"Let all my enemies be ashamed and defeated; let them turn back and be destroyed suddenly."* (Psalm 6:10)

When we read such passages, we *unconsciously* register a God who hates some of creation, who grows angry, who takes revenge. If hate, anger, and revenge characterize God, then our own response to these emotions is much more nonchalant.

We have grown accustomed to portraying God as Warrior. We pray for our side to win. *"And Joshua conquered all these kings and their countries at one time; because the Lord God of Israel was with him and it was he who fought for Israel."* (Joshua 10:43)

*"Joshua made war a long time with all those kings…. For it was the Lord's doing to harden their hearts so that they would come against Israel in battle, in order that they might be utterly destroyed and might receive no mercy, but be exterminated, just as the Lord had commanded Moses."* (Joshua 11:18,20)

We blame God for all the things we cannot explain. The biblical book of Job is an excellent example. *"God can do anything God wants to do"* is a common statement that few of us attempt to deny. Like Job, we grit our teeth and try to remain faithful: *"The Lord gave, and the Lord has taken away; blessed be the name of the Lord."* (Job 1:21)

We ponder the question *"Why do good people suffer?"* But we most often fail to reconcile our religious beliefs with our inner intuitive knowing. Job knew he was not being punished because he had broken a religious law.

The Book of Job depicts his—and our own—personal journey of reconciliation with our inner intuitive knowing. Job is Every Individual. **Have we recognized our inner knowing and sought our own Truth?** Or, have we given our power over to the religious authorities? We cannot give our power away and develop as the child gods that we are.

Do we question the biblical portrayals of God as a punishing God, a capricious God, a Warrior God? Do we ask *"How can a God of Absolute Love behave in this way?"* Do we truly believe God is Love or do we attempt to believe it while repressing those annoying questions that keep poking their camel heads into our conscious awareness, insisting upon being answered? How often I have heard ministers and Sunday School teachers say, *"Don't ask questions or you will lose your faith."*

**Recognizing and loving God is not an act of repression.**

Have we diligently sought to know Truth? For example, Job is one of the most misunderstood books in the Bible. It is actually the story of humanity's journey into enlightenment or ascension. But, in order to know that, we must delve into the deeper layers of its message and that requires a knowledge of metaphysics.[i]

There are biblical scholars who have interpreted the Bible metaphysically.[ii] The deeper messages resonant strongly with Universal Truth: **God Is Love; we live in a cosmos filled with loving beings ready to assist us in navigating our way out of the plane of duality.**

The major reason we blame God for all that we cannot explain is because the Church has denied us the opportunity to learn about reincarnation as the means of Soul progression. The Christian arrangement of the books within the Old Testament has as its concluding sentences: *"Behold, I will send you Elijah the prophet before the coming of the great and dreadful day of the Lord. And he shall turn the heart of the fathers to their children and the heart of the children to their fathers before I come and smite the earth to ruin."* (Malachi 4:5-6) The Old Testament ends with the promise that Elijah will reincarnate.

Approximately 400 years, called the Intertestamental Period, pass between the Old Testament and the New Testament. During this time, the culture of Palestine changed dramatically. By the time of Jesus, Palestine has become cosmopolitan with major trade routes running through it.

The shipping and fishing industries were flourishing. Numerous cultural and philosophical influences were present. Many were highly educated.

Jesus' maternal uncle, Joseph of Arimathea, was known as one of the most wealthy men in the world. He owned a shipping business and the tin mines in what is now England. Jesus frequently traveled with his uncle, who became the legal guardian of the family after Joseph returned to spiritual realms.

Have we considered the fact that the story of Jesus and the New Testament took place within an actual historical setting that can be researched? Or have we simply believed the simplistic narrative that the Church has propagated?

Each of the four gospels endeavor to tell the story of Jesus. All were written decades after the conclusion of Jesus' ministry.[iii] For modern Christians, the translations and interpretation of these gospels have been influenced by the writings of the Church Fathers during the first eight centuries of the Church. Numerous creeds were composed in an effort to codify the doctrines of the Christian religion.[iv] As a result, the gospels have been read within the mindset of the Christian doctrines. The passages that would be considered heretical teachings by the Church are simply ignored.

The Gospel of John is believed by many biblical scholars to best depict the actual teachings of Jesus. This gospel reveals a Jesus who came to show the Way back to the Father. In other words, Jesus came to show humanity how to evolve spiritually to the point of leaving the plane of duality and ascending to higher dimensions.

The concept of a sacrificial lamb or a blood sacrifice has been acceptable to many living on the plane of duality. It goes along with the God humanity has created—a vengeful God demanding atonement for the mistakes we have made while living on the plane of duality. **This in no way depicts the true God of Absolute Love.** On the higher dimensions, all is love and light and peace. A God of Love beholds the immaculate conception of all of humanity—made in the image of God.

Jesus incarnated as a Wayshower … he came to show us the Way out of the darkness of the plane of duality. We lost our way and needed an example to follow.

Because we are accustomed to reading the Bible in accordance with the tenets of Christianity, we do not have the eyes to see what Jesus really taught. This is especially true when it relates to the I AM sayings. Jesus taught: *"The words that I say to you I do not speak on my own; but the Father who dwells in me does his works."* (John 14:10) *"I have not spoken on my own, but the Father who sent me has himself given me a commandment about what to say and what to speak…. What I speak, therefore, I speak just as the Father has told me."* (John 12:49-50)[v]

Jesus channeled the Father who dwells within each of us. Therefore, when Jesus speaks the I AM sayings, he is channeling the Father. I AM the light of the world means the Father within each of us is the Light of the World. I AM the bread of life means the Father within each of us is the bread of life. During this Lenten Period, read the Gospel of John from the perspective of Jesus speaking the words of the Father.

Jesus repeatedly shifted the attention from himself to the Father. *"The Son can do nothing on his own, but only what he sees the Father doing; for whatever the Father does the Son does likewise."* (John 5:19)

*"My teaching is not mine but his who sent me. Anyone who resolves to do the will of God will know whether the teaching is from God or whether I am speaking on my own. Those who speak on their own seek their own glory; but the one who seeks the glory of him who sent him is true, and there is nothing false in him."* (John 7:16-18) *"Whoever believes in me believes not in me but in him who sent me."* (John 12:44)

Jesus never placed himself above humanity … he came as Elder Brother, Teacher, and Wayshower. He wanted us to follow his example. He taught the people *"Your Father knows what you need before you ask him. Pray, then, in this way: Our Father in heaven…."* (Matthew 6:8-9)

Jesus' expects his disciples to do more than they think they can and grows impatient with them for not doing so. *"When it grew late, his disciples came to him and said, 'This is a deserted place, and the hour is now very late; send them away so that they may go into the surrounding country and villages and buy something for themselves to eat.' But he answered them, 'You give them something to eat.' They said to him, 'Are we to go and buy two hundred denarii worth of bread and give it to them to eat?'"* (Mark 6:35-37)

*"Teacher, I brought you my son; he has a spirit that makes him unable to speak… I asked your disciples to cast it out, but they could not do so. He answered them, 'You faithless generation, how much longer must I put up with you? Bring him to me.'"* (Mark 9:17-19)

*"The one who believes in me (Jesus speaks the words of "our" Father) will also do the works that I do and, in fact, will do greater works than these, because I am going to the Father."* (John 14:12)

*"The Jews took up stones again to

stone him. Jesus replied, 'I have shown you many good works from the Father. For which of these are you going to stone me? The Jews answered, 'It is not for a good work that we are going to stone you, but for blasphemy, because you, though only a human being, are making yourself God.' Jesus answered, 'Is it not written in your law, I said, you are gods?'" (John 10: 31-34) Jesus is telling the men who plan to stone him that they are gods.

Jesus tells his disciples a parable about a vine: *"I am the vine, you are the branches."* Vineyards are a familiar scene in Palestine. Everyone knows that **the branches are outshoots of the vine—made of the same substance.** In fact, it is the branches that bear the fruit.

Have we understood who we truly are? Have we allowed our elder brother, Jesus, to teach us to do the works that I do?[vi] Or, have we simply followed Christian doctrine and worshipped him as a being we cannot become?

Four hundred years later, Jesus verifies Malachi's prophecy. Following his transfiguration, during which he talked with Elijah and Moses, the disciples asked Jesus, *"Why, then, do the scribes say that Elijah must come first? He replied, 'Elijah is indeed coming and will restore all things; but I tell you that Elijah has already come, and they did not recognize him, but did to him whatever they pleased…. Then the disciples understood that he was speaking to them about John the Baptist."* (Matthew 17:1-16)[vii]

The acceptance of reincarnation while living on the plane of duality allows us to understand ourselves and others on a much deeper level. **Earth has been our schoolhouse;** it is here that we have been given opportunity after opportunity to live our lives in accordance with the Universal Laws of Love and Peace, to practice the Law of Attraction, and to awaken to our true identities as child gods—made in the image of God.

A metaphysical interpretation of the New Testament reveals that the major events in Jesus' life were actually physical plane demonstrations of our own initiatory process toward ascension. These five events are: **birth, baptism, transfiguration, crucifixion, and ascension.** You may read my article entitled "Ascension" on my website at:

http://tinyurl.com/cvus4e3

It is important to understand that a metaphysical interpretation of the Bible deals with **layers of meaning** beneath the literal translation of the Aramaic, Hebrew, Greek and/or Latin words. Metaphysics means beyond the physical. A knowledge of metaphysics is required. It is also helpful to know the history of the Church, simply because so much has been covered up. Just as reincarnation was declared heretical in the 6th century, so was astrology in the 15th century. Yet, both are foundations on which the Bible is built.

In the words of Rabbi Joel C. Dobin in his book, TO RULE BOTH DAY & NIGHT: Astrology in the Bible, Midrash, & Talmud: *"Astrology helps man to understand God's will and to put himself in balance with Divine and universal forces, thus enriching his life and experience. Astrology revealed to me His order and His beauty, and His place for me in the Divine balance that links God, man, and universe into One Balanced Process which never ends in this life or on other planes of awareness of life."*

Below are photos of ruins of the floor of the synagogue of Hamath Tiberias. This synagogue was in use during the 6th through the 8th centuries. The mosaic floor depicts the Astrological Zodiac and thus, its importance in the religious life of ancient Judaism. [viii]

Photos by Nancy Detweiler

2012 marks the end of the cycle of duality upon Earth. There is so much we have failed to learn about the Bible—information that adds immensely to its richness and depth. As we ascend to the higher dimensions, we receive full consciousness and possess ready access to all knowledge. No longer will we be fooled into thinking we are less than who we truly are—child gods made in the image of God.

Our sacred text for the cycle of duality closes as it announces:

*"Then I saw a new heaven and a new earth; for the first heaven and the first earth had passed away, and the sea was no more. And I saw the holy city, the new Jerusalem, coming down out of heaven from God, prepared as a bride adorned for her husband. And I heard a loud voice from the throne, saying,*

*"See, the home of God is*
*Among mortals,*
*He will dwell with them as their God;*
*They will be his peoples,*
*And God himself be with*
*Them;*
*He will wipe every tear from*
*Their eyes,*
*Death will be no more;*
*Mourning and crying and pain*
*Will be no more,*
*For the first things have passed away."*

Revelation 21:1-4

The Endnotes offer additional information and articles on the subjects mentioned in this article.

May your Lenten Period be one of much spiritual growth and newfound knowledge!

[i] My book, *WHERE ARE YOU, GOD?* A Metaphysical Interpretation of the Biblical Book of Job is available free on my website:
http://tinyurl.com/bmgudwu

[ii] Charles Fillmore's METAPHYSICAL BIBLE DICTIONARY is most helpful in interpreting the Bible metaphysically. Geoffrey Hodson's THE HIDDEN WISDOM in the Holy Bible supplies additional information. Corinne Heline interpreted the entire Bible metaphysically in her series NEW AGE BIBLE INTERPRETATION.

[iii] The Gospel of Matthew was written around 90 C.E. (A.D.) by an unknown Jewish Christian of the 2nd generation. The Gospel of Mark is attributed by early church tradition to Mark, a companion of Peter in Rome, during the persecutions of Nero around 64 C.E. (A.D.).

Tradition attributes the writer of the Gospel of Luke to be Luke, a companion of Paul in Rome around 80-90 C.E. (A.D.)

It must be remembered that all the Gospels were written anonymously. It is tradition and scholarship that has attempted to discern the author, place, and time.

Although still considered one of the Gospels, the Gospel of John is significantly different from the synoptic gospels. Mystery surrounds the Gospel of John both as to the time period in which it was written and to the author.

The Beloved Disciple is never identified as John, the son of Zebedee. *"The identity of the author of the Fourth Gospel remains a mystery, perhaps deliberately concealed."*

(Above information was taken from: Harper's Bible Commentary) A thoroughly researched article by Ramon K. Jusino, entitled *Mary Magdalene: Author of the Fourth Gospel?* may be found at:
http://tinyurl.com/blslan8

You may also read what the Ancient Texts have to say about Mary Magdalene at: http://tinyurl.com/bqs73mp

[iv] CREEDS OF THE CHURCH: A Reader in Christian Doctrine From the Bible to the Present, Edited by John H. Leith.

[v] You may read "An Analysis of the Nicene Creed In Comparison With Jesus' Teachings" at: http://tinyurl.com/c7kqb77

[vi] You may read a series of articles on "If Jesus Is A Wayshower, What Did He Show Us?" at:
http://tinyurl.com/5vtd39

[vii] You may read my article on Reincarnation in the Bible at:
http://tinyurl.com/7slaylq

[viii] You may view a photo/commentary of the Middle East at:
http://tinyurl.com/d9kkpcn

Also See
*THE REVELATION OF ST. JOHN: IN METAPHYSICAL OUTLINE FORM*
by the publisher of this Alert
http://tinyurl.com/7byrujr

# Maine Republic Email Alert

No.051

"... that I should bear witness unto the truth." — John 18:33 // David E. Robinson, Publisher

"... if the trumpet give an uncertain sound, who shall prepare himself for battle?" — I Corinthians 14:8 —     04/08/12

## The Resurrection signifies humanity's awakening from the illusion

The Resurrection signifies humanity's awakening from the illusion – from Jesus through John Smallman, April 8, 2012

Easter is an excellent day on which to bring to mind God's Love for all His children. It is a reminder of His Intent that all of them return to Reality – eternal life with Him in the heavenly domains – as demonstrated by the Resurrection.

In Christianity, the Resurrection signifies Christ risen from the dead, but in fact it signifies humanity's awakening from its extensive sojourn in the illusion, because within you all the Light of Christ Consciousness is burning to light your way Home, and it is now becoming impossible for you to continue ignoring it as you have done for so long.

The time you have spent in the illusion has been arduous and painful, causing you much fear and suffering. It is the divine Will that you awaken from that unhappy state. And so you will.

It is becoming increasingly apparent that your present mode of existence on Planet Earth is unsustainable, and yet those who could start to make the necessary changes to alleviate the situation and help to move you away from the brink of self-destruction are apparently insufficiently concerned with the seriousness of it to do anything about it. However, that ongoing irresponsible behavior, demonstrated by those who are in a position to start humanity's move away from what appears to be an inevitable world-wide ecological catastrophe, and who are refusing to act, will soon cease as they are persuaded to resign, and those with the ability, the competence, the technological means, and the intense desire to correct this untenable state of affairs replace them.

You came to Earth as guardians of the planet, but due to confusion and disagreements among you about who were the chosen ones of God, you became mightily distracted and forgot your role. Many began to believe that God showed favor to some and condemned others, and so you began to compete quite viciously for His favor. And right up to the present many continue to follow this insane but well-worn path towards mutual destruction.

As you have been told, and told, and told, God loves you all; there are no exceptions. And yet this message of divine Love has been constantly ignored as you fought among yourselves for His approval. The time for that behavior to end is finally upon you, and awareness is growing rapidly that your insane, and frequently traumatic ways of dealing with one another, person to person or nation to nation, must cease if you are to survive.

It is this awareness that makes it possible for essential alteration of attitudes and behaviors to be implemented on a planetary scale, thus enabling you to live together as always divinely intended – in loving, harmonious, and respectful cooperation.

These changes are now being implemented most effectively all across the planet, and the wonderful results that are occurring are being seen and reported on. Intend to become aware of this information, share it, and become part of it as you release all the blocks and inflexibilities of mind that have prevented you, on occasion, from acting as lovingly and fearlessly as your honesty and integrity demands.

To live in integrity, honesty, and loving harmony is to follow the path out of the illusion. And this is what more and more humans are realizing. A groundswell of awareness is flowing across the planet as more and more of you inform yourselves of the devastation that has been taking place – almost always in the name of progress and with the suggestion that it is leading to prosperity for all, poisoning your air and water and destroying parts of the ecosystem without which life on Earth cannot continue.

This awareness is God-sent to arouse you from your slumber, and its success is assured because of its origin. To awaken is your destiny, and therefore you will awaken, and with the help that is now available to you, you will resolve the many major issues facing humanity, and repair the devastation that the planet and its ecosystems have suffered. A new age of enlightened living is approaching when all will truly understand and appreciate the beauty of your planet as you re-assume your role as planetary guardians. You are securely on the path to a life of joy, peace, and harmony, and the Earth will rejoice in her abundant health and fruitfulness.

Your loving brother Jesus.

John Smallman | April 8, 2012
URL: http://wp.me/p1B8dY-3B

*"ad Christi potentium et gloriam"*
*(for the power and glory of Christ)*

# Maine Republic Email Alert

*No.052*

"... that I should bear witness unto the truth." — John 18:33 // David E. Robinson, Publisher

"... if the trumpet give an uncertain sound, who shall prepare himself for battle?" — I Corinthians 14:8 —   04/08/12

## Obama Orders Press Blackout After US Credit Rating Cut

Posted by EU Times

A shattering report from RIA Novosti's Washington D.C. bureau appears to prove that the mainstream press in America has become nothing more than a propaganda arm of the Obama regime when during a White House news briefing this past week they were effectively ordered not to report on this past weeks credit rating cut of US government debt.

The Russian International News Agency (RIA Novosti) is a Russian state-owned news agency based in the capital Moscow whose clients include the presidential administration, Russian government, Federation Council, State Duma, leading ministries and government departments, administrations of Russian regions, representatives of Russian and foreign business communities, diplomatic missions, and public organizations.

The White House news briefing referred to in this report occurred this past Thursday (5 April) when Obama regime officials were queried about the latest shock downgrade of the United States credit rating stating that to the American people this critical event should be kept in the category of a "non-story" so as not to confuse and/or shock them.

Most surprisingly, this report continues, the mainstream US news media, including their most important television networks and major newspapers, dutifully followed the directives of the Obama regime and failed to uniformly inform the American people of this momentous event.

Vermont Retirement Secret - No 401k Needed to Retire Rich.

Credit rating agency Egan Jones (EJR) downgraded the United States Thursday on concern over the sustainability of public debt. Egan Jones

is one of the most important ratings firms in the world; they lowered the US credit level from AA+ to AA. The firm reduced the US from AAA to AA+ in July 2011, just before Standard & Poor's did the same.

Egan Jones further warned: "Without some structural changes soon, restoring credit quality will become increasingly difficult." They added that there was a 1.2% probability of US default in the next 12 months. The company cited the fact that the US's total debt, which now equals its total GDP, is rising and soon will eclipse the national GDP; the company sees the debt rising to 112% of the GDP by 2014.

So dire have economic conditions become in the United States that American freelance alternative press on-line columnist Allen Roland stated to Press TV this past week that the United States is experiencing a deep depression and cited the following facts:

"Reality is finally coming to the surface. The stock market is not the American economy. Eighty percent of the stock market is basically high frequency trading of the big boys playing games with their money.

And 61 percent of the American debt is being bought by, guess who? The Fed (US Federal Reserve Bank) – So we're printing money. So let me give you the raw economic numbers, which basically what this is telling us – raw economic numbers about the American economy:

38 percent of all Americans are either considered to be low income or living in poverty; 57 percent of all children in the US are living in homes that are either considered to be low income or impoverished; the average amount of time a worker stays employed in the US is now over 40 weeks and according to the Bureau of Labor Statistics, 16.6 million Americans were self-employed in 2006; today that number is 14.5 million."

Most astounding to note in these horrible statistics about the US economy are that they are apparently welcomed by Obama who yesterday stated about the weekly jobs report: "We welcome today's news that our businesses created another 121,000 jobs last month, and the unemployment rate ticked down..."

Failing to be mentioned by Obama, or his propaganda mainstream press corps lap-dogs, was that the only reason the US unemployment rate was able to be tagged lower was due to the record number of 88 million Americans dropping out of the work force because there are no jobs for them.

To how the Obama regime is really dealing with the catastrophic rate of unemployment, aside from keeping the American media from telling the truth, appears to be through mass arrests of those who dare to protest, and as of 29 March showed nearly 7,000 US citizens jailed for protesting in at least 113 separate cities.

Even worse, new reports from the United States are further warning that a new wave of home foreclosures is underway that will rival the upheaval seen by those who lived through the Great Depression of the 1930's.

To how the Obama regime will deal with future instability caused by unprecedented economic dislocation and chaos Americans are being warned that their police forces have now adopted Israeli techniques which, in essence, labels all protesters as terrorists while at the same time the US Department of Homeland Security is still refusing to say why they ordered 450 million rounds of ammunition.

One of the rare exceptions to those American media organizations doing lap-dog service for the Obama regime is the highly respected lawyer and New York Times best selling author Glenn Greenwald who in his latest article in Salon Magazine writes: "The uncritical relationship and overlapping functions of government officials and establishment media organs are more severe than ever."

Most sadly in all of these events, the once great United States, whose press freedoms were once legendary, has been placed at No. 47 on the world's press freedom index by the internationally respected Reporters Without Borders (RSF) organization in a stunning move reflecting how deprived of real truth the American people truly are.

The great American Founding Father Thomas Jefferson once warned his fellow citizens, "Our liberty cannot be guarded but by the freedom of the press, nor that be limited without danger of losing it."

With that warning going unheeded, however, the quote of the great American author Mark Twain seems to be the more appropriate one to use for this American generation, "There are laws to protect the freedom of the press's speech, but none that are worth anything to protect the people from the press."

# Maine Republic Email Alert

No. 053

*". . . that I should bear witness unto the truth." — John 18:33 // David E. Robinson, Publisher*

*". . . if the trumpet give an uncertain sound, who shall prepare himself for battle?" — I Corinthians 14:8 —*  04/09/12

## Sheriffs Bushwhacked

- **Delaware attorney general strips county sheriffs of arrest powers**

**By Pat Shannan**

Sheriff Jeff Christopher of Sussex County, Delaware, when he was elected to the office in 2010, thought he was handpicked by the people to represent them as the highest-ranking law officer in the county. Instead, he has found himself in the middle of a fight for the future of American law enforcement as a result of a nationwide effort to abolish the sheriff's office altogether.

This is one more example of federal and state governments ignoring the will of the people as well as state laws. In the case of Delaware, the state's own constitution stipulates that the office of the sheriff is a constitutionally created position just like the secretary of state and the attorney general. Delaware's Constitution states: "The sheriffs shall be conservators of the peace within the counties . . . in which they reside."

This time it is Delaware Attorney General Beau Biden, son of Vice President Joe Biden, sending out mandates to commissioners informing them that their sheriffs no longer have arrest powers. In an opinion released Feb. 24, State Solicitor L.W. Lewis said that neither the state nor the common law grants arrest powers to the county sheriffs.

It would appear that Lewis is a little confused. The office of sheriff was created more than a century before the official founding of the United States. Delaware's first sheriff took office in 1669.

Christopher tells AFP that the two administrations prior to his—as far back as 2000—began to notice a reduction in funding and the chipping away of powers of the office in general.

Sussex County Sheriff Jeff Christopher

"Now my deputies and I have been relieved of all arrest powers and can't even make a traffic stop," he said. "Delaware has only three counties... The other two sheriffs . . . will not stand up with me" to prevent the elimination of county law enforcement, he said.

During an interview at the Las Vegas Sheriffs Conference in January, Christopher told AFP that the impotence of his office was brought home to him when he was hit in the eye and kicked by County Councilman Vance Phillips but was unable to arrest him.

Beau Biden's questionable ruling against the longtime tradition of the sheriff being the highest ranking law enforcement officer in the county because of election by the people means the state's usurpation of the office appears to be a forthcoming fact.

County spokesman Chip Guy announced, "The opinion from the attorney general's office reinforces what has long been the position of the county [that] Delaware sheriffs and their deputies do not have arrest powers and are not in the same vein as state police or municipal officers."

———

Pat Shannan is a contributing editor of *American Free Press*. He is also the author of several videos and books including *One in a Million: An IRS Travesty, I Rode With Tupper* and *Everything They* Ever Told Me Was a Lie*.

All are available from FIRST AMENDMENT BOOKS. Call 1-888-699-6397 toll free to charge.

YOUR COUNTY SHERIFF IS THE HIGHEST LAW ENFORCEMENT OFFICER IN YOUR COUNTY
YOUR COUNTY SHERIFF WORKS FOR YOU !!!

*Office of The Maine free State, 3 Linnell Circle, Brunswick, Maine 04011*

Available at retail bookstores and AMAZON.com

The Sheriff is the only elected law enforcement officer in the United States - and therefore in his county. He's the only official who reports directly to "we the people" on the land.

He is sovereign in this regard because he reports directly to the Sovereigns. That is why the Sheriff is the ultimate authority on the land. He's not a bureaucrat from Washington, D.C.

# Maine Republic Email Alert

No. 054

"... that I should bear witness unto the truth." — John 18:33 // David E. Robinson, Publisher

"... if the trumpet give an uncertain sound, who shall prepare himself for battle?" — I Corinthians 14:8 —    04/09/12

## Update from "Drake"

People want to be free and they're hungering for it." He predicts that Eric Holder will be "thrown under the bus." I'm not sure if that's accurate, myself.

There is a plan, it is being put into place, it is being worked on. In conjunction with that there are a whole lot of things going that people may not be aware of. A lot of it you will not see in the mainstream media. ...

Right now we're in a wait-and-hold pattern and I don't like it any more than anyone does. But right now there is more going on than people realize. ... Things are closer than people realize.

There has been a great deal of shuffling of a combination of resources, both personnel, material, records, you name it. And it's been going pretty much like a beehive if you took one up and shook it. Consequently I'm looking for something to happen very shortly.

When they're in position to do it, it will be done."

I am a position where I have arranged communication with some of these people. If something extraordinary starts to happen, we will contact everybody and their mother-in-law and make sure everybody is aware what's going on.

The process is simple. Get as ready as you can. Commonsensically, gather together what you've gotta have. Meds, diapers for the kids, toilet paper, a little food, and so on. Figure in the neighborhood of 2-6 weeks.

It's not supposed to be that long, according to the plan, in terms of any disruptions that may come about.

This effort works in conjunction with a combination of the military and our local law enforcement. That's the only way it can correctly be done. The idea of civilian authority is in play. It is in force.

At this point we're looking at a transition, where the people who have been causing the general populace the problems that we are facing presently are to be removed, as peacefully and without any violence as possible.

The basis of all this has been laid out on the website (FreedomReigns.us).

It is my understanding that as it becomes available, there is going to be be a Q&A section added to the website, if it isn't already up. This is going to give the general gist of what I've just stated and answer some of the questions.

So basically the update is that things are moving and all of a sudden there is a lot of scrambling and this usually takes place just prior to some sort of action. And I hope we all know what that action is going to be.

To be part of the birth of a nation, or rebirth in this case? My goodness. It gives me goose bumps. ...

There is one country whose prime minister told the Rothschild central banking system to take a flying leap at a rolling donut. The debt that they incurred was fraudulent and illegal and they weren't going to pay it.

I sent a hard copy of that when I saw it to Greece and my understanding is that it went pretty viral in the Greek newspapers so they are aware of it. And I would expect that these people will start handing the back to those people who made it up and see if they will pay it.

Bundesbank ... put a restraining order on [Germany's Prime Minister] Merkel. That means she can't touch a dime. That means that all of these deals are done. That means there won't be bailouts. I'm looking for some fun and games in Europe.

That pretty much puts the icing on the cake in terms of the ideology of control through finance. The other part is that there is an alliance of nations that has cut off the corporate cabal or central banking system, as it is known, in terms of the Rockefellers and Rothschilds, from being able to go to small countries and loot their treasuries.

They can't do that because even if they are not a member of the alliance, they have offered protection to anyone who's interested.

# Maine Republic Email Alert

No.055

"... that I should bear witness unto the truth." — John 18:33 // David E. Robinson, Publisher

"... if the trumpet give an uncertain sound, who shall prepare himself for battle?" — I Corinthians 14:8 —    04/07/12

## A 'Teri Hinkle' Tough Talk

Since Drake's interview with David Wilcock, and seeing dozens of posts, claims, and idiotic comments concerning Tim Turner's psyop Republic, I want to go on record, loud and clear, that any claim that Turner is involved in that has taken place regarding our return to Civil Authority, connection with the military, the White Knights, or ANY LEGITIMATE SOURCE OF FUNDING - IS AN OUTRIGHT LIE!

This process was completed by the people, many of them ex RuSA people, but not exclusively ex RuSA.

This process has nothing to do with forming a parallel or interim government. None is needed and such would be considered treasonous by the people as well as the rest of the world.

There is no group, no organization, and there are no leaders.

This is exactly what we were instructed to do by our founders if and when we found ourselves in the grips of a criminal rogue government.

Many have speculated that I was the leader, but as I said, there is none.

Yes, I *was* involved in so much that I did coordinate the completion of the process for my state, and I did help with communications, and help with *other* states, but I am not in charge of anything; the people are, and that means all of you our there, as it should be.

Today's subject is Unalienable Rights and the fact that most Americans haven't a clue what this means.

I warn you, I am known for saying exactly what I think, and sharing what I find to be true... so let's explore that subject now.

**On July 4, 1776, Congress such as it existed then adopted our most sacred founding document: "The Unanimous Declaration of the Thirteen United States of America".**

Today we refer to this founding document simply as the Declaration of Independence. But how many of us truly understand what this document's purpose means, and what it contains? And why not?

Today, most people will simply tell you that it was our countries' declaration to the King of England that the Colonists didn't want to be part of his Kingdom anymore.

While that was certainly true, it doesn't actually describe the contents of the declaration, nor the principles contained therein.

The first clue that we don't, as a nation, have the slightest understanding of our founding documents, is in the title — The Unanimous Declaration of the Thirteen United States of America.

But wait a minute! Weren't we taught that before the Revolutionary War this nation was comprised of Thirteen Colonies of Great Britain?

Weren't most of you out there taught that this country only became a country with the writing of the Constitution and the formation of a central government?

How many of you out there even realize that the Constitution was never presented to the people, nor were the people consulted as to its contents?

How many of you understand the reason why this is so, or that the Constitution is not the "law of the land"? Nor does it pertain to the people?

How many of you know that it is the Unanimous Declaration of the Thirteen United States of America (not the United States Corporation) that declared and guarantees your freedom?

How many of you know that even before the Constitution was written, *another* document had been written for the collective governance of the limited areas of the already established United Thirteen States — the Articles of Confederation that (unlike the Constitution) *did* pertain to the people?

How many of you know that your rights do not come from the Constitution, and cannot by given or taken away from you by any government?

What exactly does The Unanimous Declaration of the Thirteen United States of America say that we have been taught to ignore?

What exactly was Thomas Jefferson (as the author of that document) trying to convey to the people and secure for our posterity?

The hearty of The Declaration is contained in its second paragraph:

*We hold these truth to be self evident, that all man are created equal, that they are endowed by their Creator with certain unalienable [**un-a-lien-able**] rights, that among these are life, liberty and the pursuit of happiness. That to secure these rights, governments are instituted among men, deriving their just powers from the consent of the governed. That whenever any **form** of government becomes destructive to these ends, it is the right of the people to alter or to abolish it, and to institute new government, laying its foundation on such principles and organizing its powers in such **form**, as to them shall seem most likely to effect their safety and happiness. Prudence, in deed, will dictate that governments long established should not be changed for light and transient causes; and accordingly all experience hath shown that mankind are more disposed to suffer, while evils are sufferable, than to right themselves by abolishing the **forms** to which they are accustomed. But when a long train of abuses and usurpations, pursuing invariably the same object evinces a design to reduce them under absolute despotism, it is their right, it is their **duty**, to*

Office of The Maine free State, 3 Linnell Circle, Brunswick, Maine 04011

*throw off such government, and to provide **new guards for their future security.** (emphasis mine).*

Thomas Jefferson took great care to include a most fundamental basic truths which we have been systematically and deliberately taught to over look. The fact that our rights come from our Creator and not from any form of government. Jefferson says that among these rights are:

**Life.** ...only the Creator has the power to grant life to all creatures great and small.

**Liberty.** ...all creatures great and small are free to be, to exist, to live in the manner enabled by the nature of their species.

**The Pursuit of Happiness.** ...just as an animal strives to exist in the manner most suited to its kind, in the way in which it is most content, so too does humanity have that right from birth.

Yes, there was actually some heated debate at the time over this one right, because Jefferson first intended for it to read "**Property**" instead of "**Happiness**", but many of the other founders were afraid that since slaves (both owned and indentured at the time) were considered property, it might render it impossible to abolish slavery at some future time. They knew that slavery was an issue which would inevitably divide the states instead of unite them, and that they needed to leave a door open to address this issue at a more opportune time.

Thomas Jefferson pointed out that these truths are self evident. In other words, anybody should understand them. Man did not create them, and man cannot take them away.

In the next sentence, Jefferson says that governments are made by men, only to secure the rights given to us by the Creator, and even then only by the consent of those to be governed.

When was the last time you were consulted and asked for your consent to be bound by any law which our out-of-control government simply decided to pass and enforce?

How many secret laws have been passed under the "guise" of government which you did not agree with, had no say in, but are expected to know about, understand, and comply with?

Are you even aware that every day of your life you inadvertently violate some law you didn't even know about, which makes you a felon in the eyes of the law?

Today, we have quite literally been taken over by an out-of-control Socialist Regime. Not be accident. Not by natural progression. But by a cunning plan and patient application of insidious laws, statutes, codes, and decrees, most of us are unaware of, until we find ourselves suddenly the victim of the purpose of one or more of them.

Those involved in this twisted agenda would have us believe that the self evident truths Thomas Jefferson spoke of include a lengthy list of material items and services which are totally the product of human endeavor.

We are *now* told through absolute idiocy that the following things are rights. Things like:
**Education**
**Housing**
**Jobs**
**Health Care**
**Food**
**Energy**
**(etc.)**

And my personal favorite: ***Not having our little feelings hurt and being offended.***

And a host of other goods and services we are now told are rights, instead of things to aspire to, or privileges to be earned.

I recently came across a document entitle, *"Silent Weapons For Quiet Wars"* — an introductory programming manual being used at the CIA Training Center.

All of its contents are *beyond* disturbing, but the section on the use of education to wage **class warfare** is particularly disturbing and of interest here.

On page 7, I bring your attention to the following, directly quoted:

*"In order to achieve a totally predictable economy, the low-class elements of society must be brought under total control, i.e., must be housebroken, trained, and assigned a yoke and long-term social duties from a very early age, before they have an opportunity to question on the propriety of the matter. In order to achieve such conformity, the lower-class family unit must be disintegrated by a process of increasing preoccupation of the parents and the establishment of government-operated day-care centers for the occupationally orphaned children. The quality of education given to the lower class must be of the poorest sort, so that the moat of ignorance isolating the inferior class from the superior class is and remains incomprehensible to the inferior class. With such an initial handicap, even bright lower class individuals have little if any hope of extricating themselves from their assigned lot in life. This form of slavery is essential to maintain some measure of social order, peace, and tranquility for the ruling upper class."*

This Quiet War, using Silent Weapons, was declared by the international Elite at a meeting held in 1954. Even though this silent weapons system was exposed 13 years later, the evolution of this *new weapon system* has never suffered any major setback, even today.

For more information in this regard visit http://freedomreigns.us/

This website is the home for the 'Freedom Reigns radio show' – a cutting edge production that will tackle any aspect of life where our freedoms are under attack.

*'Freedom Reigns'* is not just a name for a radio show.

Freedom is the thread that weaves itself through every aspect of our lives – **freedom to travel – freedom to provide for ourselves and those we choose to provide for – freedom to say what we'd like – spend time as we choose – associate with whom we choose** – and **freedom to defend ourselves and others** – unencumbered by anything but the responsibility to do those things without harming others.

Without freedom, all the wealth in the world would be worthless. With freedom, comes the responsibility to protect others who might not be able to protect even themselves.

# Maine Republic Email Alert

No.056

"... that I should bear witness unto the truth." — John 18:33 // David E. Robinson, Publisher

"... if the trumpet give an uncertain sound, who shall prepare himself for battle?" — I Corinthians 14:8 —  04/10/12

## Bernanke and Geithner are still trying to cash bad checks

Posted by Benjamin Fulford

It appears that both the so-called "dragon family," and the "harmonious world banking system," are just the same criminal godfathers that Ben Bernanke and Timothy Geithner have always worked for. They are running around now claiming they have 600 trillion dollars inside the Federal Reserve Board computers ready to be used for "humanitarian projects worldwide."

Indeed both Eijiro Katsu, top bureaucrat at the Japanese Ministry of Finance and Bank of Japan Governor Masaaki Shirakawa have confirmed that the money is sitting there inside the Federal Reserve Board computers. The problem is that the same crooks who have been spreading biological mass murder weapons and carrying out countless other unfathomably evil acts are now saying they will be doing good.

The fact of the matter is that the owners of the Fed are a bunch of gangsters who murdered, bribed and lied their way to the top of the planetary power system only to preside over the a largest mass extinction event (including both humans and nature) since the dinosaurs were wiped out. Here is what the world has to say to you murdering crooks: "you are fired!"

This latest twist in the ongoing financial war came as two individuals (whose names we promised to keep off the record) came to Japan claiming to represent the "dragon family royal society." They said they had $600 trillion waiting to be distributed to the world and that this could be confirmed by punching a certain access code into the Fed "Black Screens" or "Euroclear screens." We used considerable political capital to get Bank of Japan Governor Masaaki

Shirakawa and top MOF honcho Eijiro Katsu to confirm the money was indeed sitting inside the Fed computers.

The problem is that the representatives from the "dragon family royal society" claimed to represent Asian royal families. They said a man by the name of Hiroshi Nakano was the real power behind the Japanese throne and that he could confirm this. We asked that they get a formal letter from one of the public members of the royal family such as the Emperor or the Crown Prince to prove they were speaking the truth. They apparently could not because their representatives dropped out of sight.

After that, these people changed tactics and approached Shirakawa and Katsu via some individual by the name of Akihiko Deguchi and Asahi Shinbun newspaper slave propagandist Yoichi Funabashi. They managed to get a whole bunch of ex-bureaucrats to sign on to their band-wagon. Their claim to Asian royal family pedigree was reduced to saying their royal family representative was princess Masako, daughter of Trilateral Commission gangster and Rothschild controlled international court judge Hisashi Owada.

These people were so arrogant they thought they could buy off Japan, their largest creditor, with $10 trillion, a mere 1/60th of the money they were planning to spend. Even that tiny share of the money could only be spent pending approval from a secret committee that reports directly to "celestial beings." Message to David Rockefeller et al: "you are gangsters not celestial beings."

The "dragon family royal society," that has been putting its name out there refers mainly to the Merovingian European Royal bloodlines, not Asian royal families.

Then of course there is the ongoing fight over who really has the rights to the global collateral accounts. The Vatican and the P2 Freemason lodge together with their allies claim it is a Cambodian by the name of R.C. Dam who has the rights.

The CIA's own research and historical treaties indicate the rights were originally given to Indonesian President Sukarno and are now held by his nephew Eddy Sukarno. We also have various Chinese and Japanese and Philippine royal dynasties making plausible claims to historical ownership of much of the gold. Most people would agree that the gold of the world ultimately belongs to the people of the world and that the true historical owners were entitled to a share.

Here is a counter-proposal based on BIS international banking guidelines. The Japanese have earned $8 trillion cash (they have paper receipts for all of this) based on selling cars, TVs, appliances, etc., to the rest of the world for the past 60 years or so.

According to the BIS rules, any cash deposit can be leveraged 10 times. That means Japan could legally offer $80 trillion, or over $100,000 to every man, woman and child on the planet. Obviously just handing out that much cash would simply result in a financial bubble, but the money could be delivered in the form of schools, scholarships, nature preserves, infrastructure, consumer goods and other tangible things that exist in the real world.

The White Dragon Society is proposing doing this by setting up a transparent new agency, manned by an international staff of some of the most intelligent people on earth.

This plan would in no way contradict other plans by other groups to carry out similar endeavors using other organizations. The advantage of this plan is that Japan's legal claim to the money is water-proof and does not require extensive litigation to prove. It can be acted on right away.

The government of Japan has already signaled its willingness to set up such an agency. A lot of the money released would go towards rebuilding the gutted industrial bases of Europe and the US. Much more would go towards ending poverty, stopping environmental destruction and financing an exponential expansion into the universe.

In any case, the fact that the Federal Reserve Board finally sent somebody directly to the White Dragon Society in Japan is a clear sign they want to negotiate peace.

As this is being written the White Dragon Society is awaiting a counter-proposal from the Feds. The initial response was that they would offer more money but they were still reluctant to hand over any independent control of how the money was spent.

Hopefully there will be further progress in negotiations this week. However, if not, the Feds had best remember that Friday, April 13th is coming up this week. In Asia the month April is pronounced "shi," which means death. That means it may turn out to be an especially inauspicious day for the Western banking cabal.

*"ad Christi potentium et gloriam"*
*(for the power and glory of Christ)*

Office of The Maine free State, 3 Linnell Circle, Brunswick, Maine 04011

# Maine Republic Email Alert

No.057

"... that I should bear witness unto the truth." — John 18:33 // David E. Robinson, Publisher

"... if the trumpet give an uncertain sound, who shall prepare himself for battle?" — I Corinthians 14:8 —    04/07/12

## Epic Paradigm Shift Poised to Unfold Within US and World Imminently

**Are militaries around the world preparing for final take down of New World Order cabal?**

Major events across the US continue to accelerate towards a momentous breaking point with each passing week in the first quarter of the year 2012.

We are fast approaching a paradigm shift of epic proportions that will result in the total freedom of all US and world citizens. Many spectacular developments, long in the planning stages, are set to unfold that will alter the course of history forever and will place humanity permanently on the path towards the Golden Age.

Behind the scenes, heroic battles wage the likes of which have never been seen on this planet before yet go completely unnoticed by the people who will ultimately benefit from them the most. Along the way, intense negotiations are and have been underway within all sectors of our modern society to break an intricate control system that has been in place for a hundred years or longer. In some cases — for thousands of years.

These include the stranglehold upon our monetary systems, our governmental organizations, media empires, religious institutions, energy resources, science and technology spheres, food productions and health care industries. All are about to be lifted out a state of suppression to be transformed into a state of dynamic activation for the benefit of **all** of mankind.

**FINANCIAL WAR THE MOST INTENSE**

Most particularly intense at this stage of the game is the war to wrest control of the world's financial power structures with major victories occurring at a near daily basis. **This unseen war is the precise reason why we have yet to see any major news of currency revaluations in foreign countries, particularly with the Iraqi dinar which has long been anticipated.**

Although the revaluation of the Iraqi dinar was originally intended to be a secret held by a few insiders devised during the first George Bush, Jr. administration, current estimates are that as many as six million people around the world have discovered and subsequently invested in this classified plan.

Even a few select mainstream news media outlets are now beginning to report on foreign currency revaluations such as Bloomberg News and Fox Business News.

On another note, the alliance between Brazil, Russia, India, China and South Africa, also known as BRICS, has taken the bold steps to dump the US dollar as their primary trading currency and create its own bank. This is yet another nail in the coffin for the privately-owned Federal Reserve banking cartel as more and more nations seek to increasingly marginalize the dollar for a take down.

BRICS recently held their annual summit in New Delhi, India in late March 2012 where they made a series of major announcements. Along with the White Dragon Society, BRICS is now emerging as perhaps the most forceful global resistance vehemently opposed to any further aggressive overtures by the NWO cabal, such as World War III in the Middle East.

One significant person who continues to stand tall is Russian Prime Minister Vladimir Putin, who has miraculously managed to rescue his country from a total downfall to the New World Order banking cabal. Mr. Putin survived two assassination attempts in his home country recently in his bid for re-election and is now set to lead the Russian people into the promised land.

On Friday, March 28, 2012, Barack Obama appointed Jim Yong Kim, a physician and President of Dartmouth College to lead the World Bank. The irony of placing an Asian in charge of this major financial institution was not lost and was likely strongly endorsed, if not enforced, by the White Dragon Society.

Apparently, Jim Yong Kim has no ties to the criminal cabal as previous World Bank Presidents have such as Robert Zoellick and Paul Wolfowitz. His appointment is yet another sign the world's financial systems are dramatically changing for the better.

Further indications that the criminals are turning upon one another are another series of unprecedented reports arising from the Vatican — the richest, most powerful institution and the very heart of darkness on planet Earth. The US State Department announced it has placed the Vatican bank on the "concerned list" for money laundering, while JP Morgan suddenly decided to close all of the Vatican's accounts it holds. Astonishing news, to say the least!

And finally, no less than the Queen of England's own bank, Coutts Bank, was fined 8.75 million pounds for failing to carry out correct checks on "politically exposed persons" and prevent money laundering. And in an even more dramatic development, the Queen's fortune has now has been officially linked to drug trafficking.

**UNSUNG HEROES ABOUND**

Meanwhile in the shadows, many, many

heroic people are battling in the trenches with little recognition yet they possess the most noble and altruistic intentions for all of humanity, often risking life and limb to do so. They have remained true to their purpose of fighting against darkness and evil with a strong sense of will and determination to see the job through to the bitter end.

In the not-too-distant future, we will need to recognize and honor these individuals for their courage, bravery and service towards not only to our country, but to the whole of the human race. These heroes come from the military, economic fields, various governmental departments, legal professions, intelligence services and average, ordinary walks of life — all linked by a high moral fiber that propels them to serve.

Still others making a profound difference in our world include a large number of people in highly conscious states who are proactively meditating, consciously co-creating and envisioning a grand future for humanity. They can be found in far flung regions across the planet such as India, Tibet, China, etc. and they are literally birthing a new reality for us all to step into.

Together, all of these diverse cross-section of people have worked tirelessly to bring the Golden Age to planet Earth as rapidly and as expeditiously as possible. And they have made tremendous strides since the dawn of the year 2012.

If you can, imagine not having to worry about the basic necessities of life such as feeding your family, putting clothes on your back, affording your housing or having access to first class medical care. Soon, all the people of world will be provided with these basic necessities as a birth right, once the resources, technologies and monies have been freed up to be dispersed among all.

Perhaps this kind of scenario may sound fanciful and untenable. Yet many are seeing and *feeling* the real possibility of this kind of lifestyle emerging for all of the human race sooner, rather than later.

**We are indeed living in the most exciting times ever seen in the history of the Earth!**

**MASS ARRESTS WITHIN U.S. BORDERS ABOUT TO BEGIN**

Soon, our news media will finally begin reporting on an unprecedented number of mass arrests that will sweep up many well known political, religious, economic and social leaders, as well as other high profile individuals whose names will be familiar to us all. While many other unknowns who have stood in dark corners wielding great negative power and influence upon the world will be removed from their hiding places.

According to the latest report from Benjamin Fulford, these arrests will include those at the very top of the pyramid including within organizations as powerful as can be found on the planet. These groups that will be targeted are: the Committee of 300; the Bilderberg group; the Council on Foreign Relations; the Club of Rome; the Trilateral Commission and the European Commission.

A whistleblower by the name of "Drake", a former member of the US military who served in Vietnam has emerged recently to act as a sort of quasi-spokesman for the U.S. Pentagon and was interviewed by David Wilcock on March 28, 2012.

In this extensive nearly three-hour long phone interview, Drake and David Wilcock discussed a wide-range of topics including the impending mass arrests, the military's role as backing law enforcement and Federal Marshals, and the return of the U.S. to a sovereign nation state.

Particularly interesting was the final hour of the interview where David Wilcock and Drake discuss some of the suppressed technologies that will be emerging in the very near future, as well as the dimensional shift about to occur.

Once these arrests begin in earnest, it is possible that some areas of the country may experience slight delays in services such electrical power, or perhaps even telephone or internet utilities. Although, Drake stressed that the military will make every effort to insure that all Americans do not experience undue hardships during this momentous transition.

Therefore, it is recommended to have a three-day supply of food and water on hand for any possible short-term emergency situation.

Of further note, a major shift is already occurring within our corporate news media as people in the US move away in record numbers and turn towards alternative news sources found on the internet.

Reports are suggesting that viewership for the CNN channel has dropped by 50% this year alone. Other media empires such as News Corp, owners of Fox News, have seen numerous of their employees arrested in the United Kingdom.

Polls are indicating that the majority of the American people no longer trust mainstream media sources such as newspapers, magazines and cable news networks, which spells doom for those in the compromised news media.

Meanwhile, the hacker activist group known as Anonymous continues to grow stronger by the month. In their boldest move yet, the group recently released a sensational video that called for the outright overthrow of the the corrupted, corporate U.S. government.

Anonymous continues to prove that is more than the authorities can handle at this time and has became a valuable PR machine for the Occupy Wall Street movement. Occupy Wall Street itself is gearing up for a massive round of protests beginning this Spring that will last until the big changes start to roll out and perhaps longer. Anonymous is also to be featured in an upcoming documentary film entitled, "We Are Legion: The Story of the Hacktivists".

And finally, Foster Gamble, the creator and host of the landmark documentary film, "Thrive" recently announced his company will be making the film available for free, beginning April 5, 2012.

It will be available for viewing on their website so as to spread their message to as may people as possible, without any hindrances.

**DIVINE INTERVENTION IN FULL FORCE NOW**

**And while we are at it, cancel all plans for Martial Law, FEMA enslavement camps, a devastating worldwide financial collapse, World War III and Armageddon. They are**

*officially* off the table! We are full steam ahead for Heaven on Earth now.

What seems like an extraordinary synchronicity of events all occurring at once, is merely the human race responding en mass to an enormous influx of energy emanating from the galactic center of the universe.

Assisting humanity along every step of the way, these energy waves streaming in are upgrading everything in their path including human consciousness, human DNA and the very nature of human reality which is being transformed from a third-dimensional to a fifth-dimensional existence. All of these upgrades are part of a grand Divine plan now moving into hyper-overdrive, preparing humanity's ascent into the Golden Age.

What may seem absolutely impossible and unfathomable one month, will suddenly become highly probable the next month. **Therefore, it is vital not to cast doubt or dispersions on any of these seemingly unrealistic scenarios that many are envisioning for our immediate future. In other words, you may be quite surprised what becomes magically available to you from one day to the next.**

**At this point in time, *anything and everything* is possible and we should not limit our selves in any way, shape or form. Go ahead and dream the impossible dream.**

### YOUR CALL TO SERVE

As these monumental historic events begin to unfold, it is important to be mindful to not go into a state of fear or panic. In point of fact, many of us will be called upon to assist others with understanding the true ramifications of these epoch-making developments.

Many of you reading this update are probably familiar with many of these planned changes because you have heard rumors or you have done your research on them for many years.

Perhaps you have even grown rather weary and impatient, knowing within your heart that changes of this magnitude were inevitable, yet the wait for their implementation has felt like an eternity. You will soon be rewarded for your patience and persistence.

**However, we must be ever mindful that the average American has absolutely no clue of what is coming down the pike.** Many may have just recently become awakened to the horror that our government, banking institutions and media sources are completely corrupt yet they feel incapable of seeing any kind of solutions available to right the ship.

Your role will become more clearly defined as a mentor, an educator, a psychologist or even as a spiritual advisor as these historic events unfold upon your television and computer screens. In other words, you will need to explain to your family, your friends and acquaintances, or your co-workers what is really going on simply because you may have a better understanding of the overall big picture.

You will become an invaluable asset to those around you who may feel bewildered or completely overwhelmed by the sheer number of changes that will occur, one after another, after another.

**Above all, remember –– stay calm, stay positive and stay strong. Trust that all that is unfolding is part of a vast amazing, miraculous Divine plan that will result in your personal freedom, as well as, the freedom of your loved ones.**

**The Golden Age is here, ladies and gentlemen, now it is time to get down to work.**

*"ad Christi potentium et gloriam"*

# Maine Republic Email Alert

No.058

"... that I should bear witness unto the truth." — John 18:33 // David E. Robinson, Publisher

"... if the trumpet give an uncertain sound, who shall prepare himself for battle?" — I Corinthians 14:8 —   04/14/12

## What if the Government rejects the United States Constitution?

**By Judge Andrew Napolitano**

What if the government never took the Constitution seriously?

What if the same generation -- in some cases the same human beings -- that wrote in the First Amendment, "Congress shall make no law ... abridging the freedom of speech," also enacted the Alien and Sedition Acts, which made it a crime to criticize the government?

What if the feds don't regard the Constitution as the Supreme Law of the Land?

What if the government regards the Constitution as merely a guideline to be referred to from time to time, or a myth to be foisted upon the voters, but not as a historic delegation of power that lawfully limits the federal government?

What if Congress knows that most of what it regulates puts it outside the confines of the Constitution, but it does whatever it can get away with?

What if the feds don't think that the Constitution was written to keep them off the people's backs?

What if there's no substantial difference between the two major political parties?

What if the same political mentality that gave us the Patriot Act, with its federal agent-written search warrants that permit unconstitutional spying on us, also gave us ObamaCare, with its mandate to buy health insurance, even if we don't want or need it?

What if both political parties love power more than freedom?

What if both parties have used the Commerce Clause in the Constitution to stretch the power of the federal government far beyond its constitutionally ordained boundaries and well beyond the plain meaning of words?

What if both parties love war because the public is more docile during war and permits higher taxes and more federal theft of freedom from individuals and power from the states?

What if none of these recent wars has made us freer or safer, but just poorer?

What if Congress bribed the states with cash in return for their enacting legislation that Congress likes, but cannot lawfully enact?

What if Congress went to all states in the union and offered them cash to repave their interstate highways, if the states only lowered their speed limits? What if the states took that deal?

What if the Supreme Court approved this bribery and then Congress did it again and again?

What if this bribery were a way for Congress to get around the few constitutional limitations that Congress acknowledges?

What if Congress believes that it can spend tax dollars on anything it pleases and tie any strings it wants to that spending?

What if Congress uses its taxing and spending power to regulate anything it wants to control, whether authorized by the Constitution or not? What if anyone other than members of Congress offered state legislatures cash in return for favorable legislation?

What if Congress wrote laws that let it break laws that ordinary people would be prosecuted for breaking?

What if the Declaration of Independence says that the government derives its powers from the consent of the governed?

What if the government claims to derive powers from some other source that it will not -- because it cannot -- name?

What if we never gave the government the power to spy on us, to print worthless cash, to kill in our names, to force us to buy health insurance or to waste our money by telling us that exercise is good and sugar is bad?

What if we never gave the government the power to bribe the poor with welfare or the middle class with tax breaks or

Office of The Maine free State, 3 Linnell Circle, Brunswick, Maine 04011

147

the rich with bailouts or the states with cash?

What if we don't consent to what has become of the government?

What if the Constitution has been tacitly amended by the consent of both political parties, whereby instead of ratifying amendments, all three branches of government merely look the other way when the government violates the Constitution?

What if the president cannot constitutionally bomb whatever country he wants?

What if the Congress cannot constitutionally exempt its members from the laws that govern the rest of us?

What if the courts cannot constitutionally invent a right to kill babies in the womb?

What if the federal government is out of control, no matter which party controls it?

What if there is only harmony on Capitol Hill when government is growing and personal liberty is shrinking?

What if the presidential race this fall will not be between good and evil, between right and left, between free markets and central planning or even between constitutional government and Big Government; but only about how much bigger Big Government should get?

What if enough is enough? What do we do about it?

What if it's too late?

Andrew P. Napolitano, a former judge of the Superior Court of New Jersey, is the senior judicial analyst at Fox News Channel.

Judge Napolitano has written six books on the U.S. Constitution. The most recent is "It Is Dangerous To Be Right When the Government Is Wrong: The Case for Personal Freedom."

To find out more about Judge Napolitano and to read features by other Creators Syndicate writers and cartoonists, visit:

http://www.creators.com/home.html

*"ad Christi potentium et gloriam"*

Office of The Maine free State, 3 Linnell Circle, Brunswick, Maine 04011

# Maine Republic Email Alert

No.059

"... that I should bear witness unto the truth." — John 18:33 // David E. Robinson, Publisher

"... if the trumpet give an uncertain sound, who shall prepare himself for battle?" — I Corinthians 14:8 —    04/14/12

## God is in the Details

Have you ever examined a flower closely? Really looked at it and studied it, and asked how could an infinite number of little mindless atoms get together and decide to grow a beautiful, fragrant flower with such creativity as found in a rose? How could these mindless balls of energy originate an expression of such beauty and perfection? How could they organize and give life and beauty to such a lovely thing?

To illustrate: What if you frequently passed by a vacant lot that had a messy pile of old bricks on it. And then one day you discover the lot now had a beautiful wall around it built of old bricks, a perfect wall made with such skill, you would have to conclude that someone with experience, intelligence and creativity had built it.

Certainly there was no life or creativity or intelligence in the bricks to do so. The bricks couldn't get together and vote to organize and build the fence.

As with the fence, so with the rose. There had to be some outside intelligence giving this flower such exquisite manifestation. The design of the rose is hopelessly original, its details, the color, the form, the fragrance. Considering its beauty and perfection, Could we not say, **God is in the details** of the rose?

Today there seems to be a great effort to deny the presence of God in the universe, to push Him out of His own creation and out of our lives. This comes at a time when the scientific community is discovering that there seems to be a "supreme intelligence" as the real cause behind the creation of the universe.

Isn't that what Mrs. Eddy was telling us when she wrote in *Science and Health*, "Perfection underlies reality. Without perfection, nothing is wholly real." (p.353)

And consider how perfectly His universe is, right down to the last detail. As the natural scientists have discovered an extremely close tolerance in the physical laws in the universe, laws that make everything fit together and work to perfection, God is in the big picture and He is in the smallest details of a creation so vast, so incredibly beautiful and perfect, how can we doubt His presence underlying it? Mrs. Eddy assures us, "Creation is ever appearing, and must ever continue to appear from the nature of its inexhaustible source." (p.507)

As students of Christian Science, we are beginning to learn the hidden laws, qualities and structure of this realm of "supreme intelligence". And we are experiencing the healing power hidden in it, and coming forth to bless us and enlighten us as we come to understand and obey its laws.

We will find that the laws and elements in this realm reveal the power behind Christ Jesus' healing work, his dominion over the elements, over lack, and even over death itself.

It would appear that **God is in the details** of every minute of his life.

His first baby-bed was a manger. And his need for a tomb after the crucifixion was waiting for him, as well as the friends needed to take him down from the cross and put him in it.

It was Christ Jesus who said, "Your Father knoweth what things ye have need of, before ye ask him." Certainly he proved what he taught.

When day after day good things happen to us, we feel God's presence in our day-to-day details: when we are in a great hurry and we suddenly remember not to lock our keys in the car; when we remember to get every thing at the store we came there to buy; when we find the perfect thing to wear to a very special occasion; when we take time to put God first in our day, we find He is in the details throughout our busy hours. Mrs. Eddy tells us, "God creates and governs the universe, including man." (p.295)

Lovingly,
Ann Beals

# The Bookmark
### Early and Contemporary Works on Christian Science
### Learning from the Past, Preparing for the Future

This month, the Bookmark is offering two outstanding books, that will help you understand how the natural scientists are discovering that there is no matter, and how you can understand this meta-physically in Christian Science.

Reading these two books will reveal that Christian Science will eventually become the most advanced scientific discovery of the centuries. The book by Richard Claude Haw, was written to be used as an association address, but he never used it. Eventually he gave it to The Bookmark, to share it with everyone.

Mr. Haw wrote prolifically for the periodicals and eventually he wrote and published his book, *Mind Power and the Spiritual Dimension*.

He could see so well how Christian Science would eventually be seen as a scientific revelation and how we need to treat it as the Science that it is.

Both of these books, on special this month, draw, to a large degree, from the present books being written by physical scientists showing how scientific discoveries are leading us toward a spiritual cause underlying the whole of creation.

**Purchase *The Myth of Matter*, by Ann Beals, for ONLY $19.95 and receive *The Spiritual Nature of Reality* FREE**

**Includes shipping and handling**
Offer Expires May 15, 2012.
**Contact The Bookmark** - 800-220-7767
The Bookmark | PO Box 801143
Santa Clarita | CA | 91380

*"ad Christi potentium et gloriam"*

# Maine Republic Email Alert

*No.060*

"... that I should bear witness unto the truth." — John 18:33 // David E. Robinson, Publisher

"... if the trumpet give an uncertain sound, who shall prepare himself for battle?" — I Corinthians 14:8 —     04/14/12

## Major Event: Liens Filed against all 12 Federal Reserve Banks

New article by David Wilcock just came out. I am posting a portion of it here, and giving a link to his site at the end. I can only say that I sense this is a significant point in our Earth's history.

David's article needs to get out to the world quickly, so this is why I post this now. By the way, if you do not know the definition of a lien, here it is.

lien: *n.* The legal claim of one person upon the property of another person to secure the payment of a debt or the satisfaction of an obligation.------------------

### MAJOR EVENT: Liens Filed Against All 12 Federal Reserve Banks

The next major milestone for Mass Arrests of the corporate cabal has now arrived. Liens have now been filed against all twelve Federal Reserve banks.

A Cease and Desist Order has also been filed — to prevent the world's wealth from continuing to be stolen.

PRELUDE TO MASS ARRESTS

If you have been following this and certain other websites, then you have already heard the eyewitness testimony suggesting that thousands of conspirators in finance, media, defense, military, corporations and government are about to be arrested.

The mass resignations of CEOs, worldwide — now numbering well over 450 in the last few months alone — is a tangible sign that a major event is anticipated within the insider community.

Let's be clear, again, that this is NOT a coup, NOT martial law, and NOT a takeover of the government in any way.

IT ALREADY HAS BEEN TAKEN OVER

Our financial system, media complex, defense industry, corporate world and government has already been taken over. It is not being run for the people and by the people. It has been systematically manipulated by a secretive, occult Cabal.

We cannot sit back and wait for their next attempt to generate mass chaos and destruction, and say "let's just leave everything the way it is," simply because this group has been so circumspect in revealing its true intentions.

This system threatens the welfare of everyone on Earth.

In their plan to secure global control, they have repeatedly attempted to create mass casualties — by a variety of different means — and significantly reduce population.

Many, if not most of these efforts have been thwarted. Much of this is thanks to the will of the people; great heroes who take a stand. This includes countless hundreds of millions of people doing their best to spread the word — and inform others.

More recently there appears to be Divine Intervention, for lack of a better term — which is utterly destroying the Cabal's ability to do any further harm on a mass level.

This does not, in any way, reduce or eliminate our need to act. For now, we focus on the practical, tangible, on-the-ground steps we must take to free our planet from Financial Tyranny — within this very opportune set of circumstances.

THE PLAN REQUIRES THE WILL OF THE PEOPLE

The plan for mass arrests appears to have been in development since the 1960s, as my interview with a new insider named 'Drake revealed'.

Drake was asked by the "good guys" in the Pentagon to provide a public voice for a plan that, up until then, had almost entirely been disclosed by Benjamin Fulford, since 2007, and myself since November 2011 — when I was personally briefed on it.

This plan requires the will of the people to succeed. Otherwise, our supporters within the military and the justice system do not have the legal precedent to perform such actions.

After many years, the public outrage is now sufficiently high that the will of the people has become more than sufficient to take these steps. Elements within our civilian and military sectors alike have had enough — and are taking a stand.

US marshals from the Department of Justice and peace officers will carry out the arrests, with the assistance of military personnel — in the event of any unforeseen disturbances.

By assisting a legal civilian authority and operation in this manner, the military personnel are following their Oath of Enlistment — *"to protect and defend the US Constitution against all enemies, foreign and domestic."*

THIS WILL BE A POINT OF NO RETURN FOR THE CABAL

Again, to reiterate, the mass arrests will generate a situation from which there is no turning back for the Cabal.

Once the truth is exposed, there will be no further walls of secrecy for them to hide behind.

Every genuine fact you've ever read on the Internet about this problem will quickly become common knowledge. The "learning curve" is steep, but this is what everyone will be talking about.

The rules of logic are absolute in a case like this. Full disclosure of this group guarantees that no such actions will ever be tolerated again by the public. It is a full-stop Game Over for the cabal.

This is why they are so terrified right now. There are plenty of headlines showing this — such as Muppetgate, the public divorce of JP Morgan and the Vatican, the mass resignations of over 450 CEOs, and the passing of ridiculous and tyrannical executive orders.

This cannot and will not be a "cleaning out of middle management" only. The upper levels will be clearly exposed. These people's lives will never again be the same.

No one will tolerate the continuation of their plans.

Read more...
http://tinyurl.com/cq4n7uk

*"ad Christi potentium et gloriam"*

# Maine Republic Email Alert

No. 061

*". . . that I should bear witness unto the truth."* — John 18:33 // David E. Robinson, Publisher

*". . . if the trumpet give an uncertain sound, who shall prepare himself for battle?"* — I Corinthians 14:8 — 04/14/12

## Notice to the world was delivered to the Office of Private International Law at the Hague!

Just before the end of last year, Pennsylvania — *as a state* — removed itself from the RuSA organization. After they did this, they put together a **Declaration of Notice to the World** stating that the Commonwealth of Pennsylvania had returned itself and its people back under its *de jur* Constitution, *of the 1700s,* and declared the People of Pennsylvania, Free! — no longer recognizing *unlawful corporate government* within their state.

They did this *legally and properly.* They did not ask for permission, they simply went ahead and did it. And they received their receipt back from the Office of Private International Law at the Hague.

And shortly after that, an informed contact — who had been in touch with the various groups who had come forward in the beginning, concerning funding for RuSA and Rap, before changes were made and they withdrew their support — was contacted and given a simple message, and that message was this:

*"It has come to our attention, what Pennsylvania has done. How long would it take you to put together a simple majority of states to duplicate what Pennsylvania has done, for at such a time there could be monetary and military support?"*

They asked for a copy of the original documentation that Pennsylvania had submitted to the Office of Private International Law at the Hague, *so they could see who had been involved.*

Our contact had no problem with that, and neither did Pennsylvania. So they forwarded on the documentation that Pennsylvania had submitted. The answer was *"Yes! we'll just see how fast we can get that done!"*

So they sent out emails to everyone across the country that they knew, and had worked with all this time, that they knew to be capable, honorable, and honest Patriots, who would roll up their sleeves and actually ,get the job done, once they were told what had to be done.

And by the following day, at least one contact in 20-22 states had stepped up and volunteered to be a lead person in their state, to get it done!

The goal was for at least a simple majority — meaning 26 or more states to duplicate *exactly* what Pennsylvania had done.

It was later decided by those involved, to add *more strength* to the action by making the **Declaration of Notice to the World**, collectively as a united effort, so that the world will know we are not just free people in the various free states, but a Free People, *united as we were meant to be.*

We need no permission, recognition or opinion from foreign bodies or corporations to be what we are — Americans who claim our rightful heritage that was given to us by our founders in 1776.

This action should be seen as a *Declaration;* not just a notification — this is primary.

This action is interim; and we can't emphasize that enough.

A small group of elite people, have already screwed things up — and in order to make sure that this doesn't happen again, all of the temporary aspects of this will be in writing.

After a period of about 120 days, free elections will be held. Paper ballots only; machines can be played with; paper ballots are a lot more difficult.

We've been told that old money people from before the Revolutionary War have been in contact with our military, and that some 80-90% of the military agree with the ideology found in our founding documents.

Everything we do is based on the principles in our 1787 Constitution and the Bill of Rights — including the *original 13th Amendment* that prohibits any foreign association, title of nobility, etc. — and the Oath of Service that everybody must take to *"support and defend the Constitution of the United States against all enemies, foreign and domestic."*

The U.S. Military has indicated to the financial people that they are willing to back us and that we have their recognition and support.

This gives the Military — *probably for the first time* — power to be used as a backup to federal Marshals who will take into custody all of the crooks and "fun-and-games people" on Wall Street, and so forth. There is going to be a tremendous house-cleaning.

The reorganizational portions of the government itself should be concluded in about 120 days. This 120 day period will begin with a formal announcement from the press-room of the White House.

This will give every reporter a clean shot at broadcasting the transition.

So these measures — *in terms of what the military wants* — they want to be the good guys. They're tired of being the bad guys. They would much rather be invited into a foreign country as a friend, and an assistant.

You need some help? What do you need? Manpower? Bull-dozers? Food? We can come in and help you out.

Yes! we're the United States Military! but we're the *new* one. We're the good guys. BINGO!

*Office of The Maine free State, 3 Linnell Circle, Brunswick, Maine 04011*

We think this new approach will work quite well.

We are not putting together any interim government. We are not trying to overthrow anything. We are trying to revert back to law and order, and create the smallest amount of chaos, *in the most peaceful fashion that we can*.

Our military cannot do this on their own for the simple reason that under the current structure, Obama is considered to be the President — *we all know that he is not* — he is the CEO (Chief Executive Officer) of a Corporation called THE UNITED STATES.

The majority of the American people do not understand this.

So as long as the American people recognize a criminal corporation in Washington D.C. as having jurisdiction over them — *and they do not stand up and say otherwise* — our military's hands are somewhat tied. They have been taking orders from a fake Commander in Chief.

As far as the financial people are concerned, they will never bring forth the money that's been intended for this country, these many years, until Washington is cleaned out, because if they did, it would disappear down the black hole of theft, almost immediately.

If the military are to once again take their orders from we the people, we have to be ready with a list of what we require it to do.

As pointed out above, this is temporary, and what gives the people the power and the authority and the standing to do this is simply that a majority of states filed the same paperwork that Pennsylvania filed, putting the world on Notice that they have gone back under their *de jur* Constitution.

They have reclaimed the Articles of Confederation, which have never been rescinded.

The Declaration of Independence and the Articles of Confederation are the basis of our freedom.

These arrests will mean the removal of the final obstacles that will allow for the implementation of the *new abundance systems* that are ready to free humanity from the current economy and its falsely imposed conditions of poverty and debt.

There are many men and women dedicated to this cause who have been working diligently in secret for years to bring us to this moment, who are eager to present to humanity the new system that will redistribute abundance to all, and release humanity from the mundane life it has known.

Freedom is being returned to the people.

The release of withheld technologies and other suppressed elements will follow to assist this transition.

The news of these mass arrests will come sudden and come hard, and many who are unprepared with an understanding as to why, may feel shocked and confused to see so many people taken into custody.

These people, how ever, have served to perpetuate our enslavement, and all have actively taken part in serious crimes against the people.

Certain big media groups have agreed to cover these events and assist in the disclosure timeline.

These arrests will be televised and fully shared with you, for it is owed to the people of the world that they witness the very moments and actions taken that will mean our release from the control of these people who have for so long worked to exploit and control humanity.

This manipulation will end and all humanity will enter into a new life.

---

The full text of the Notice can be found on the next page

---

# FedEx Express

February 7, 2012.

Dear Customer:

The following is the proof-of-delivery for tracking number **798019154282**

---

**Delivery Information:**

---

Status: Delivered
Signed for by: L. MOLENA
Service type: International Priority Service
Delivered to: Receptionist/Front Desk
Delivery location: SEE: RECIPIENT DETAILS
THE HAGUE 2517
Delivery date: Feb 7, 2012 14:45

---

**Shipping Information:**

---

**Tracking Number:**
798019154282
**Ship Date:**
Feb 3, 2012
**Weight:**
28.0 lbs/12.7 kg
**Reference:**
Nation/States project
**Shipper:**
M C MANAGEMENT SERVICES OF S FL
19411 NW CT
PEMBROKE PINES, FL 33029 US
**Recipient:**
PERMANENT BUREAU
HAGUE CONFERENCE ON PVT. INTL. LAW
SCHEVENINGSWEG 6
THE HAGUE 2517 NL

# Notice

We the people, the flesh and blood inhabitants, of the several nation states on the continent of North America, known as the united states of America, hereby declare and give **Notice** to the World herewith that;

We have assembled in our individual states and given **Notice** that by the authority of jural assembly in each state, having ratified a sovereign constitution for its own governance, declaring its own civil authority of independence, freedom and every power, jurisdiction and right which is not expressly delegated to the united states in honourable Congress assembled, by the will of the people.

We have assembled as a majority of the states with the purpose to return our Nation to its original design **according to the true belief and intention of the free people** under the Articles of Confederation, the original Constitution for the united states of America, the Declaration of Independence, the Northwest Ordinance, and the Bill of Rights, whereby we are a nation by the people, for the people and of the people.

These nation states assembled as a majority of the states hereby give **Notice** we **mandate our right of civil authority** to reclaim our freedom of governance from all usurpation of our Common Law structure so as to eliminate forevermore the existence of federal, state and local corporate entities in any position impersonating the original sovereign structure of government.

The nation states assembled as a majority of the states give **Notice** we intend to disavow any national affiliations with IMF, World Banks, United Nations, Federal Reserve and all other such organizations, as well as all alleged encumbrances and claims associated with the corporate United States, which were never created, sanctioned, or authorized according to the will of the people of the united states of America.

This assembly of the majority of nation states of the united states of America, including a quorum of the original thirteen states in Union, as empowered in Article 11 of the Articles of Confederation, do also hereby agree to the admission of, lay claim to, and empower all states not having completed documentation of Notice for inclusion in this **Notice** document, to be included nonetheless, either as nation states in Union, pending completion of documentation, or as developing Territories, unless specifically and individually declined by them.

*Office of The Maine free State, 3 Linnell Circle, Brunswick, Maine 04011*

## FREEDOM'S KEY

"We hold these truths to be self-evident, that all men are created equal, that they are endowed by their Creator with certain unalienable Rights, that among these are Life, Liberty and the pursuit of Happiness.--That to secure these rights, Governments are instituted among Men, deriving their just powers from the consent of the governed, --That whenever any Form of Government becomes destructive of these ends, it is the Right of the People to alter or to abolish it, and to institute new Government, laying its foundation on such principles and organizing its powers in such form, as to them shall seem most likely to effect their Safety and Happiness. Prudence, indeed, will dictate that Governments long established should not be changed for light and transient causes; and accordingly all experience hath shewn, that mankind are more disposed to suffer, while evils are sufferable, than to right themselves by abolishing the forms to which they are accustomed. But when a long train of abuses and usurpations, pursuing invariably the same Object evinces a design to reduce them under absolute Despotism, it is their right, it is their duty, to throw off such Government, and to provide new Guards for their future security.-- Such has been the patient sufferance of these Colonies; and such is now the necessity which constrains them to alter their former Systems of Government."

*Office of The Maine free State, 3 Linnell Circle, Brunswick, Maine 04011*

# The Declaration of Independence

IN CONGRESS, July 4, 1776.

The unanimous Declaration of the thirteen united States of America

When in the Course of human events, it becomes necessary for one people to dissolve the political bands which have connected them with another, and to assume among the powers of the earth, the separate and equal station to which the Laws of Nature and of Nature's God entitle them, a decent respect to the opinions of mankind requires that they should declare the causes which impel them to the separation.

We hold these truths to be self-evident, that all men are created equal, that they are endowed by their Creator with certain unalienable Rights, that among these are Life, Liberty and the pursuit of Happiness.--That to secure these rights, Governments are instituted among Men, deriving their just powers from the consent of the governed, --That whenever any Form of Government becomes destructive of these ends, it is the Right of the People to alter or to abolish it, and to institute new Government, laying its foundation on such principles and organizing its powers in such form, as to them shall seem most likely to effect their Safety and Happiness. Prudence, indeed, will dictate that Governments long established should not be changed for light and transient causes; and accordingly all experience hath shewn, that mankind are more disposed to suffer, while evils are sufferable, than to right themselves by abolishing the forms to which they are accustomed. But when a long train of abuses and usurpations, pursuing invariably the same Object evinces a design to reduce them under absolute Despotism, it is their right, it is their duty, to throw off such Government, and to provide new Guards for their future security.--Such has been the patient sufferance of these Colonies; and such is now the necessity which constrains them to alter their former Systems of Government. The history of the present King of Great Britain is a history of repeated injuries and usurpations, all having in direct object the establishment of an absolute Tyranny over these States. To prove this, let Facts be submitted to a candid world.

*Office of The Maine free State, 3 Linnell Circle, Brunswick, Maine 04011*

He has refused his Assent to Laws, the most wholesome and necessary for the public good.

He has forbidden his Governors to pass Laws of immediate and pressing importance, unless suspended in their operation till his Assent should be obtained; and when so suspended, he has utterly neglected to attend to them.

He has refused to pass other Laws for the accommodation of large districts of people, unless those people would relinquish the right of Representation in the Legislature, a right inestimable to them and formidable to tyrants only.

He has called together legislative bodies at places unusual, uncomfortable, and distant from the depository of their public Records, for the sole purpose of fatiguing them into compliance with his measures.

He has dissolved Representative Houses repeatedly, for opposing with manly firmness his invasions on the rights of the people.

He has refused for a long time, after such dissolutions, to cause others to be elected; whereby the Legislative powers, incapable of Annihilation, have returned to the People at large for their exercise; the State remaining in the mean time exposed to all the dangers of invasion from without, and convulsions within.

He has endeavoured to prevent the population of these States; for that purpose obstructing the Laws for Naturalization of Foreigners; refusing to pass others to encourage their migrations hither, and raising the conditions of new Appropriations of Lands.

He has obstructed the Administration of Justice, by refusing his Assent to Laws for establishing Judiciary powers.

He has made Judges dependent on his Will alone, for the tenure of their offices, and the amount and payment of their salaries.

He has erected a multitude of New Offices, and sent hither swarms of Officers to harrass our people, and eat out their substance.

He has kept among us, in times of peace, Standing Armies without the Consent of our legislatures.

He has affected to render the Military independent of and superior to the Civil power.

He has combined with others to subject us to a jurisdiction foreign to our constitution, and unacknowledged by our laws; giving his Assent to their Acts of pretended Legislation:

For Quartering large bodies of armed troops among us:

For protecting them, by a mock Trial, from punishment for any Murders which they should commit on the Inhabitants of these States:

For cutting off our Trade with all parts of the world:

For imposing Taxes on us without our Consent:

For depriving us in many cases, of the benefits of Trial by Jury:

For transporting us beyond Seas to be tried for pretended offences

For abolishing the free System of English Laws in a neighbouring Province, establishing therein an Arbitrary government, and enlarging its Boundaries so as to render it at once an example and fit instrument for introducing the same absolute rule into these Colonies:

For taking away our Charters, abolishing our most valuable Laws, and altering fundamentally the Forms of our Governments:

For suspending our own Legislatures, and declaring themselves invested with power to legislate for us in all cases whatsoever.

He has abdicated Government here, by declaring us out of his Protection and waging War against us.

He has plundered our seas, ravaged our Coasts, burnt our towns, and destroyed the lives of our people.

He is at this time transporting large Armies of foreign Mercenaries to compleat the works of death, desolation and tyranny, already begun with circumstances of Cruelty & perfidy scarcely paralleled in the most barbarous ages, and totally unworthy the Head of a civilized nation.

He has constrained our fellow Citizens taken Captive on the high Seas to bear Arms against their Country, to become the executioners of their friends and Brethren, or to fall themselves by their Hands.

He has excited domestic insurrections amongst us, and has endeavoured to bring on the inhabitants of our frontiers, the merciless Indian Savages, whose known rule of warfare, is an undistinguished destruction of all ages, sexes and conditions.

In every stage of these Oppressions We have Petitioned for Redress in the most humble terms: Our repeated Petitions have been answered only by repeated injury. A Prince whose character is thus marked by every act which may define a Tyrant, is unfit to be the ruler of a free people.

Nor have We been wanting in attentions to our Brittish brethren. We have warned them from time to time of attempts by their legislature to extend an unwarrantable jurisdiction over us. We have reminded them of the circumstances of our emigration and settlement here. We have appealed to their native justice and magnanimity, and we have conjured them by the ties of our common kindred to disavow these usurpations, which, would inevitably interrupt our connections and correspondence. They too have been deaf to the voice of justice and of consanguinity. We must, therefore, acquiesce in the necessity, which denounces our Separation, and hold them, as we hold the rest of mankind, Enemies in War, in Peace Friends.

We, therefore, the Representatives of the united States of America, in General Congress, Assembled, appealing to the Supreme Judge of the world for the rectitude of our intentions, do, in the Name, and by Authority of the good People of these Colonies, solemnly publish and declare, That these United Colonies are, and of Right ought to be Free and Independent States; that they are Absolved from all Allegiance to the British Crown, and that all political connection between them and the State of Great Britain, is and ought to be totally dissolved; and that as Free and Independent States, they have full Power to levy War, conclude Peace, contract Alliances, establish Commerce, and to do all other Acts and Things which Independent States may of right do. And for the support of this Declaration, with a firm reliance on the protection of divine Providence, we mutually pledge to each other our Lives, our Fortunes and our sacred Honor.

The 56 signatures on the Declaration appear in the positions indicated:

| Column 1 | Column 2 | Column 3 |
|---|---|---|
| **Georgia:** | **North Carolina:** | **Massachusetts:** |
| Button Gwinnett | William Hooper | John Hancock |
| Lyman Hall | Joseph Hewes | **Maryland:** |
| George Walton | John Penn | Samuel Chase |
| | **South Carolina:** | William Paca |
| | Edward Rutledge | Thomas Stone |
| | Thomas Heyward, Jr. | Charles Carroll of |
| | Thomas Lynch, Jr. | Carrollton |
| | Arthur Middleton | **Virginia:** |
| | | George Wythe |
| | | Richard Henry Lee |
| | | Thomas Jefferson |
| | | Benjamin Harrison |
| | | Thomas Nelson, Jr. |
| | | Francis Lightfoot Lee |
| | | Carter Braxton |

| Column 4 | Column 5 | Column 6 |
|---|---|---|
| **Pennsylvania:** | **New York:** | **New Hampshire:** |
| Robert Morris | William Floyd | Josiah Bartlett |
| Benjamin Rush | Philip Livingston | William Whipple |
| Benjamin Franklin | Francis Lewis | **Massachusetts:** |
| John Morton | Lewis Morris | Samuel Adams |
| George Clymer | **New Jersey:** | John Adams |
| James Smith | Richard Stockton | Robert Treat Paine |
| George Taylor | John Witherspoon | Elbridge Gerry |
| James Wilson | Francis Hopkinson | **Rhode Island:** |
| George Ross | John Hart | Stephen Hopkins |
| **Delaware:** | Abraham Clark | William Ellery |
| Caesar Rodney | | **Connecticut:** |
| George Read | | Roger Sherman |
| Thomas McKean | | Samuel Huntington |
| | | William Williams |
| | | Oliver Wolcott |
| | | **New Hampshire:** |
| | | Matthew Thornton |

Revelation xii. 10-12. *And I heard a loud voice saying in heaven, Now is come salvation, and strength, and the kingdom of our God, and the power of His Christ: for the accuser of our brethren is cast down, which accused them before our God day and night.*

Revelation xxi. *And I saw a new heaven and a new earth: for the first heaven and the first earth were passed away; and there was no more sea.*

*"The march of mind and of honest investigation will bring the hour when the people will chain, with fetters of some sort, the growing occultism of this period."* — Mary Baker Eddy (*Science and Health with Key to the Scriptures,* page 571.)

This is not the END
This is a new BEGINNING!

"IN GOD WE TRUST"

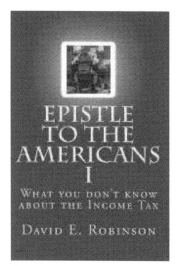
https://createspace.com/
3398018

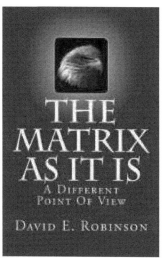
https://createspace.com/
3495158

https://createspace.com/
3715660

https://createspace.com/
3398756

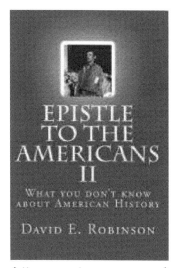
https://createspace.com/
3398019

https://createspace.com/
3650756

https://createspace.com/
3407070

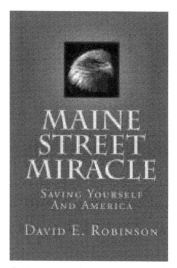
https://createspace.com/
3397262

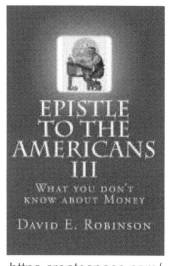
https://createspace.com/
3398020

https://createspace.com/
3610190

https://createspace.com/
3412422

https://createspace.com/
3406527

*Office of The Maine free State, 3 Linnell Circle, Brunswick, Maine 04011*

https.createspace.com/
3761587

https.createspace.com/
3676730

https.createspace.com/
3694967

https.createspace.com/
3724222

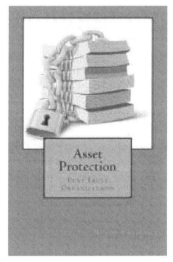
https.createspace.com/
3700522

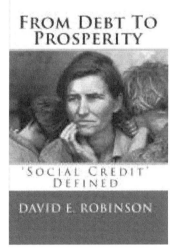
https.createspace.com/
3485734

https.createspace.com/
3397150

https.createspace.com/
3475497

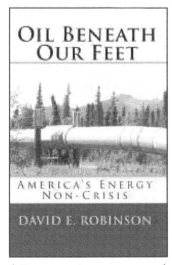
https.createspace.com/
3420496

https.createspace.com/
3462990

https.createspace.com/
3464566

https.createspace.com/
3432946

*Office of The Maine free State, 3 Linnell Circle, Brunswick, Maine 04011*

Made in the USA
Coppell, TX
04 November 2024

39618464R00094